PLATO ON JUSTICE AND POWER

SUNY Series in Philosophy
Robert C. Neville, Editor

Plato on Justice and Power

Reading Book I of Plato's *Republic*

Kimon Lycos

State University of New York Press

First published
in U.S.A. by
State University of New York Press
Albany

For information, address State University of New York
Press, State University Plaza, Albany, N.Y., 12246

Printed in Hong Kong

Library of Congress Cataloging-in-Publication Data

10 9 8 7 6 5 4 3 2 1

Library of Congress Cataloging-in-Publication Data
Lycos, Kimon.
Plato on Justice and power.
(SUNY series in philosophy)
Bibliography: p.
Includes index.
1. Plato. Republic. 2. Justice. I. Title.
II. Series.
JC71. P6L93 1987   321'.07   86–19166
ISBN 0–88706–415–9
ISBN 0–88706–416–7 (pbk.)

To the memory of Mari Kuttna
and John Lycos

Contents

Preface

The idea for this book would not have occurred to me if I had not been confronted over a number of years with generations of puzzled, resisting, and, even, irritated students. Though these were not the only responses to being introduced to Plato's *Republic*, they were the most fruitful for me. For the probing criticisms and imaginative suggestions of such students I am deeply grateful. They made me realise that though the basic ideas in the *Republic* are clear enough, what a modern audience finds somewhat difficult to grasp is the intellectual motivation underlying the perspective on justice that inspires the work. It gradually dawned on me that the best way of making this clear was through a particular way of reading Book I—one which sought to bring forth its positive force as a philosophical intervention in the socio-political climate of Plato's time.

Existing commentaries on the *Republic*, though sound and sometimes outstanding, read Book I as consisting of a set of negative arguments against existing views of justice, thus emphasising the argumentative aspect of Socrates' philosophising. These arguments are often found to be implausible and inconclusive. As a consequence the deeper, reflective, aspects of Socrates' philosophising remain unexposed, especially to students. The task, I thought, was to try to remedy this, hoping to achieve two interconnected objectives: to render intelligible and plausible the reasons why Socrates and Plato were critical of the state of thinking about justice in their culture; and to introduce a style of reading Plato's text that elicited the value and import of the *questions* it led to, rather than assessing the merit of the theories found in it. This method of reading could, of course, have been applied to the whole of the *Republic*, as well as to other dialogues. My decision to confine myself to Book I was dictated by the idea that, being a record of how Plato chose to introduce his major thought on justice, it would contain traces of what enlivened that thought as a reflective response to features of his own culture. My hope, in concentrating on that Book, was to revive in contemporary readers a sense of how relevant to our present situation is that type of response. I was concerned to make manifest the type of thinking and attitude that led to Socratic questioning; I was less concerned with Plato's positive theory of justice which, in any case, has been the subject of much excellent comment in recent times.

My considerable intellectual debt to such comment, in particular to that of Irwin, Annas and White, will be evident to all those who consult the notes. I am also grateful for the comments and criticisms of all those colleagues, in Australia and elsewhere, who heard different versions of some of the chapters and who forced me to reconsider my views. A great debt of gratitude is also due to anonymous readers whose meticulous suggestions about many aspects of the book I wish I had been better able to follow. I owe a very special debt to my colleague Dr Genevieve Lloyd who kindly read the first draft of the book and who made comments which have been invaluable; without her encouragement I doubt whether I would have completed the work.

Finally, my warmest thanks go to Jean Ryan for the enormous patience and understanding with which she approached the daunting task of converting my scribble into clear typing, and to Catriona MacKenzie and Petra Gilfedder for invaluable assistance with proof-reading and general help with the book.

K.L.

1

Introduction: 'Turning the Soul Around'

THE OBJECTIVES

The subject-matter of the *Republic* is the nature of justice (*dikaiosyne*), and its relation to human well-being (*eudaimonia*).[1] It is widely recognised that the work belongs to the 'middle' period of Plato's writing career, even though Book I, the concern of this study, bears all the characteristics of an 'early' or 'Socratic' dialogue. Indeed, some scholars in the past thought it was an early dialogue, the 'Thrasymachus', which Plato had tacked on to the rest of the *Republic* as it has come down to us.[2] Whatever the vicissitudes of the composition of Book I, it cannot be denied that it differs markedly in style from the rest of the *Republic*. Though the dialogue form is retained throughout, it is only Book I which presents strongly characterised interlocutors and elaborate dramatic setting. From Book II until the end, Socrates, the principal character of the dialogue, presents a positive account of justice, showing why, understood in the way he proposes, justice must benefit the individuals and communities which possess it. By contrast, Book I is fundamentally 'Socratic': it contains highly dramatic characterisation of Socrates' interlocutors as they react to his method of critical examination (the *elenchos*). It ends on an inconclusive note: Socrates questions certain ways of thinking about justice because they cannot explain why it is a mark of excellence in individuals and communities. An understanding of the 'true' or 'real' nature of justice is required to show its links with excellence and human well-being. Yet, in Book I Socrates and his interlocutors fail to articulate such an understanding. The *Republic*, from Book II on, may be seen as making a fresh, positive, start to deal with this issue; resulting in a work which came to play an enormously influential role in the moral and political thinking of the West.[3]

Looked at this way, the relation of Book I to the rest of the *Republic* is that of an introduction or preamble to the main discussion (it is called so by Socrates at 357 a2). Themes, ideas and sketches of arguments are introduced which receive their full elaboration and explanation later on; the main function of the first Book being to clear the ground of mistaken or inadequate accounts of justice in order to make room for the new theory.[4] This fits in well with standard estimations of Socrates'

1

contribution in Book I, which, when sympathetic, regard it as containing over-abstract and compressed arguments whose plausibility depends on too many unobvious and unargued assumptions.[5] Other commentators, less sympathetic, find the arguments inadequate and invalid—regarding Socrates' procedure as verging on the unfair and as dishonest towards his opponents.[6] Yet other scholars judge Socrates to be playful and ironic; his assertions are not meant to be taken literally. Alternatively, Socrates' argumentation is taken seriously, as representing the commitments of Socratic ethics, while its inadequacy is viewed as signifying Plato's dissatisfaction with some of his master's ideas.[7]

I believe that most treatments of Book I, even when they are illuminating, do it less than justice in not recognising that it contains its own positive theme. A theme which not merely anticipates the ideas propounded in the rest of the work, but which prepares the reader for the unorthodox theory that is to come.[8] Book I is certainly an introduction—but it is one whose special function is to reshape thinking about justice in a certain direction. It not only attempts to show that certain beliefs and attitudes are inadequate or inconsistent, it also suggests how the inadequacies of traditional Greek views about justice are to be overcome. Plato does this by exposing to the reflective consciousness of his contemporaries what it is in the traditional views they hold which he regards as an obstacle to a true understanding of justice and its value. It is because his contemporaries systematically mislocate where, and how justice operates that they are unable to perceive it as an unqualified excellence. Consequently, they have no adequate reply to the sort of challenge about the benefits of justice which Thrasymachus, Socrates' main opponent in Book I, vigorously puts up.

The argument of this study is that the central theme of *Republic*, Book I is the relation of justice to human power. The underlying aim of much of Socrates' critical examination of his interlocutors is to 'convert' upholders of traditional ideas away from the notion that justice is 'external' to that which enables individuals and communities to achieve the best use of their capacities and talents. Socrates wants to urge that justice cannot be seen as an unqualified good unless its 'internal' links with human 'powers', with their best and fullest development, are understood.

Traditionally justice was, of course, regarded as one of the 'cardinal' virtues: to avoid injustices, and to deal equitably with both equals and inferiors, was seen as part of what was expected of the good man (the *agathos*).[9] But it was not clear how the benefits of justice or, indeed, of any of the other cardinal virtues were to be understood. The standard view would have been that no quality could be a virtue, an *aretē*, if it did not benefit its possessor. But this belief is consistent with two radically different ways of understanding how virtue confers benefit. It may be understood 'externally' from the perspective of social norms and expectations associated with the concept of some particular virtue. Given, for example, a society frequently engaged in war and competitive conflict with other communities, the willingness and ability to stay at one's post, to endure hardship, and not to succumb to the fear of danger—courage, in short—comes to be a socially highly valued attribute. Similarly with the virtue of temperance or self-restraint. In the context of a harsh physical environment and of relative scarcity of resources, over-indulgence, excess, the stepping beyond 'due' measure (the *metron*), greed and acquisitiveness (*pleonexia*), will be frowned upon, and the opposite attributes will be highly valued. The 'external' assessment of a virtue consists in primarily valuing the behaviour, the types of action and response, in which people said to exhibit the virtue are generally expected to engage. Though it is assumed that such conduct is normally the outcome of a settled disposition (a *hexis*), and that people should be encouraged or trained to develop the traits of character which correspond to the virtue, it is the behaviour, not the state of mind or 'psychic constitution' of the person acting (say, courageously) which is primarily valued.[10] This way of assessing virtue leaves open two questions. One is that someone can act in the socially desired ways (and, thus, be socially praised, benefited and honoured) without possessing the quality of 'soul' or mind which constitutes the 'power' to be courageous—that is, the desire and the ability not merely to perform actions conventionally regarded as courageous, but to act 'out of courage' or for the sake of courage. One can do 'the courageous thing' without being courageous. This links with the other feature of 'externally' assessed virtue: a person may perform 'the courageous act' out of social conformity, or out of fear of dishonour, and so on—motives which may not only differ from those of the genuinely courageous person but be antithetical to them. One may do the 'courageous' thing out of cowardice.[11] The main thing about an 'external' assessment of virtue is that it leaves indeterminate whether it values the genuine possession of virtue or merely its social 'appearance'. So long as a type of socially desirable behaviour occurs, it does not seem to matter whether the virtue is 'real' or 'apparent'; that is, whether the relevant actions are an *exemplification* (not merely the outcome) of a specific quality of mind, or whether they are, instead, the consequence of an indeterminate plurality of disparate and possibly conflicting desires.

By contrast, Socrates wants to persuade his contemporaries to adopt an 'internal' way of estimating the benefit of virtue. From this perspective what matters is primarily the quality of mind, the psychic organisation which enables a person to act virtuously: a quality which can be valued for itself, in the way one may value a healthy constitution or the possession of a physical or intellectual skill. Such 'goods' can be valued as well for what they enable their possessors to achieve in life. The achievement that was uppermost in the Greek mind was to lead a life of *eudaimonia*; a life free not only from major misfortune, but characterised by a pattern of acting well (*eu prattein*) in the pursuit of activities whose combined effect is to enable an individual to live well (*eu zēn*). By leading a life which is appropriate to the type of being humans are, a person achieves fulfilment and satisfaction—one becomes successful as a human being. *Eudaimonia* being the supreme Greek value, Socrates' attempt to 'convert' his contemporaries to an 'internal' assessment of virtue requires that he show how such an assessment justifies the view that virtue either leads to, or is a component of, *eudaimonia*. The task is a major one, and it lies at the heart not only of Socratic ethics but the moral theories of both Plato and Aristotle.[12]

To appreciate the scope of this enterprise we should note that the 'external' assessment of virtue allows its upholder to think of virtue as relating to *eudaimonia* in a rather contingent way. If the material and social circumstances of one's life are secure and propitious, virtue will gain for one the praise and approbation of one's fellows—the life of the virtuous is thus enhanced and 'enobled'. The virtuous are good (*agathoi*) and fine (*kaloi*). Virtue will also safeguard one against excesses of passion and action which may well ruin or jeopardise one's chances of leading a good life. This belief in the interaction and mutual support between material prosperity and virtue is well captured by Plato in the character of Cephalus, Socrates' first interlocutor in the *Republic*. But material circumstances can go wrong. Though, in general, it is good to be virtuous for the reasons just stated, it does not follow that virtue is in any way logically tied to *eudaimonia*. Not only may one's virtue prove powerless to avert misery; doing the 'right' thing may, in some contexts, prove harmful. It may be wrong to act 'rightly'. The 'internal' assessment of virtue cannot allow this. Though a measure of good fortune is necessary for the fully eudaimonic life, it can never be wrong to act virtuously, since the quality of mind that *is* the virtue is a good and enjoyable thing in itself. The fact that, due to untoward circumstances, virtuous people may not be able to achieve the best possible result through their action does not mean that the exercise of their virtue did not yield its essential benefit. The demonstration that virtue has such benefit must convince not only the sceptic about virtue, but also the ordinary person whose belief that virtue is beneficial is based on an 'external' assessment of that benefit.

This opposition between two types of assessment of virtue is one of the major themes explored in Socrates' examination of his interlocutors about justice. But there is a further, more specific, theme concerning the relation of justice to power. Making a case for assessing virtue 'internally', is difficult enough in the case of the more self-orientated virtues such as courage, temperance and wisdom. Whatever the difficulties in showing that the benefits these virtues confer to their possessor issue from the excellence of certain mental states, the idea is, at least, not at odds with the conventional view. Though individuals possessing these qualities were socially valued, it was thought that a person had good reasons, from the point of view of his own good, to possess them. Being courageous, temperate, and wise is not merely useful to those interacting with the agent; these virtues are of direct benefit to agents to the extent that they prevent them from engaging in shameful, degrading or personally harmful acts. More positively, they also contribute to their achieving the things they value most—honour, status, esteem, influential position, material and spiritual comfort, and so on. It is much more difficult to show this in the case of justice. For even if being just is a quality of character, it is in one's transactions with others and with society, or with the social group taken as a whole, that one's justice is thought to manifest itself. Unlike the other virtues, justice is essentially *other-orientated*. Thus, the benefit of justice to the agent is indirect; it derives from the general social benefit to which the justice of individuals contributes. By being just one can gain the good-will and co-operation of others. And by not committing injustice one may avoid incurring the wrath, indignation, and retaliation of others, or of the official instruments of the state.

But there is no guarantee that one's justice will secure these benefits, or that one's injustice will damage one's interests. Indeed, it may well turn out that acting unjustly, if undetected, is to one's advantage, and that in acting justly one benefits others at the cost of what is advantageous to oneself. Thus, even if Socrates were to succeed in showing that justice, like the other virtues, is a mental quality good in itself, could he show that its exercise or manifestation enabled its possessors to achieve something excellent in their life? Justice may benefit others, and a just society may be more beneficial to its members than an unjust one, in that it secures concord and avoids dissension. But this by itself would not show that the benefit of justice could or should, be 'internally' assessed. How does my justice, the 'power' of justice in me, enable me to achieve the highest realisation of my capacities and the best use of my talents? Surely, what is more likely to succeed in this regard is my possessing power. Personal success depends on being in a position to control those whose interests and desires may frustrate my efforts, and whose subordination is, consequently, necessary if I am to be free and master of my own destiny. But acting justly may be an obstacle to possessing or achieving power. How, then, can it enable a person to achieve personal excellence? As we shall see, this attitude is captured by Plato in his portrayal of Thrasymachus, Socrates' main opponent in Book I.

The crux of Socrates' strategy against Thrasymachus turns upon a redefinition or re-examination of power. If Thrasymachus is to be answered, not only must the 'powers' of justice be shown to be beneficial to its possessor, the possession and exercise of power in its ordinary, social and political, sense must also be shown to be logically related to the 'internal' assessment of justice. Socrates must convince his interlocutors that, contrary to the conventional view, it is not being in a position of power which makes people truly powerful and truly able to control their environment so as to avoid the frustration of their desires; they cannot achieve this end unless they possess the mental quality of justice.[13] It is this paradoxical and novel idea, or, at least, the need to embrace it, which forms the specific theme of *Republic*, Book I. The rest of the work is Plato's attempt to elaborate and to provide a metaphysical defence of his idea. Thus, the role of Book I is to 'turn' the minds of readers with conventional ideas away from their customary evaluations of justice and towards this new vision.

In this respect the relation of Book I to the rest of the work corresponds somewhat to the powerful and highly influential image of the Cave Plato describes in Book VII. There Socrates suggests that education is the art of turning around, or converting the soul, already possessed of sight, from looking in the wrong direction, and at the wrong things, to where it ought to look.[14] The image is that of prisoners in a cave, so shackled (perhaps by the bonds of custom and tradition) as to be able to look at the shadows projected on a wall facing them by puppets illuminated by a fire behind them. The allegory concerns the release of such a prisoner, and his arduous progress (the path to knowledge) to the contemplation of the genuine realities outside the Cave. It is not my purpose to interpret this rich image—surely one of the most uncompromising conceptions in Western culture of the power of intellectual activity to liberate and enlighten.[15] My reference to it is simply to indicate how I propose to read Book I.

In this book Socrates' *elenchos*, the examination of the beliefs of his interlocutors, corresponds to the forcible 'turning around' of the soul of the prisoner. This implies that in his characterisation of Socrates' interlocutors Plato will incorporate aspects of traditional attitudes he sees as resistances to a true theory of justice. The prisoners' attachment to the shadows on the wall of the cave makes them unwilling to look in the direction towards which their heads are being turned. At the same time, Plato's presentation of the sort of intellectual activity required to achieve this forceful 'conversion' has to convey more than the ability of Socrates' questioning to expose confusion. It must also persuade the reader that Socrates' effectiveness derives from the fact that, unlike his interlocutors, his gaze is directed at what the 'realities' of justice might be rather than merely considering its conventionally recognised 'appearances'. I have, accordingly, divided this study into two 'movements': the first explores the relation between Plato's characterisation of Socrates' interlocutors and the general cultural and ethico-political attitudes of his contemporaries which Plato sees as containing resistances towards a correct theory of justice. The second 'movement' attempts to extract from Socrates' argumentation the ideas that make up his new vision of justice. I am less concerned to assess for validity the arguments Socrates uses to test and reject the views of his interlocutors, and more with how effective he is in establishing the *need* for his contemporaries to rethink their attitude to justice. Though it is important that Socrates' arguments should be sound, the thoughts contained in his premises must also be such as to make those who reflect upon them realise that there are gaps in the ordinary conception of justice, and that these gaps require a thorough reassessment of ordinary notions. Thus, this reading of Socrates' contribution regards it as a new form of the activity of cultural critique which, in Greece, had been mainly the function of poets.[16] Socrates' arguments, which to many have appeared abstruse and implausible, emerge as part of a powerful and sustained strategy to force a revision in how people should understand a commitment to virtue and justice. The arguments, particularly to a modern audience, will certainly seem bizarre, or even perverse. But, as we shall see, the puzzle about them is, more often than not, their true import rather than their logic. It is to a critical assessment of this import that the concluding chapter is devoted.

THE BACKGROUND

What were the features of political and ethical thinking about justice which Plato saw as resistances to the Socratic vision? What were the shadows on the walls of the Greek or, for that matter, the Athenian cave? As a background to the discussion in the following chapters, I shall conclude this introductory chapter with some sketchy remarks about socio-political concerns in Greek city-states, as well as highlighting certain shifts in how Greeks came to think about justice. The two are related, in that changes in ideas about justice tend to accompany shifts in socio-economic and political structures.

The history of Greek city-states provides ample evidence that social cohesion was a problem for them. The problem was how to ensure the high level of social unity required by the strong identification of citizens with their *polis*. This difficulty had persisted throughout the period of political experiment which had followed the socio-economic changes in the seventh century BC.[17] These changes had precipitated a divisive class-structure which, to begin with, impelled the Greeks to move from a quasi-tribal form of social organisation towards the *polis* form. Subsequently, it imposed a severe strain on the *polis* structure itself.[18] The political experiments of tyranny and democracy as alternatives to aristocratic oligarchy may plausibly be seen as 'solutions' to the problem of social unity.[19] In both cases, however, the solution was predicated on conceiving the causes of social conflict and disunity to be narrowly political rather than perceiving such conflict and disunity as a cultural reflection of the arbitrary and irrational manner that wealth, power, status, and social tasks, were distributed in the community. The struggle to achieve for all citizens equal participation in the affairs of the *polis*, which had marked the development of democracy in Athens and elsewhere, at best could only achieve a delicate balance between the 'few' and the 'many' in the attempt to avoid *stasis*, civil disruption. It is important to remember that the political success and economic prosperity of Athens during the second half of the fifth century, responsible for its becoming an imperial force in Greece, would not have been possible without such a balance. Its maintenance had, to a large extent, been the work of democratic reform. Things would remain stable so long as the state provided the 'many' with material benefits and with a substantial say in the running of the affairs of the *polis*. It did not matter that it was only the 'few' who received the honour, esteem, and power that went with political and military leadership. After all, such 'few' would be prepared to shoulder the heavy burden of financial and military charges that went with leadership only so long as the 'people', the *demos*, accepted that it was the 'few' who provided leaders. The system worked well enough. So much so, that in spite of her defeat in the war with Sparta, Athens in the fourth century was able to find within herself 'resources to maintain the political and civic organization which the empire had helped erect in the previous century'.[20]

But this political balance between the 'many' and the 'few' depended on the fact that the leaders' policies could appear to the *demos* as maintaining a high level of material and cultural benefit. This, in turn, meant that economic expansion and commercial success in competition with other states was necessary for political stability within. Given the political supremacy Athens had achieved in the Persian Wars during the fifth century, the forces pushing Athens to become an empire, to secure the expansion of its sphere of economic activity by making sure that its imperial position was not threatened, were almost irresistible. And, yet, the political and social structure of the *polis* was ill-adapted to handle the complex problems of diplomacy and fiscal policy thrown up by the rise of Athens as *the* commercial and naval power in Greece. With hindsight we can see that the development of Athens into an empire entailed the downfall of the *polis* structure. For Athens really to succeed in the struggle with Sparta she would have had to bring the whole of Greece within her empire. This was evidently beyond her reach; it would have required a radical change in her social and political structure.[21] The remarkable fact that it did not happen for another 100 years or so testifies to the high degree of communal integration in the *polis*, and the ability of democracy, through its leaders, to withstand threats to the *polis* structure. Nevertheless, it could not have survived.

It is not my purpose to analyse the factors responsible for social change in Greece. This is the task of historians and social theorists.[22] Rather, I want to note the *ideological* transformations which accompanied this social change; the shifts in conception of what is the right and best way for a society to live. The question of justice is central to this conception. It may well be that the evolution of the idea of justice in Greece reflected, in moral and political terms, the largely unconscious efforts of a society to adjust to the forces pushing for structural social change. Viewed from this perspective, Socrates' and Plato's critique of Athenian culture, and their proposal for a new conception of justice, may be seen as part of this process of adjustment. It is customary to separate Socrates' primarily ethical concern from Plato's apparently more political interest in how Athens was conducting its affairs. No doubt there were important differences in temperament and outlook between the two men—not to mention the fact that Plato had to reflect upon a deeper issue which had only arisen as a result of the confrontation between Socrates' philosophic activity and the restored democracy in Athens. This issue was how to make persuasive the idea that a special mode of inquiry (exemplified by Socrates' activity) was *politically* relevant—not merely the expression of the zeal of a moral reformist. It is difficult to be certain whether in Socrates' case we can distinguish all that easily between morals and politics. It is difficult enough to do so in the case of poets such as Aristophanes or the historian Thucydides. Indeed, it could be argued that though Plato himself would have been deeply opposed to such a separation, the *effect* of such a work as the *Republic* was to suggest the possibility of distinguishing political theory from philosophical ethics. Nevertheless, in making justice his chief concern, Plato was evidently attempting to incorporate reflective dialogue about virtue, in which Socrates had sought to engage his contemporaries, into a comprehensive proposal for social reform. A proposal, moreover, which gave political pride of place to philosophical activity, and made it a matter of justice in a *polis* that reflection upon questions of human excellence and social well-being become the proper concern of philosophers.[23]

Such an idea is, to put it mildly, difficult for us to accept, not least because of its elitist implications. However, I believe that we misconstrue what is important about the idea if we dwell excessively on its elitism. Elitism was not the preserve of Plato's rationalist politics. Socrates' moral innovativeness as well as Aristotle's more empirically-minded political reflections were tinged by it.[24] Nor was a tendency to political elitism in Athens confined to those with aristocratic sympathies. Democrats like Pericles could betray it, though in a suitably transmuted form fit to appeal to adherents of democratic ideals.[25] The roots of elitism in Greece lay in the very nature of the *polis* structure and in the pervasive influence the sense of community in the *polis* had on the actions, emotions and thoughts of its citizens. The political behaviour of rulers and popular leaders, the policies they promoted, and the way decisions were arrived at within a *polis*, could come into conflict with or betray the goals and ideals which the citizens associated with the specific identity of their community. Though personal and factional interests were often at stake, the ideological coin of debate was basically whether what was done, or was proposed, harmonised with or undermined the citizens' *polis*-consciousness. The fundamental anxiety of the ordinary citizen (though not fully shared, perhaps, by the 'modernising' young men of good families vying for political power in democratic Athens) was whether the political process preserved what they felt their *polis* stood for.[26] It is this essential conservatism of the concern for social identity, a conservatism undermined but never abandoned by democracy, which accounts for the ease with which the Greek mind can accommodate elitist thoughts even when ideologically committed to democratic ideals.[27]

It is against this background of the essential conservatism generated by the *polis* structure itself, rather than in terms of conservative political ideals, that we should understand the Platonic proposal. What underlies both Socrates' and Plato's intervention against their contemporary cultural values was not merely the perception of moral corruption in Athenian political practices and institutions. Rather, they had sensed a growing cultural deterioration: the point of a social organisation such as the *polis*, to preserve a coherent and stable social identity, was in danger of being lost by the turn of events in Athens. To the 'Socratics', therefore, philosophical inquiry came to seem as a method of safeguarding the point of living in a *polis*; a method that would rival the practice of public persuasion conventionally regarded as the province of political leaders. So, for the philosophers the political concern for social cohesion and the preservation of the *polis*-identity takes a more intellectual and rationalist form. Different forms of political behaviour are viewed teleologically, according to whether man's natural moral ends are subverted by decisions of rulers based on class-interest.[28] This suggests that for these philosophers the point or functional purpose—the *telos*—of a *polis* is to enable human beings to achieve moral ends set by their 'nature', and that such ends can be subverted by the political process whereby decisions affecting the *polis* as a whole are arrived at. But though intellectualised, this concern for social cohesion is not far removed from the strong sense of communal identity which inspired the ordinary citizen of a Greek *polis*. And though the philosophers universalise and 'naturalise' the ends the *polis* is meant to achieve, they have the same aversion towards *stasis* (dissension, factionalism, sedition) as the non-philosophical citizens with their more conventional conception of the goals of their *polis*. This horror of *stasis* attests strongly the full extent of the influence that the sense of community exerted on Greeks.[29] *Stasis* was seen as a chronic evil in Greek society which might at any moment plunge a *polis* into ruthless civil war. As Finley points out, so strong was this aversion that even tyranny—a political solution that had become unpopular by the latter part of the fifth century—would be tolerated if it was seen as a way of averting *stasis*.[30]

By its nature a small and exclusive community like the *polis* generates an intense and proud desire to participate in its affairs. But great inequalities in the distribution of wealth and power were bound to clash with the sense of community which constituted this type of social arrangement. Because of these inequalities the desire to participate often became frustrated. Whenever this happened those whose demands for a political say were denied or curtailed not only felt that they were unjustly treated, they were also bound to think that those in power were not ruling the *polis* as if it were *polis*; that they were treating it as if it were a barbarian kingdom, as part of their estate. Factional strife was particularly bitter because the clash of interests *also* appeared as an assault on communal identity. The problem in the Greek *polis* was to reconcile diversity of interests with the citizens' strong sense of identity with their *polis*. Within such a context the idea of justice and, more especially, that of injustice will convey something beyond the unfair treatment of some at the hands of others, or by those in power. To the extent that the behaviour of citizens or leaders undermined the communal identity and the power of social cohesion such behaviour would be unjust, whether or not it was also (as it often was) the effect of unjust relations between the citizens. A *polis* which, because of the conduct of those in power within it, was not governed *as* a *polis* was unjust—the character of its political life being a reflection of the character of its rulers.[31]

Thus, the debate about justice and the right political arrangement took in Greek antiquity a different form from modern debates. The issue then was not whether a type of political organisation was the most equitable, or efficient, in distributing social benefits to the citizens. Rather, it was whether the political arrangement could lay claim to being the one most *appropriate* to preserve the citizens' sense of identity with their *polis*. What caused the most serious division was not so much policy, as the question of who should rule—'the few' or 'the many'.[32] But while the character of the *polis* had evolved considerably in response to changing circumstances during the sixth and fifth centuries, the majority of Greeks did not perceive their constitutional debates as due to the crises the very structure of the *polis* was undergoing. They were attempting to preserve an almost tribal sense of community in a social organisation which, at least in Athens, encompassed commercial, naval and imperial activities. If the *polis* was 'a people acting in concert, and therefore . . . able to assemble and deal with problems face to face', then organisational complexities demanded at least a reduction in the expectation that political action could preserve every citizen's sense of community.[33] Such a reduction was achieved, though not consciously, by the democracy. It was this reduction which formed the aristocrats' complaint. Nevertheless, it was not difficult for the democrats to believe that their solution in terms of equality of participation in political decisions was the one which could best preserve the traditional view of the *polis* as the source of all rights and obligations whose authority extended over every aspect of human behaviour. Traditionally the *polis* was inescapable.[34] Under the democracy a considerable portion of the behaviour of individuals must have been *de facto* freed from the collective consciousness of the *polis*, but such a separation was not constitutionally recognised. The administrators of justice, the jurors, were still selected from the body, the Assembly, engaged in legislative decision.[35] Hence, the paradox that a democracy claimed to represent, while it simultaneously undermined, the collective consciousness of the citizens.

This emphasis on collective consciousness comes out in the Greek idea of freedom. Freedom as an assertion of a right *against* the state or the majority in it—so much part of the modern conception of a polity—was inconceivable for a citizen of the *polis*. Freedom lay precisely in leading an orderly existence as a member of a community ruled by a long-established code revered and respected by all. Rulers who were suspected of departing from it were seen as unjust and as enemies of freedom. To fight for freedom was to struggle to maintain, or to return to, one's status as a member of a culture in the face of threats to change its code, or in response to acts which disregarded it.[36] This fierce allegiance to the principle of 'the Law is King' represented the outcome of a long struggle throughout the archaic period, during which first the traditional hold on privilege and power by the nobility, and then the unchecked power of the tyrants, was undermined.[37] But even under democracy this principle did not entail the notion of obeying legal-political arrangements as distinct from obeying the communal moral precepts governing the conduct of individuals. However 'progressive' the political struggles had been, and however much moral tension they had generated, they had not managed to eclipse the deep conviction that the good or bad behaviour of the citizens was the concern of the *polis*, and that the political behaviour of its leaders was subject to the same code.[38] So, when Plato suggests that in characterising virtue or justice in the *polis* one will be able to determine how these qualities manifest themselves in the individual, he is relying on the old traditional idea that every aspect of the life of the citizens, both of the people and their leaders, *mirrors* the extent to which the code of the *polis* is being observed.[39] Democrats and aristocrats alike would have agreed with this, even though much strain had been placed on this conception by the development of democracy in Athens.

To appreciate the sort of 'conversion' Socrates hoped to effect on his contemporaries with respect to justice we need to see it as a re-interpretation of the ordinary view that justice has the power to achieve social cohesion in the *polis*. At the same time, this 'conversion' marks, in Plato's eyes, a return to a conception of justice which, however dim and unphilosophised, lurked in the memory of the culture—a conception which the political developments in Athens had done much to undermine and confuse. I turn, therefore, to look at some aspects of the development of the Greek notion of justice. They reveal the ways in which political evolution in the sixth and fifth centuries—itself a response to the changing socio-economic circumstances of Greek states—had generated tensions in the very manner Greeks thought about justice. In two important and stimulating books, A. W. H. Adkins has explored what he regards as a deep-rooted problem in the Greek value-system from Homer to the fourth century.[40] The problem, as he sees it, is that given their competitive and success-orientated aristocratic ethic, the Greeks had great difficulties in fitting co-operative and 'quiet' virtues such as justice into their ethical scheme. The outcome was the lack in Greek ethics of anything like our notion of moral duty or responsibility.

It is not my purpose to trace the complicated story of the shifts in moral conception which accompanied the efforts of the Greeks to adapt their ethical outlook to the new conditions of the *polis*. Rather, I want to stress another point which does not receive sufficient attention in Adkins.[41] Though he rightly emphasises the fact that the Greeks had difficulty in bringing justice as a virtue into line with the other virtues which formed the standard Greek conception of excellence, *aretē*, virtues such as manly courage, 'great-spiritedness', self-control, wisdom, piety, and so on, he does not make much of the fact that justice in ancient thought and myth, as well as in the more 'naturalistic' thought of the sixth century, was conceived as a cosmic force of power. The power of justice was thought to be so pervasive that it governed the ways not only of men and their communities but those of natural elements, of plants and of animals.[42]

Given this pervasiveness, it would seem rash to confine one's assessment of how Greeks thought about justice to literary contexts where comparisons between just behaviour and other virtuous behaviour were made. If justice, or, more importantly, injustice, is viewed as a cosmic dimension of life in general, the fact that if occupies a relatively lower place in the scale of *personal* excellences is hardly surprising. Nevertheless, from the fact that justice did not easily fit into the system of personal excellences it would not follow that it did not occupy a high place in the overall scheme of things according to which human beings comprehended their lives and destiny. If justice is 'the way of things', and injustice concerns the disturbance of what is laid down by nature as fitting or appropriate, then justice can be valued as an awesome and mysterious force, commanding everybody's respect (even that of Zeus), however difficult it may have been to see it as a goal an individual might set out to achieve. By its very nature justice will be an awesome power transcending individual wills, whose benefit derives from the sort of limitations it imposes on ambition and on the insatiable desire for self-aggrandisement of individuals—limitations which will seem *external* to the desires, passions and interests with which an individual identifies at any given moment.[43]

As we shall see in the chapters that follow, Plato's critique of contemporary conceptions of justice relies heavily on this traditional dimension and is unintelligible without it. His solution, at once radical and conservative, consists in 'internalising' this supra-personal dimension of justice, in identifying it with the power obtained when intellect and reason rule over appetite and passion in the minds of individuals. This power becomes social justice when such supremacy is adopted as the guiding principle of social arrangements in the *polis*. It is with this alternative that Plato hopes to combat the moral dangers he detects in the way democracy had 'socialised' justice in the *polis*. It is one thing to make justice the business of every citizen as Solon had proposed;[44] it is quite another to make it an effective force in the lives of the citizens.

It cannot be denied that the Greeks were ambivalent about justice as a personal virtue. Though they were aware—certainly by the fifth century—of its value as a power in the community to maintain stable and harmonious social relations, it was not clear to them how much the excellent man, the *aristos*, should make it a personal ideal.[45] True enough, as we saw earlier, the well-being and freedom of the citizen depended on peace and prosperity reigning in the *polis*. But did the latter require that the relations between individuals in a *polis* were dictated by a just frame of mind, a frame of mind thought to constitute, in part, personal excellence? Or could social peace and prosperity be thought of as merely a matter of hitting upon the right sort of social and political arrangements? On the one hand we have the total pervasiveness of the *polis* in the life of its citizens. On the other, we have a conception of excellence that is fiercely competitive, unqualifiedly stressing doing well for oneself and for one's friends and dependants in the eyes of one's peers—a conception which tends to relegate questions of social cohesion to extra-personal factors or forces. Clearly, we have here all the ingredients for dramatic conflict and tension.

What is particularly of note is that the ingredients themselves are such as to make impossible a clear separation of moral from political or social issues. The debate about democracy in Athens cannot be understood in merely political terms. For, even though democracy required that the citizens recognise justice as everyone's concern, that there is a justice *of* the *polis*, it did so by generating a bifurcation between such political justice as a natural self-regulating social process, and the justice of wealth—the justice which governs the fortunes and successes of individuals. This bifurcation, deeply evident already in Solon's thought, left it as an unfathomable mystery what it was that regulated the processes whereby wealth, power and privilege were distributed among citizens.[46] As Vlastos points out, though Solon castigates (in Frag. 13) the injustice of money-grabbing individuals in language similar to that he used to describe the class-covetousness and *hybris* of the nobles (in Frag. 4), he is unable to show *how* the original act of injustice with respect to wealth leads to disaster, though he was able to show how political injustice leads to bondage, and this, in turn, to strife.[47] Solon is forced to admit that wealth got unjustly will get its deserts 'in the end'. Punishment descends biologically upon the sinner's posterity. Over the justice of acquisition or distribution Solon remains a traditionalist, having to fall back on the inscrutable *moira* which gives and withholds punishment in ways that transcend man's comprehension.[48]

In contrast, Solon is able to think of political justice 'as an intelligible order of reparation', freeing the conception of retributive justice from ideas of religious pollution and purification, and showing how justice for crimes committed within the state are the concern of all. He did this by arguing that (a) 'a direct injury to any member of the *polis* is indirectly, but not less surely, an injury to every member of the *polis*; for though the initial injustice affects only one or a few, the eventual effects on the common well-being imperil everyone's welfare; hence, everybody's wrong is everybody's business', and (b) that the freedom of the *polis* cannot survive the bondage of anyone within it.[49] He is able to argue the latter point on the basis of history. Just as the subjection of the whole *polis* to a tyrant is due to its being divided within, so the enslavement of the poor peasants robs the whole *polis* of its freedom. The poor peasants had enough power to make *stasis* even though they were oppressed by the rich landlords. Therefore, '[Freedom] must either be enjoyed in common, or else it would be lost in common. The *polis* is one, and its freedom is indivisible'.[50]

To the extent that this bifurcation between retributive and distributive justice remained embedded in the way justice was viewed in the democracy, to that extent a tension would persist in the reconciliation of political action with the ethical ideals of personal excellence. Democracy had certainly curbed the political supremacy of the aristocrats; it had not introduced any effective means for limiting the desire to excel among its citizens. Indeed, it could be argued that by sloughing off political from social and economic justice, Solon was adding his own contribution to the weakening of the traditional religious restraints in terms of *hybris*—the stepping beyond one's appointed 'share' or lot in the scheme of things—which, however shakily, had served as the only curb on the ambition of individuals. Democracy had not replaced these curbs with any new powerful moral precepts.[51] This not only left unsolved the problem of what motivates people to respect justice; it exacerbated the moral issue by creating the impression that a political solution to the problem of retributive justice was all that was required for peaceful existence within the *polis*, a belief still prevalent today in some circles. As a consequence, the idea that (political) justice was a prerequisite of social peace was a departure from another and very ancient strand in the Greek conception of social harmony: that justice was something generated by the forces of social ordinance. In Greek mythology *Dikē* (Justice) was the daughter of *Themis*, the power of the social imperative which even the Olympians needed to bring them into assembly.[52]

In dealing with Plato's examination of justice we are thus confronted with a conception in which a number of disparate layers of meaning had accumulated; layers which corresponded to different stages in the evolution of Greek society, and, more especially, to different unconscious representations of social structure and of man's relation to nature. We cannot, of course, encompass in this short work the complex ways in which the shift from a primitive tribal formation to a *polis*-like structure brought in its train changes of perspective on the nature of justice and its relation to the forces of social cohesion. As Jane Harrison suggested some time ago, the worlds of religion, of social structure, and of morality are complexly interwoven in the collective representations of Greek culture.[53] For our purposes we need to note the following point. Underlying the Solonian conception of political justice is the effort to isolate a concept of social causality which though parallel to natural causality is distinct from it. Thus, he says (Frag. 12), 'The sea is stirred by the winds; if someone does not move it, it is the justest of all things.' For Solon the change of the sea is not arbitrary. 'Disturbance is not the natural ("just") state of the sea, if it gets into this condition there must have been a disturbing cause'.[54] Similarly with the *polis*. If it is racked by *stasis*, it is the outcome of unjust acts. As he puts it,

> Men are tempted to enrich themselves by unjust acts; they snatch and steal from one another without sparing sacred or public property and without safeguarding themselves against the dread foundations of justice, who takes silent note of what is happening, and what was before, and what comes in time to exact vengeance without fail. Then at last the whole *polis* is visited with an incurable sickness and soon falls into servitude, which awakens wars and internecine conflict, so that many perish in the flower of youth.
>
> (Frag. 4,11–20)

Here we have a retention of the idea of the divine power of justice which, as in Homer and Hesiod, can mete out disaster. But while in the latter poets the disasters are natural, famine, plague, barrenness of land, and so on, Solon's injustice brings about a social disease, a disease which affects the community conceived of as a moral order.[55] It would seem, therefore, that *Dikē* in Solon's hands takes over the vengeful tasks of the ancient *Erinyes*, the Furies who punished transgressions against the *Moirai*, the appointed 'lot' or share of everyone in the scheme of things. But with an important corollary. *Dikē* does not only pay the transgressions of man against man in *social* coin—civil strife and loss of freedom. Because *Dikē* indicates 'the way of things', of the universe of all living things, to make it stand as guardian over the community's moral order has the effect of conceiving justice as the way, the *due* habit, of the *polis*. Disturb that and you get social disease, the way in which to disturb the natural, the 'just', ways of living organism leads to illness and death.

Yet, the effect of this recognition that the *polis* as a distinct entity has its specific kind of justice is to blur the differences between *Themis* and *Dikē*. For, the former stood for the fixed conventions, the common ways of human beings as sanctioned by the collective conscience and responsible for all the Greek held as civilised.[56] The latter, *Dikē*, when applied to human beings indicated a right or due habit. In Homer, for example, 'to lie soft' is the *dikē*, not merely the *habit*, but the *due* habit, of old men.[57] As Jane Harrison points out, 'The word *themis* has more of permission to do, human sanction shadowed always by *tabu*; *fas* is unthinkable without *nefas'*.[58]

But in Solon's hands *Dikē*, as justice, designates what stands guard over the ways of the *polis*. It indicates that the punishment of acts which threaten the peace and order of the *polis* is a right and a duty of every citizen. Does this mean that the survival of the *polis* as a social entity can no longer rely on the ordinances, the utterances of social consciousness, that people in a *polis* cannot live together through group-customs alone? If this is so, if the *themis* of the *polis* is not sufficient to ensure peace and harmony, what force will it be that shapes the identity and character of the *polis*? If, now that *themis* has been swallowed up in the *polis*, *dikē* regulates the affairs of men, what will be the gentle force which regulates the hearts and minds of the citizens to generate a just frame of mind?[59]

That the nature of justice should become an ethical problem was inherent in the very conception of political justice introduced by Solon to meet the crisis in the *polis*. By weakening the magico-religious conception of justice which, in the new economic circumstances, was failing to curb the hunger of the nobles for wealth and power, he made possible a conception of it as something for which every citizen was responsible. But the very factors which rendered his innovation ultimately successful and acceptable also created an empty space, previously occupied by religious ideas, as to what the moral criteria of justice were. What could make it a moral ideal for individuals and city-states, as distinct from a set of norms whose observance was in the interest of every citizen?

Solon's own suggestion that justice punishes violations of *metron*, transgressions of 'due measure', of moderation, of proper limits to acquisitiveness, and so on, is more successful as an ideological reflection of the socio-economic changes of the latter part of the seventh century, and of the sixth, than as a solution to a moral problem. Clearly, the replacement of the Furies by *Dikē* meant a shift of attention from what falls to the lot of a person in accordance with his place in the natural scheme of things, to the idea of a limitation imposed on individual activity within a community because of the social implications of such activity. But to say that justice stands over the new order, the community as a moral order, in the way the Furies stood guard over the old order, the community as a natural order, is to say not only that the citizens should control justice in the *polis*, but also that they possess the *moral* knowledge to determine what it consists in. A far-reaching thought which, in the absence of any indication as to how conflicting interests and desires will permit the achievement of such knowledge, makes Solon's .

appeals to the observance of *metron* an ideological tool in the hands of those who wish to maintain the status quo in the distribution of power and wealth in the *polis*.

As we saw earlier, Solon remained a traditionalist on the subject of distributive justice, though he sensed that his new ideas about political justice could not stop at retribution. His idea was in essence both new and general: that not only in nature, but also in the social order, there might be a right limit to productive and personal relations, knowledge of which would maintain the community in harmony and cohesion. 'How hard it is', he says, 'to perceive the hidden measure of intelligence which alone holds the limits of things' (Frag. 16). Yet, that it *must* be perceived was a logical consequence of Solon's new thought enshrined in his social reforms. It is the question of how such perception is to be achieved which, among other things, Plato addresses to Athenian democracy. It is as if he asked, 'if justice is to be the business of every citizen in the *polis*, by virtue of what social and educational instrumentalities will the *polis* ensure that its citizens identify correctly what it is?' With this question we stand at the threshold of the *Republic*. Socrates' emphasis, in Book I, on knowledge and skill in connection with justice echoes Solon's worry which, the political developments in Athens notwithstanding, had not been squarely faced. In Socrates' uncompromising commitment to, and desire for, wisdom, Plato saw a new social role for the philosopher: to stake a claim on behalf of reflective reason as being the only appropriate and authoritative agency one could entrust with the determination of justice.[60] But since justice concerns how social and political power is shaped in a community, the philosopher as representative of reflective reason becomes inevitably enmeshed in the political process. The empty space left by the relative demise of the mythico-religious idea of *Dikē* as a super-human force, which had been created partly by the emergence of the new idea of a *polis*-justice, is now to be filled by the power of Reason (that is, by the rule of the philosopher). But while the earlier idea made justice a power external to and, possibly, beyond human comprehension, the new, philosophic, conception of it locates it in the very heart of the human capacity to apprehend intelligible order. Justice becomes *internal* to the power of Reason to grasp such order. What makes justice an unqualified good thing, and how it benefits its possessor, cannot be understood except as an aspect of the proper exercise of human intelligence to control life. From Socrates onwards the perfection of the intellect becomes an essential component of moral and political perfectibility. The suggestion I explore in the following chapters is that the Socratic insistence on an 'internalist' conception of justice is made both intelligible and plausible if we see it as a strategy of how to respond to the moral impact of the socio-cultural factors sketchily outlined above. At the end of this study I take up the question of whether this insistence contains any valuable insights relevant to our contemporary situation.

Part One
Dramatic Characterisation

2

Old Recipes about Justice

Nothing in Book I of the *Republic* quite prepares the reader for the large-scale and ambitious work into which it develops from Book II on. In a manner typical of the 'Socratic' dialogues, the book opens in a quiet, unassuming way: Socrates tells of a conversation he had with a number of people at the house of the rich merchant Cephalus.[1] Returning to Athens from the port of Piraeus, where they had been attending a religious festival, Socrates and Glaucon are intercepted by Cephalus' son, Polemarchus, who playfully 'forces' them to come to his father's house. A large company is assembled there. Socrates asks the old man what advice he has to give to the youth now that he has reached the vantage point of old age.

The simplicity and the civilised atmosphere of these opening pages conceals a good deal of irony on Plato's part. Cephalus is the head of a family of 'resident aliens'. They are not Athenian citizens, and the old man's considerable fortune was accumulated from trade and manufacture. Only a few years after this conversation with Socrates is supposed to have taken place, Athens fell to Sparta. The family fortune was seized and Polemarchus put to death.[2] To Plato's contemporaries, well acquainted with these events, the peaceful mood of the conversation would be in bitter contrast to the seething unrest that had followed the Peloponnesian War. The traces of that war were probably still being felt at the time Plato was writing. Though written a considerable time after that war, the scene of the *Republic* is set well before it.[3] But it is not merely this contrast in mood that would have struck Plato's readers; they would also have been dismayed by the complacency of father and son in their choice of some codes of conduct as recipes for a good and flourishing life. People acquainted with the cruel reversals of fortune of the disastrous war were not likely to welcome with equanimity Cephalus' simplistic reliance on wealth as a condition which enables the good person to lead a life of justice. Nor were people who had seen how utterly contingent the foundations upon which social relationships and alliances were revealed to be in the shifting attitudes of a city in war likely to be impressed by Polemarchus' dogged adherence to the view that justice consists in doing good to friends and harm to enemies.

Advocating honesty, fair-dealing, the discharge of debts and obligations, as a recipe for living well in a community may appeal to those who are materially prosperous and enjoy stable relationships. But what considerations could the advocates of these simple precepts use to persuade those who had lost material prosperity and social stability? Would the advocates themselves have stuck to their codes of conduct under adverse conditions? And if they did, would their *reasons* be good? Plato's purpose, I suspect, is to show that conventional adherence to codes of conduct is fundamentally non-reflective about what makes a life lived according to these codes unqualifiedly good and fine. It is not so much the simplistic and unsophisticated nature of how Cephalus and Polemarchus think that is at fault. They are not, after all, philosophers. This would not be in itself a ground for complaint against them if they lived and acted well. Unless, of course, being unreflective about the goodness of one's life is *itself* a bad thing; or, at least, something that diminishes in important respects the excellence of that life. Underlying the moral complacency Plato builds into his characterisation of Cephalus and Polemarchus there is a determined effort to show that what matters most with them is not the inadequacy of their view of justice; the whole discourse in terms of which they understood the good and moral life needed to be replaced by one in which the value of reflection was given a supreme and explicit place.

Commentators disagree about whether Plato's portraits of Cephalus and Polemarchus are sympathetic. Certainly, they lack the rudeness and arrogance of Thrasymachus, who later bursts into the discussion. But some have felt that there are enough malicious touches in the way even old Cephalus is presented to suggest that Plato means his readers to grasp the enormous moral bankruptcy contained in the simple attitudes to justice typified by Cephalus and Polemarchus.[4] However, exposing the complacency with which certain moral views are held is only of value if the complacency is still prevalent and the view still likely to elicit agreement. Would this have been the case with Plato's contemporaries? Though there may well have been some people at the time Plato is writing who thought and felt like Cephalus and Polemarchus, it is not likely that Plato is writing for them. Whose attention, then, is Plato attempting to capture, and what purpose is served by the choice of the particular characters that comprise the discussion in Book I? Assuming that the book is an introduction to what, in fact, turns out to be a radically novel approach not only to the moral, but to the social, political and psychological implications of justice, one would expect a specific strategy to inspire the structure of Book I of the *Republic*. But what is it? The views put forward by the three characters are shown by Socrates to involve inadequate conceptions of justice, and, though we may be less than convinced by some of Socrates' arguments, we cannot fail to be struck by how narrow and simplistic the views are—and how incompetent philosophically their adherents are in defending them. Plato's readers would have been aware of more sophisticated views about justice such as those of Protagoras, so brilliantly articulated by Plato in the dialogue of that name.[5] One also senses a sharp shift in level of sophistication when the two brothers, Glaucon and Adeimantus, re-present Thrasymachus' challenge to Socrates in Book II of the *Republic*.[6]

Philosophers are likely to be impatient with such questions of literary analysis. They are interested in Socrates' *arguments*, whether they show certain beliefs and their justification to be inadequate. The rest, it may be felt, belongs to the history of thought or culture. The danger with this attitude is that, by failing to appreciate the nature of Plato's targets, we misconstrue the force and plausibility of what Socrates is trying to do. In particular, exclusive attention to the validity of arguments may make us insensitive to the possibility that the major function of *Republic*, Book I, is to prepare the ground for a new and different discourse about justice. To assess how effectively or convincingly this is done, we need to concentrate not so much on the formal validity of Socrates' arguments but on the suggestive richness and ambiguity of the way concepts are employed in the premises. It is there that the cultural and intellectual space is created for Socrates' novel way of discoursing about morals. Many have found the discussion in Book I of the *Republic* unsatisfactory and, philosophically, a bit of a 'mess'.[7] But, as we shall see, this is partly due to their looking upon its arguments as attempts to knock out certain views of justice, rather than as a systematic replacement of one sort of discourse by another. At the end of Book I Socrates confesses his dissatisfaction with the way the discussion has proceeded. But, even so, certain key ideas about how to think of the relation between justice and human well-being have been introduced—ideas which are elaborated and given theoretical justification later in the *Republic*.[8]

Naïve simplicity, complacency, shallowness, aggressive cynicism—these are the features Plato weaves, successively, into his presentation of Socrates' three interlocutors. What lifts the standard of the discussion is Socrates' persistent effort, not merely to bring out the difficulties in the views put forward, but to search for intellectually adequate ways of thinking about justice; ways which can be dialectically extracted from what his interlocutors believe. Leaving aside for the moment (cf., below, Chapter 5) the aims of Socrates' method of question-ing— the *elenchos*—let us note briefly some of the dramatic indications embed-ded in the 'material' he has to deal with. As was noted in the previous chapter, the Greeks had some difficulty in accommodating justice into their idea of the excellent person, the *agathos*. Throughout Book I, Socrates clings with single-minded tenacity to the notion that justice is a virtue—a 'power' or capacity within people or communites which enables them to lead good and flourishing lives. By contrast, none of the ways the other three characters think of justice permits them to speak of it as such an enabling quality. Cephalus, while recognising that justice is an attribute of the good person, sees it as the law-abiding conduct which is the fortunate outcome of an inner disposition together with sufficient material prosperity. Polemarchus believes that it consists in meting out 'fair' treatment to others in the context of various social relationships, and that it is a good and proper thing to do this. As emerges from the discussion with Thrasymachus, neither of these views can meet the challenge of the claim that to act justly is to play into the hands of those who are politically powerful, of those who are capable of laying down what is 'right' for the weaker to do. According to Thrasymachus it is not justice which enables people to lead beneficial and flourishing lives; in being just they merely promote the advantage of the powerful. It is the latter's 'grand injustice', their rejection of the motive to act justly, which enables them to lead excellent and flourishing lives. Justice is not an excellence, a 'virtue', at all—it keeps people in a dependent position and is a mark of servility. It is left to Socrates to try and rescue from Thrasymachus' onslaught the conviction that justice is a central feature of human excellence. Cephalus and Polemarchus share that conviction but their way of thinking about justice does not help them to justify or explain it. Socrates' new discourse hopes to remedy this deficiency.

To make the need for this new discourse felt, Plato must not only show certain views to be inadequate; he must also bring out how they are based on mistaken conceptions of excellence. Plato hits upon an ingenious dramatic device to achieve this—one which distances his readers from contemporary ideological rhetoric and aims to rouse political consciousness to philosophical reflection. The *Republic* is, after all, the first thorough attempt by a philosopher in the West to enter the field of political theory.[9] Plato makes Socrates' interlocutors non-citizens, and non-Athenians. As 'resident aliens' they cannot have been presumed to have had the sort of concern an Athenian citizen would display towards the affairs of his *polis*. Furthermore, they would engage in the sort of activities (money-making, armaments manufacture, speech-writing and the teaching of rhetoric) which no Athenian citizen of good family would consider as a worthy pursuit.[10] It is no accident that Book I concentrates almost exclusively on the value of justice in the lives of individuals without once raising the question of what constitutes the justice *of* institutions or political arrangements. Thrasymachus does refer to the variety of conduct different constitutions lay down as 'just', but he does not consider whether these constitutions themselves display just arrangements. Neither Plato, nor his contemporaries, were likely to forget how much the notion of justice was, and continued to be, part of the rhetoric of the ideological conflict between oligarchs and democrats.[11] Nevertheless, it is only when Socrates' discourse becomes an Athenian 'family affair'—the brothers Glaucon and Adeimantus, who become the main interlocutors in the rest of the *Republic*, are Plato's half-brothers—that the political dimension comes to the fore. But by that time the need for a new way of discoursing about justice has been introduced.

Plato's dramatic device in Book I enables him to achieve two important effects: to isolate questions about the nature of justice, considered as a moral quality, from the conventional terms in which citizens of a *polis* praised the just conduct they expected from their fellows; and to reverse the tendency among his contemporaries to subordinate justice, and the 'virtues' of a citizen generally, to the processes of political rule. In doing so, Plato is indirectly identifying two sources of resistance to Socrates' new way of thinking about human excellence. One is the conceptual inability to articulate what makes the possessor of a moral quality a good and excellent person, independently of how the conduct of that person affects, or is regarded by, others. This corresponds to the question: 'how does a person's justice benefit, *by itself*, its possessor?'. The other source of resistance to Socrates' new ways is also socio-cultural, but it has a more political dimension. The excellences of a person or a *polis* are thought to be tied to their capacity to achieve beneficial and excellent things. To do this a person, or a *polis* through its political leadership, must have the power to come out on top in a competition for supremacy. If justice forms part of such excellence, then one should be able to point out in the conduct of the just how their justice is a source of such power. But things do not look this way. The motives required for achieving power seem antithetical to just motives. The latter appear to be part of the mechanism for achieving self-control and self-limitation, not rule and supremacy over others. How, then, can justice be thought of as a politically enabling power? Certainly, no one really takes it to be that, even though the ideology of conflicting political recipes lays rhetorical stress on its importance. But this only reflects a realisation on the part of those seeking power that a belief in the value of justice is functionally necessary as a tool of social control. They do not think of it as a source of excellence.

The fact that Socrates' interlocutors are foreigners and non-citizens helps Plato construct a plausible setting in which he can expose to philosophical scrutiny the attitudes and perceptions that shape the above resistances. The setting is plausible because, being foreigners and non-citizens, the interlocutors can say things and express attitudes which are free from the protective covering that a citizen's supposed total involvement with his *polis* and its political institutions imposes. A 'resident alien' like Cephalus or Polemarchus can be forgiven the crudity and simplicity of their view of justice, since their regard for it is 'innocent' of their seeking the honour (*timē*) the citizens accord to their equals for behaving justly. Being non-citizens, Cephalus' and Polemarchus' approval of honest, law-abiding behaviour, or of 'fair-dealing', need not be seen as aimed at public honour and reputation. It can simply be an expression of an attitude they hold as persons, independently of their social status. A citizen, however, cannot speak about justice without at least appearing to give cognizance to the fact that it is something properly 'owed' by a citizen to his *polis*, without recognising it as a *civic* 'virtue'. A resident alien does not have to see it this way. He thus becomes an apt representation of how one may think about justice in abstraction from the political context.

Moreover, a non-Athenian can engage in activities which are not quite proper for an Athenian to make the core of his life-style. Making a living through commerce or manufacture, or by writing speeches for a fee for litigants and political hopefuls, may provide a perspective on what 'doing well' means that is not affected by notions of what is thought of as 'fine' in the political arena. An 'outsider' is, plausibly, 'permitted' to view issues about justice and excellence in terms of considerations that altogether prescind from values tied to political success. The citizen cannot do this without appearing shameless. He cannot afford to be seen to talk about justice and excellence in ways which neglect what counts as social success in the super-critical eyes of his fellow citizens. To do so would give the impression that he did not care for the things his *polis* stood for, and for the benefits he obtained by virtue of belonging to it.[12] A non-citizen is not thus constrained in his outlook. He is, therefore, an apt symbol for ways of talking about justice and excellence that prescind from the standard assumptions that govern the way a citizen should talk about these topics. But an 'outsider' can also supply a measure of 'objectivity' about the motivations which govern the practices of those entitled to engage in political activity—motivations shorn of the ideological appeals to what is 'just', 'right', 'advantageous', 'beneficial', and so on, which the politically ambitious cannot altogether dispense with. An outsider does not need such appeals. He can thus 'voice' unashamedly the cynical considerations at play in the drive to power; considerations which, though unlikely to be the sole motivating factors in politically ambitious citizens, nevertheless form an inevitable aspect of political conduct in actual city-states.

In the hands of a literary artist of Plato's calibre this simple dramatic device becomes a weapon of cultural criticism. For those who are willing to look, Plato holds up a mirror in which his contemporary Athenians can see themselves: how their attitudes to justice, and their beliefs about power and excellence, appear when stripped of the protective blinkers their customs and conventions provide. As we shall see, in this and the next two chapters, the effect is at once stunning and depressing: the reader is overwhelmed by a sense of moral and intellectual bankruptcy, barely relieved by the promise of illumination provided by the strange ways of Socrates' relentless discourse.

CEPHALUS

Viewed as an element in Plato's philosophic diagnosis of Athenian culture, the portrait of Cephalus is neither exclusively sympathetic, nor merely aimed at exposing the limitations of moral complacency.[13] Cephalus is certainly limited and somewhat self-satisfied with his conduct in life. But is not Plato using the moral complacency of the old man to draw attention to a deep resistance towards reflective awareness embedded in the very life of law-abidingness? If at the end of the exchange with Cephalus it emerges that his idea of the life of justice is limited, the reasons for this are subtly linked earlier to the limitations of how the old man assesses the factors which enable a person to keep to the straight and narrow path. Possessing the right disposition, and equipped with adequate wealth, a person can satisfy the requirements of a just and good life. This is all that his life experiences have shown Cephalus. But will reflection yield the same conclusion? Suppose Cephalus was lucky in possessing a quiet, even, temperament, and in inheriting wealth. Can the capacity to lead a just life be merely an outcome of such luck? And if we regarded the ability of a person to be just as subject to fortune in this way, what sort of value would we attribute to justice itself?

Cephalus is not a reflective person. Though he allows a respect for thought and discussion, he mislocates the worth of philosophical investigation. Rather patronisingly he suggests that the attraction of its pleasures increases as the capacity for bodily pleasures abates with old age (328d 2–4). Philosophy (that is, Socrates) can come to us now that we are old and we have escaped the pressing demands of youthful passion ('the savage and fierce master'—329c 3–4). The implication is that though philosophising has its place in the scheme of things it is not a life-long and pervasive concern. Cephalus, quite unlike Socrates, is not a man for whom 'the unexamined life is not worth living'.[14] Socrates' response to Cephalus is important here. He does not confront directly the old man's implicit attitude to philosophy; rather, he observes that the value of talking to old men is that they may teach us something about the life they have traversed. They may be able to tell us their estimate of the benefits of old age (328c).

Is old age a source of wisdom? Is the man who has lived a life free from iniquity and injustice enabled by his advancing years to give an account of what made that life worth living? There is a parallel question concerning the longevity of traditional ideas about the decent life. Is the antiquity of such ideas a guarantee of moral wisdom? Can the ancient collective experience encapsulated in the governing precepts of a culture provide it with an account of its own worth? Plato subtly exploits Cephalus' musings about old age to suggest that the answer to the latter question may be negative. The calm wisdom which enables Cephalus to see his advanced years as a beneficial condition, as a condition free from the distorting demands and stresses of the passions of youth, need not come with old age. To most men, as Cephalus recognises, old age is a source of misery and resentment. Only those 'who have order and peace within themselves' can accept old age with equanimity (329d 4–6). It turns out, then, that neither youth nor old age are conditions which enable people to perceive the true worth of how they live; it is character and a right disposition. As with individuals so, perhaps, with a culture. The ideas in terms of which a culture assesses its own worth owe their soundness not to their venerable antiquity, but to the fact that forces within the culture itself generate the correct moral dispositions and thoughts at all stages of its development. But what precisely is the connection between the soundness of ideas and the social factors which generate and sustain these ideas?

Could Cephalus be wrong in thinking that right disposition is responsible for the correct perception of what makes a life good? Suppose that material success and possessions compensate for the limitations of old age and render it palatable. Analogously, it may be that what leads people to accept the limitations and sacrifices imposed by traditional moral demands is not the quality of the culture to which those demands contribute but the plain fact that the society happens to be blessed with good fortune and that they benefit from belonging to it. If this is so, the real source of people's well-being will be external to the moral worth of the precepts which guide their behaviour. Take the consolations of wealth away and see whether right character ensures the same peaceful acceptance of old age. Analogously, the belief that it is the moral dispositions generated within a culture that are responsible for the sound assessment of what is excellent about life in that culture needs rational justification. The mere conviction—exemplified by Cephalus—that it is character which helps people understand the benefits of old age is not sufficient. It may be that they are under an illusion. Acceptance of old age may be due to material success, not to the possession of right character. Similar illusions may govern people's perception of what makes their own culture good and acceptable.

Socrates' probing of Cephalus' attitude to his own wealth (329e 1–5) is thus significant. Upon the latter's response to this probing will depend whether Cephalus sees good character as a necessary condition for *understanding* the goodness of an action or condition. Perhaps Cephalus thinks that character in conjunction with good fortune and wealth, are necessary conditions which are jointly sufficient for behaving decently. If, as it emerges (330a 3–6), Cephalus believes that the achievement of inner peace and harmony is the result of a combination of good disposition and wealth, a crucial philosophic question is left unanswered. Are the morally good those who (let us agree) merely act in accordance with and accept the norms and actions prescribed in their culture as proper and fitting? Or, are they those who understand the goodness of these norms and actions? Only if the latter is the case will the goodness of the 'right' disposition be part of moral intelligence. For if we think of character as responsible for a good and 'happy' life the way wealth and good fortune may be, we will be clear neither about the moral differences between character and fortune, nor about the morally correct assessment of their relation to each other. Plato is, perhaps, implicitly criticising here the way Greeks traditionally estimated the relative value of character and good fortune. But his criticism is not directed at character being thought of *instrumentally*; he himself saw character, the proper ordering of the elements of the soul and of society, as the correct means to, and a safeguard of, the joys and happiness afforded by justice as he understood it.[15] Rather, he is signalling an insensitivity in traditional thinking. The tradition is blind to a possible distinction in the ways one thinks of factors which favour, or even generate, good conduct in an individual or in a city-state. One can think of them as patterns of habit and disposition fashioned in accordance with certain norms and goals, or one can think of them as part of the capacity in individuals and states to understand what makes them and their goals good. Cephalus talks of right disposition and good fortune as equally effective in producing just behaviour. He is not over-bothered about what generates moral understanding.

As we saw in the previous chapter, the effect of Solon's dichotomy between 'political' justice and the justice pertaining to the attitude of individuals towards material possessions gave rise to, but did not rationally justify, a distinction between the socially intelligible aspects of just conduct and those that are not so. But though Solon can recommend his 'political' justice as beneficial to those who observe it because it averts civil strife, it is not clear whether 'political' justice is anything more than a 'recipe' for achieving the social benefit in question. There is nothing in Solon's recommendation which could explain to those who accepted it that the *structure* of political justice is something good in itself, apart from having the effect of avoiding social conflict. Missing from the Solonian picture are the factors which make justice morally desirable as distinct from its being socially necessary. For, if the social benefits of 'political' justice can be obtained in other ways, these ways will be as good as justice; there will be, thus, no moral requirement to be just derivable from the nature of 'political' justice itself. The moral requirement to be just, like the sanctions governing transgressions of 'measure' (*metron*) in matters of human greed and ambition, will be divine and lie outside human understanding. Socrates' questioning of Cephalus about how he thinks of character and wealth in relation to the life 'well-lived' brings to the surface serious inadequacies in traditional ways of thinking about what can intelligibly be seen as the source of a moral outlook. The question is not what causes conduct which one may reasonably approve or disapprove; rather, the problem is to identify what gives a person, or a society, the power to fashion a distinctively ethical understanding.

However decent Cephalus' life may have been, the ideas in terms of which he apprehends its goodness do not allow him even to sense the problem just stated. His moderate attitude towards wealth ('a mean between his grandfather and father with respect to acquiring wealth') betrays, as Socrates says, a commendable lack of the unseemly attitude which leads those who do not inherit but make their money to value it as their creation—'the way poets love their poems and fathers their children' (330b,c). Cephalus appreciates wealth for its uses. Though he has made money he does not regard himself as a money-maker, a person for whom the activity has become a social role, and who consequently can expect to be recognised and honoured as such in the *polis*. Is Plato ironic here? After all, as a 'resident alien' Cephalus' role, and that of his family, in Athenian society would have been pretty much tied to commercial concerns—whence, then, comes his 'moderation' towards money? The fact that he is content to maintain the family fortune between the much greater fortune his grandfather left to his father and the reduced wealth Cephalus had inherited from the latter, does not by itself show that Cephalus holds this attitude to wealth because he understands what is good about moderation. If he did, he would, perhaps, have been able to answer Socrates' next, almost abrupt question: what is the greatest good which the acquisition of great wealth enables a person to enjoy (330d 2–3)?[16] The implication of the question at this point ought to be clear. If Cephalus understands why and how his life is a good one he should be able to justify his estimation of the ways wealth and character contribute to the goodness of a life. Furthermore, one would expect his justification to show what particular aspects of that goodness were promoted by the acquisition of wealth or, indeed, by the possession of the right character. Plato is pressing hard the question whether traditional moral precepts of moderation can deliver any morally significant insights about what makes the precepts rational and intelligible.

Cephalus' last speech (330d 4–331b 7), before he departs to continue his life of observing socio-religious duties, is a thoroughly disappointing response to Socrates' question. Money is most useful, Cephalus considers, to the person who believes that one can face death and the after-life without fear only if one is guiltless of even unwilling deceit or falsehood, and only if one has repaid all debts—of sacrifice to gods and of money to men. Rather sentimentally, Cephalus quotes Pindar's line that for him who has lived a pious life and a life free of injustice 'kindly hope the nurse of old age' will be with them. But they will need sufficient wealth to qualify for a visit from that nurse! Though money will only yield that benefit to 'the peaceable and orderly' person (331a 11–331b 1), it is unclear whether such a person would shun injustice in the face of want. And if the disorderly person, afraid in old age of punishment in Hades for his injustice, had failed to observe this beneficial use of wealth in his life, Cephalus does not explain how such persons come to act in the way they do. From where does their disorderly character come? After all, the relevant moral injunctions and cautions would have surrounded such people from birth. If they disregard justice and misuse an important means to it, what good do they fail to see about a just and pious life that the others, the upright, succeed in grasping? Cephalus' speech avoids this central question. He leads what he considers to be an ethical life, and he assigns value to various elements he believes essential to it. But he does not understand why it is good in itself. The thought of having led such a life is a comfort when old age and death approach. But is this motivation the right sort of motivation? And will it be strong enough to ensure a life-long commitment to justice, one which would operate even when death and old age were dim possibilities in the distant future? Perhaps Cephalus' life has been a good and a just one; but it has left him singularly unable to explain its strengths and merits. No life which cannot explain itself in this way, Socrates will hint next, can be a genuinely good and just life.

We shall consider this somewhat astonishing assumption later. As far as Plato's characterisation of Cephalus is concerned, the message is plain: traditional morality expects the good man to obey rules of justice towards other members of the community and rules of piety towards the gods. Though there are punishments for transgressors of these rules (even if it is left vague how inevitable these are and who dispenses them), the inclination in a good person to observe them comes from possessing a gentle and quiet character in conjunction with relative freedom from the burdens of ill-fortune. The mild character ensures the observance of *metron*, the shunning of acts which disregard human limitations, while the possession of sufficient wealth ensures that persons can pursue effectively what their character inclines them to do—to observe rules which bind men together in a community and which appease the gods.[17] This picture of the good life entirely fails to locate within it any *cognitive* capacity on the part of those who lead it to explain its worth. Cephalus' limitations are not simply those of a person locked in a narrow and tradition-bound perspective. For all we know, the behavioural *content* of such a perspective may be sound. What limits Cephalus morally, Plato suggests, is the fact that the perspective from which he views the law-abiding life as good has no room for the idea that one acts in certain ways because one understands and knows these ways to be conducive to something unqualifiedly good.

POLEMARCHUS

Cephalus is unable to explain why the disposition to obey the rules of justice and piety is one which exemplifies something unqualifiedly good. Plato has him retire from any further discussion in spite of his earlier enthusiasm for the pleasures of philosophic discourse. His life-long adherence to fulfilling obligations (to the gods in this case) places a higher value upon such observance than on philosophic reflection. And it does this at the very point at which the unqualified value of such adherence is put into question by Socrates. Plato is letting us know that followers of traditional morality are not basically very interested in theoretical inquiry. In this respect, of course, Cephalus is not much different from those who subscribe uncritically to traditional moral norms at any time or place. But Cephalus' departure from the scene may mark something much more specific than this. The confident acceptance of traditional values, at peace with itself and unperturbed by the events and changes that would threaten it, is no longer one Plato and his contemporaries can sustain. Plato's audience knows this. It is not implausible to view the succession of characters from Cephalus to Thrasymachus in Book I as a kind of review of the change of attitudes towards justice which Plato thought had gradually come to govern the behaviour of Athenian democracy during the war, and, especially, its tolerance of corrupt and unwise actions.[18]

Though speculative, this idea bears importantly on how we interpret Polemarchus' position and that of Thrasymachus after him. Commentators, dealing chiefly with the narrowly philosophical issues raised by Socrates' discussion with him, tend to lump Polemarchus too quickly with his father. It is thought that like him Polemarchus is morally complacent and represents 'the best common sense has to offer about justice, which, on Plato's view, is very little'.[19] This view of Polemarchus neglects some crucial differences between him and his father.[20] Cephalus does, indeed, hand over the argument to Polemarchus, and, as Socrates ironically suggests, it is only fitting that an heir should defend his inheritance (331d 6 –331e l). But from the fact that the son has this 'obligation' it does not follow, of course, that his defence will preserve the *spirit* of his father's views—any more than inheriting property and wealth means that you use them in the same way the person you inherited them from employed them.

Polemarchus is set the specific task of showing how the terms in which Cephalus understands justice—honesty and the repayment of debts to men and gods—signify something unqualifiedly good. If 'just' and 'justice' refer to such a good, then the behaviour Cephalus sees as constituting justice must exhibit this feature. If it does not, and the relevant acts produce sometimes good and sometimes bad things, this will imply that the things which it is just to do are sometimes unjust things. Polemarchus' initial response does, on the face of it, appear to meet this point. There is a formula about justice—an aphorism of the poet Simonides—which fits the bill: to render each what is owed (or due) is just (or is justice).[21] Polemarchus is prepared to grant Socrates that one and the same act may produce good or bad effects. But there is nothing wrong with this since the justice of the act depends on the description of the recipient of the act. Returning a borrowed weapon is the right thing to do when the lender is of sound mind, but the wrong thing to do if the lender is in a fit of madness. Why should this be a counter-example to Cephalus' conception of justice? If Simonides is right about justice, then we should *expect* justice to call for acts which bring about opposite effects on different kinds of 'recipients' of them. So long as an act fits the description 'rendering what is due' it is always good and just. But, this does not mean that different recipients of the act are affected in a uniform way. Depending on the type of person they are, the just action towards them will vary in character. As Polemarchus qualifies his position later (332a,b), if the recipient is a friend, what is 'owed' is a good; if the recipient is an enemy, a harm.

We are not, at present, dealing with the logic of Socrates' exchange with Polemarchus; only with Plato's presentation of Polemarchus. Clearly, Polemarchus has not taken in the point Socrates was pressing on Cephalus—are honesty and repayment of debts unqualifiedly good? Simonides could be right that 'rendering what is owed' is unqualifiedly good, but this does not make honesty and the repayment of debts of necessity exemplifications of what is 'owed'. Polemarchus has a tendency not to pay any heed to what others want to do if he feels in a strong position—witness the early banter between him, Socrates, and Glaucon (327c 7–14). The way he chooses to defend his father's position abandons an important aspect of it. Cephalus thought that being inclined to do the just and honest thing is a disposition of a mild and quiet temperament. In Cephalus' understanding of justice there is no thought of its being an attribute of the relation between people. If he thinks that honesty and fulfilling obligations is the essence of justice, he does so because he genuinely believes that being inclined to engage in such conduct is part of being a good person (an *agathos*). However, Polemarchus understands justice in a way which radically shifts the *locus* of justice: from being an attribute of a good person it becomes an attribute of relations between people.

It is difficult to determine whether Plato is incorporating in Polemarchus the shift in the conception of justice that was involved, as we saw earlier, in Solon's idea of a *polis*-justice. It may well be that with the development of democracy in Athens, and the socio-economic transformations that both preceded and accompanied it, the idea of justice as a social good had come to overshadow in importance the older idea of justice as a personal quality.[22] The two conceptions need not, or course, have been seen as antithetical. The just disposition is a fine thing when you have it; it ensures that your conduct will not give rise to strife and dissension between you and the people you have dealings with. But in a developed *polis* more is required if social and political unrest is to be avoided. The city expects that whatever the personal qualities of its citizens, each owes to the *polis* itself respect for the maintenance of justice. This will take the form of making sure that fair dealings between individuals or between sections of the community are maintained, and that one makes sure of this whether or not one is personally involved in a dispute or a conflict.[23] Thus, while for Cephalus honesty, the fulfilling of obligations, and the repayment of debts, primarily reflect a person's justice, for Polemarchus they are acts which are *instances* of a general principle of social regulation within a *polis*. Simonides' dictum, 'to each what is due or "owed", is just' serves nicely as an ideological bridge to facilitate the slide from Cephalus to Polemarchus. For the dictum may be taken in two ways: as a pithy summing up of the spirit which guides the good and just person; or, as a general formula or schema which sees justice as a function of human relationships.[24] Taken in the first sense, justice is a personal excellence, reflected not only in the treatment of others but also in how one uses one's wealth, intelligence, status, and so on. Taken in the second sense, justice is primarily a property of actions seen under the general rubric of distributing benefits and harms to others in the context of relationships within a group.

Plato makes sure to alert us to this ambivalence in the dictum. Socrates' questioning of Polemarchus (331e 5 – 332c 3) elicits from the latter the recognition that the way he understands Simonides' 'owed' (*ta opheilomena*) is best expressed in terms of a different concept, that of 'the appropriate' (*to prosēkon*). Simonides, according to Polemarchus (Socrates sums it up at 332c 1–3), meant to say that 'rendering to each what is appropriate (to him) is just', except that he called the appropriate the 'owed'. It is difficult not to suspect irony here. The two concepts are quite different, and it is clear at any rate that *Cephalus* both said and meant (331b 1–2) that the just man does not neglect what he owes to gods and men. Unfortunately he left unclear what is the source or ground of this obligation: does the good man behave in this manner because his relationship to gods and men is of the sort that makes it *appropriate* for him to do so—that this is how one ought to behave in such relationships—or does a person behave in this manner because, being just, he sees what is good about this behaviour? The difference between these two interpretations of 'owing' is that the first regards justice as a set of obligations imposed on a person by the relationships he or she finds himself or herself in, while, by contrast, the second regards justice as a quality which a person's character lends to conduct. The two interpretations give contrasting perceptions of the causal origins of justice: is it something generated by conforming to what counts as appropriate behaviour in the context of social relationships, or is it something a person brings to such relationships? Polemarchus' defence of his father converts obligations which could be thought of as demanded by justice into obligations imposed by what is deemed behaviour 'appropriate' to different types of relationship. This is to convert a moral demand into a social one. The effect of this transformation is to understand justice as a 'civic excellence'. It is the excellence of a type of conduct judged by what it renders the recipient of an act; it is not the excellence of a type of personality judged by what it enables the agent to do.

No doubt the relation between these two types of excellence is as much a difficult problem today as it was for Plato and his contemporaries. The idea of social, and, even, of economic justice, with its reference to what people (and, perhaps, even animals and other features of the environment) have a right to expect in the hands of governments and people, is at the centre of many contemporary debates. Is the good of social arrangements superior or more important than the excellence of character? How are these two 'goods' to be assessed from the moral point of view? These questions have sufficient overlap with elements in Polemarchus' view of justice to make Socrates' criticisms of it especially interesting. We shall look at them below when we examine the nature of Socrates' arguments. At present our concern is with what Plato means to incorporate in his characterisation of Polemarchus.

It was suggested above that Polemarchus' interpretation of Simonides'dictum views justice as a form of social appropriateness. But, clearly, Plato also intends his listeners to be, initially at least, impressed by the superiority of Polemarchus' account over that of his father's. Certainly, there is such a thing as a just disposition and there may be ways of telling whether anyone has it. But traditional Greek moral consciousness left extremely vague and obscure how reliable or invariant these ways were.[25] Is it not better to characterise the just disposition in terms of whether a person is inclined to act in conformity with what is expected of him or her in various relationships? This way just conduct can be given a specification derived from the nature of the relationship people are in. We can tell what is just for a person to do once we know that what is at issue is the 'appropriate' behaviour a friend, a brother, a father, a business partner, an ally, an enemy, *owes*. Unless we can specify what 'the just disposition' is a disposition to *do*, how can we characterise it intelligibly? Polemarchus' proposal gives a clear way of characterising the just disposition; it can be obtained from what the community agree is the appropriate way of behaving towards people who fall under different descriptions. The specific content of what is just to do in any given instance will be relative to the description under which the recipient is considered. Independently of such description, the disposition to be just would convey nothing of social relevance, of how people should live in a community. His father's remarks, Polemarchus feels, perhaps left this point unclear. Nevertheless, Cephalus' reference to honesty, fair-dealing and religious observances, may be treated as elliptical. Once we fill in the relevant descriptions of the recipients of such acts, the appropriateness of the conduct to the relationships involved will become evident.

It may come as a surprise to find Polemarchus claiming that justice consists in benefiting one's friends and harming one's enemies (332d 5–9). It suggests, as many have thought, that Polemarchus *defines* justice this way. Others believe that the definition of justice as the rendering of what is due (or appropriate) should be sharply separated from the other opinion Polemarchus attributes to Simonides, that it is just to render benefit to friends and harm to enemies.[26] It must be admitted that in his concluding remarks (335e 1–4) Socrates is careful to signal a possible separation of Simonides' dictum from its construal in terms of friendship and enmity.[27] But Socrates is there drawing a corollary from his argument to the effect that it cannot be the 'work' of justice to harm anyone. If that argument is correct, then whoever construed justice as harming enemies and benefiting friends could not have been a wise man. The attribution of such a view to any of the wise men must be resisted (335e 7–10). Nevertheless, the question remains why Polemarchus is made to hold that view in the *first* place—a view which Socrates disparagingly characterises as one coming from a wealthy autocrat who fancies himself in possession of great power (336a 1–8).

Plato is drawing the attention of his audience to the moral dangers implicit in Polemarchus' view of justice. That Plato thought there were such dangers we must conclude from the tenor of Socrates' remarks referred to in the previous paragraph. But what are these dangers, and why does Plato dramatise them in terms of the view that it is just to dispense benefit to friends and harm to enemies? The answer to these questions is more complex. Let us note first how Plato introduces reference to friends and enemies in the discussion. It first occurs (332a 9–10) when Socrates is establishing that by 'the owed' Polemarchus understands 'the appropriate' (332a 11–332c 3). Socrates had just ascertained that whatever Simonides meant by 'the owed' he could not mean that it is just to return what is owed, irrespective of whether it may lead to some evil (the case of returning borrowed weapons to someone out of his senses). Now, Socrates has in mind that anyone who is just cannot perform an act he knows, or justifiably believes, to be capable of producing something bad. The issue here is the character of the act itself—whether it is *aimed* at something good or bad. To be sure, in determining the likelihood of its producing something good we need to know, among other things, what holds true of the recipient of the action. But the morally relevant knowledge is not given by the *social category* in which the recipient is located. Thus, though a weapon is owed to X by Y because X is a 'lender' and Y a 'borrower', the justice of Y's act of returning the weapon (a 'rendering of what is due') to X cannot be morally decided merely on the grounds of what is 'appropriate' to dealings between 'lenders' and 'borrowers'. Acts in conformity to such 'appropriateness' may have bad aims. The point is important and the cases to which it may apply can be extremely controversial. Should one promote certain social policies on the ground that the 'recipients' of these policies claim a 'right' to them, or because they believe that they need what the policies recommend? Or should one's support for these policies be based on whether they exemplify some good? The former alternative does not rule out the possibility that those acting in accordance with it will effect something bad, or, even, that they have bad aims.

It is significant that Polemarchus' reference to owing friends benefit and no harm comes precisely at the point (332c 9–10) when Socrates has suggested that Simonides could not have meant by 'rendering what is due' acts which aim to bring about something bad. Of course not, says Polemarchus, otherwise

Simonides would not have thought that friends owe to friends only benefit and never harm (332a 9–10). Given Polemarchus' subsequent agreement that Simonides' 'rendering what is owed' is to be understood as 'rendering what is appropriate', his response to Socrates at this point commits him to this: what the recipient of a just act receives may be a good or a harm, but what makes the *act* good or bad (just or unjust) depends on the relationship the agent has to the 'patient'. Thus, as Socrates puts it (332a 11–b 3), a repayment whose receipt is harmful is not what is owed (that is, is not appropriate) if the repayer and the receiver are friends. Polemarchus has to agreee that if the relationship is one of enmity then the appropriate thing to render an enemy is some evil (332b 5–8). It follows that for Polemarchus the good thing about just conduct is that it effects what is appropriate in a relationship, irrespective of whether the content of what is appropriate is a good or an evil.

Why is Polemarchus narrowing appropriateness to friends and enemies? After all, his thesis about justice is quite general and can be read expansively to mean that justice renders not only benefits to friends, harms to enemies, and what one has received to lenders, but also what was promised to promisees, honest dealing to business partners, debts to creditors and so on.[28] This is certainly a plausible reading, even if it goes beyond the text. But the categories of 'friend' and 'enemy' are much more pervasive than the other categories. Polemarchus' view, as presented by Plato, may be that the relationships of friendship and enmity take precedence over more specific ones such as those between borrower and lender. Perhaps Polemarchus does not notice that he has committed himself to this view. He is under the impression that in order to cope with Socrates' case of returning borrowed weapons to a man gone mad he has to say that sometimes the justice of the act appropriate from borrower to lender is superseded by what is appropriate to do to a friend.[29] The trouble with this position is that it introduces a dangerous double-standard in the application of the very criterion of justice. For, if it is a *criterion* of justice to render what is appropriate to a type of relationship, then one cannot allow that in some cases the just thing is not to do what is appropriate to that relationship. If justice *also* depends on whether another person is a friend or an enemy, it renders quite uncertain what one can expect from the just person in any given case. The judgement whether someone acted justly will, ultimately, always depend on the agent's *decision* to treat the person he is dealing with as a friend or an enemy. It is utterly obscure, therefore, how extreme arbitrariness is to be avoided in determining whether a particular action is just or not.

In the character of Polemarchus we find Plato's acute diagnosis of the moral dangers that a 'political' or 'civic' understanding of justice can lead to in practice. It is all very well to think that the order, health and prosperity of the *polis* depends on the justice of its citizens. This is sound so long as we also think of that justice as somehow a manifestation of something objectively good in the people who are citizens, and in the relationships they have to each other. But if the 'justice' of the *polis* is simply conceived as behaviour in accordance with what is required by, or thought appropriate to, the relationships a citizen enters into, we will find that in practice personal associations, family ties, group loyalties and political allegiances will constantly and arbitrarily colour how people treat others. The idea of equal access by all citizens to the power afforded by participating in the process of instituting and administering laws does not by itself impose any moral constraints on how that power will in fact be wielded in the community.[30] The shifts in 'friendships' and 'enmities' in the *polis*—an unavoidable consequence of giving equal political voice to all sectional interests in the society—can turn the 'injustice' of yesterday's treatment of some people into the 'justice' of tomorrow's treatment of yet other people. In such a situation there will be no invariant content one can expect a just act to have.

This must have been common knowledge among Plato's contemporaries. Perhaps the fault was partly due to the failure of the Greeks to generate institutions for the administration of law that were genuinely independent of political and sectional interests. But whether justice in a broad sense can be safeguarded even in societies like modern Western democracies which do have such independent legal institutions is a moot point. Whatever the legal and constitutional restraints, the relations of power generated by the constant jostling of varied and antithetical interests and desires in a society will ensure that socially-orientated criteria of what is just are of their nature unstable, unreliable, and to a considerable degree arbitrary. Polemarchus' readiness to allow friendship and enmity to overrule the performance of acts appropriate to a given type of relationship not only suggests how Plato saw the manifestation of *polis*-justice among his contemporaries; it also reveals the fundamental weakness in the underlying conception, for, it is a conception which cannot bring out how and why justice means something unqualifiedly and permanently good.

In an important sense Polemarchus' attitude to justice, unlike his father's, does not recognise any quality inherent in justice. For, while Cephalus was prepared, however unclearly, to regard justice as a power which resides in a certain type of temperament, Polemarchus sees justice as a product of the human *will*, as the imposition on social behaviour of norms thought appropriate by society. There are two consequences of this view which undoubtedly Plato found deeply objectionable: it removes justice as a possible item of objective moral knowledge; and it fosters the frighteningly arrogant attitude—not even the Olympian gods were allowed to entertain it—that people's social 'experiments' can decide what justice is. The first consequence comes about because Polemarchus' view treats justice as acting in conformity with the social norms required for workable relations in a community. It does not recognise that justice may refer to a character of people or societies which has its own specific ways of working in people and in *poleis*—ways which are objectively discoverable independently of people's beliefs and 'decisions' about how to regulate their relations.[31] The second consequence of Polemarchus' view is well marked in Socrates' remark about who might be the author of the saying that it is just to help friends and harm enemies,

> I fancy that it was Periander, or Perdicas, or Xerxes, or Ismenias the Theban, or some other man of wealth and fancied power.
>
> (336a 1–7)

Plato's association of Polemarchus' understanding of justice with names of well-known tyrants marks the moral and conceptual distance which separates son from father. To think of justice as identical with the social power to dispense benefits and harms is to abandon its claim to be considered as a human excellence (*aretē*); it is to confuse its nature with the social or political locations within which it may be manifested. The seizure of political power by a tyrant leads him to think that his subjects will do his bidding out of adoration or fear. Is one's attitude to justice to be inspired by the same motives?

Scholarly opinion agrees that the rise of tyrants to power in Greece coincided with the economic growth of the city-state and the erosion of the hold of aristocratic families on political power. In Athens and elsewhere this was the prelude to the gradual establishment of democracy.[32] Is Plato associating this mistaken and arrogant conception of justice, as being a product of human decision, with the rise of tyrants? And is he hinting that just as tyranny was a political prelude to democracy, so this conception of justice was a moral prelude to the devaluation of justice in the democratic Athens of his day? It is difficult to answer these questions, but one thing is clear: the ways of achieving justice in the *polis* introduced by the tyrants gave rise to habits of thinking about it, of how to maintain it and of how to restore it, which were ultimately bound to overshadow its conception as a human excellence.[33]

3

Thrasymachus on Justice and Power: Some Problems of Interpretation

Philosophers and scholars have debated for long the nature and import of Thrasymachus' views.[1] More recent commentators have tended to concentrate on the propositional content of Thrasymachus' pronouncements, seeking to identify his doctrine by exhaustive elimination of various alternatives. This procedure can yield important insights, yet Guthrie is surely right to emphasise the danger of neglecting 'the dramatic situation and emotional tension between the speakers'. Whether he is also right in claiming that 'the driving-force behind Thrasymachus is passionate feeling rather than philosophical inquiry' remains to be seen.[2] The task of this chapter is to show that while there are difficulties in interpreting Thrasymachus' views consistently, Plato presents him as having a consistent and coherent *attitude* to justice. The rhetorical effect built into his speeches is that of rejecting the need to understand justice as an object of moral knowledge. Thrasymachus aims to cut off just conduct from the domain of the admirable, and does so by suggesting that the true nature of just conduct can only be grasped from the perspective of power. From this perspective one can see clearly why the conventional praise of justice is not an expression of genuine admiration. If Thrasymachus is right, to seek a moral understanding of justice is pointless and wrongheaded from the start: one does not have to explain why justice is an unqualified good given that those who praise it do not do so because they admire it in itself. The 'fact' which moral theory sets out to explain is not even a fact.

There are two important dramatic indications that this 'resistance' to a moral knowledge of justice is built into the characterisation of Thrasymachus. First, the emotion with which Plato marks his entry into the discussion (336b,ff.) is impatient indignation at the way Socrates and Polemarchus had been discussing justice. Secondly, Thrasymachus makes clear that his indignation is due to the conviction that Socrates' method of inquiry is wrongheaded. Socrates' pretence of ignorance, his asking questions, are but a sly technique to show off; a different approach is needed (337d 1-2). Thrasymachus believes Socrates is asking the wrong kind of questions about justice, and he forbids him the use of certain formulae when he demands that Socrates state 'clearly and precisely' what justice is. The forbidden formulae only lead to 'rubbish' (336d). Later, when Socrates persists in examining Thrasymachus' views in the usual way, the latter, though embarrassed by his defeat in argument, remains unconvinced and loses interest in the discussion (350 d−e; 351c,d; 352b; 353c). His final words to Socrates are sarcastic: 'well, this can be your holiday treat' (354a 10).[3]

What do these dramatic indications represent, and what is the basis of Thrasymachus' rejection of a certain mode of inquiry into the nature of justice? Unfortunately we do not get much help from the scanty information we possess about the real Thrasymachus of Chalcedon.[4] What we do learn is difficult to reconcile with Plato's portrait. Consequently, some scholars take this as evidence that Plato is 'manipulating' the character 'Thrasymachus' for his own philosophical purposes.[5] No doubt some degree of artistic manipulation is to be expected in Plato's handling of characters. But whether Plato 'detested' the real Thrasymachus, or whether his dislike is directed at what the character in the dialogue is meant to represent, are moot points.[6] Perhaps readers of Plato who knew Thrasymachus' *style* could derive their own conclusions about Plato's association of Thrasymachus with certain views, even though the views were not Thrasymachus'. What appears true of both the actual Thrasymachus and the character in the dialogue is a passionate interest in the question of justice.[7] In discussing Thrasymachus' speeches (from 336b to 343d) I shall assume that the beliefs and attitudes he expresses belong to what the character 'represents' rather than to the historical figure.

Thrasymachus is not said to be a Sophist, nor is his characterisation one Plato usually employs when presenting Sophists.[8] The latter are often made gentle fun of, but they are never portrayed as rude or uncouth. More importantly, Thrasymachus does not advance the sort of theoretical position one associates with Sophists; the linking of his views with the distinction between things that are 'by nature' (*physei*) and those that are 'by convention' (*nomō*) is not done by Thrasymachus but by Glaucon in Book II of the *Republic*. Nevertheless, this does not rule out the possibility that some ideas loosely associated with the Sophistic movement did form part of the background of Thrasymachus' attitude to justice. The full detail of the important and fascinating thought the Sophists had brought to bear on moral, political and social issues is beyond the scope of this study. In any case, it does not seem to have been part of that thought to urge that justice and other moral qualities were inextricably bound up with relations of power.[9] Thrasymachus does want to insist on this. It may be, of course, that Thrasymachus' views in the *Republic* represent a reaction to the cultural and political developments in Greece in the latter half of the fifth century BC, and that the theories of the Sophists were attempts to theorise the implications of these developments.[10] But it does not follow from this that Thrasymachus' view *is* such a theoretical response. People often promulgate opinions they think accord with vaguely understood theories without themselves having a theoretical interest in the matter. Thrasymachus' views may relate to Sophistic ideas only in this manner.

The socio-political developments in Greek city-states had occasioned Sophistic speculations about the nature and origin of social organisation and moral conduct. They may also have given rise to new expressions of *old* doubts about the way justice, and other 'co-operative' virtues, related to excellence. Thus, though the person of power and excellence (the *aristos* typified by the heroes in the Homeric poems) was expected to dispense justice among those inferior and dependent on him, it was not clear how much the *aristos* saw justice to be part of his own excellence.[11] But the development of the *polis* had highlighted, as we saw, the need for justice to regulate social relationships in society—the need to regard justice as required of a good citizen. The problem of how to relate the goodness of the citizen to the goodness of the person, a pressing issue as Adkins suggests, could easily be seen as a new version of an old moral problem: justice may be a requirement for life in the *polis*, but what reason does one have for thinking that it should be *admired*?[12] This applies especially to the powerful on whom the enforcement of justice in the *polis* depended, just as much as it did in the old tribal setting. The idea that justice enables individuals and communities to achieve certain ends does not by itself show these ends to be excellent, or to be part of what the powerful regard as belonging to the life of excellence.

The confrontation between Socrates and Thrasymachus, the emotional tension between them, is not primarily that which modern moral philosophers regard as the conflict between 'duty' and 'interest'. Essentially, it is a clash between two conceptions of the sources of political power.[13] Plato is well aware that behind the moral scepticism about whether justice is more beneficial to the agent than injustice lurks the suspicion that it is injustice, not justice, which makes people powerful. Paradoxically, Socrates and Thrasymachus agreee that in assessing the value of justice one cannot avoid considering whether it is an 'empowering' quality. It is because they disagree in the answers they each give to this question, and about what 'power' really is, that they disagree about justice.

Power, and relations of power, naturally introduce the political dimension of justice. This was noted by commentators a long time ago.[14] Others have talked of a contrast in Thrasymachus' discussion between the 'ideal' and the 'actual', between 'is' and 'ought', between 'fact' and 'prescription', and so on.[15] It is dubious whether such contrasts would, or could, have been in Plato's mind. Though they are important if Thrasymachus is proposing a *theory* of justice from which he obtains an evaluation of it, it does not seem that Plato intends to present Thrasymachus as primarily a theorist. No doubt it is possible to theorise what

Thrasymachus says, but this does not mean that he thinks of himself as doing so, or that Plato intends us to understand him that way.[16] The issue revolves around how we interpret Thrasymachus' reference to the 'strong' in his characterisation of justice. To understand the force of this reference we need to look at Thrasymachus' reasons for rejecting certain (traditional?) formulae about justice—they all systematically leave out any reference to power. Plato gives us a clue about the nature of this rejection by having Socrates engage in a somewhat puzzling exchange with Thrasymachus just prior to the latter's declaration 'that justice is nothing but the advantage of the stronger'. The exchange deserves closer attention than it has received.

If Socrates really (*hōs alethōs*) wants to understand justice, claims Thrasymachus, he should state clearly and precisely (*saphōs kai akrivōs*) what he thinks it is. He should avoid saying that it is 'the obligatory' (*to deon*), or 'the expedient' (*to ophelimon*), or 'the beneficial' (*to lusiteloun*), or 'the profitable' (*to kerdaleon*), or 'the advantageous' (*to sumpheron*) (336b 8–336d 4). To this Socrates protests (337a 8–337c 1) that Thrasymachus is like one forbidding answers to the question 'how much is twelve' of the form 'twice six', 'thrice four', 'six times two', 'four times three,' and so on. If one thinks these answers true, why should one not give them in response to the question? Thrasymachus sneers at the analogy, and, later, when Socrates suggests that Thrasymachus' own formula about justice employs one of the forbidden formulae (adding 'of the stronger' to it), Thrasymachus makes it clear that he takes this qualification to make all the difference (339b 1).

What is the purpose of this exchange? We may sympathise with Socrates' protest. Any of the formulae in the mathematical example, if true, are necessarily so. They all 'fix' how much is twelve. Though, as we may say, the formulae do not *mean* the same as each other, they necessarily *refer* to the quantity denoted by 'twelve'. Why could we not say the same thing about justice and the formulae Thrasymachus rejects? To say of an action, for example, that it is obligatory is not the same as saying that is beneficial, or any of the other things. Nevertheless, if it is true to say that the just thing is obligatory, beneficial, and so on, why could we not also say that all these descriptions necessarily refer to the value of the moral quality called 'justice'. Saying this would still leave unanswered the question what the 'nature' or 'essence' of the moral quality was, such that knowing it would explain why the different descriptions were descriptions (perhaps in different contexts) of the same value. The parallel point in the mathematical case would be that to give an account of the 'essence' of the number twelve which explained why the different formulae referred to the same quantity is different from the *fact* that they all refer to that quantity.

Thrasymachus must resist this suggestion if he believes that the true value of justice cannot be gleaned from its 'moral' character. He must disagree with

Socrates if he thinks that the value of justice is relative to how it functions in the context of relations of power. Socrates' mathematical example sets off nicely— by contrast—the 'resistance', represented by Thrasymachus, to treating justice as a moral quality. For, were Thrasymachus to allow Socrates the mathematical parallel, he would be committing himself to the view that it is the nature of justice *itself* (the quality attributed to acts, persons, institutions, and so on) which explains why acts exemplifying that quality are obligatory, beneficial, profitable, or any of the other terms commonly employed to recommend justice. Thrasymachus' view, as it soon emerges, is that the truth is the reverse: it is location in the power spectrum which determines 'the obligatory' 'the advantageous', 'the profitable'. So, it is only within the perspective of power that one can explain the value commonly attributed to just acts, persons, and so on. In terms of the mathematical example, it would be as if one were to claim that the quantity indicated by 'twice six' or 'three times four' was determined by the calculator's status; and that it was this fact which explained why some calculator took these expressions as factors of *twelve*, whereas, say, a 'higher' calculator might take them as factors of something else. The mathematical analogue of Thrasymachus' position is, of course, implausible. But is it so with respect to notions like justice? Numbers and number-theory, we feel, establish their own domain, and provide explanations of mathematical facts which can be isolated from psychological, social or cultural facts. But can this be the case with moral qualities? Why should we go along with Socrates' implicit assumption that the objective value of justice falls within the domain of a moral theory, the way the determination of quantity belongs to the domain of arithmetical theory? Be that as it may, Thrasymachus' rejection of Socrates' parallel represents a resistance to the idea that justice must be seen to fall within the special domain of a moral knowledge. His first statement about justice, therefore, may be interpreted as giving voice to precisely this resistance.

Whether or not Thrasymachus' statement that 'justice is nothing but the advantage of the stronger' is meant as a definition, it is clear that he intends it to fulfil the promises he had taunted Socrates with earlier at 337d 1–2:[17] namely, to instruct Socrates about the formula with which to *replace* statements such as 'justice is the obligatory', or 'the advantageous', and so on. Socrates' reaction to this—it rightly enrages Thrasymachus—is interesting. Does Thrasymachus mean, asks Socrates (338c 5–338d 2), that the advantage of, say, the physically stronger is a standard for what is advantageous (and, hence, just)? Socrates takes it, in other words, that Thrasymachus' reference to the advantage of the stronger is meant as a criterion of the (true) value of justice—justice is the good thing it is, an excellence, *because* it is the advantage of the stronger. Taken as such the statement will be one that belongs to moral theory, even though it is a patently false explication of the value of justice. If it were a true explanation then the fact that a diet was advantageous to a pugilist, superior in strength to the rest of us, would make the diet an excellent thing for all. Thrasymachus accuses Socrates of interpreting his remark in the most damaging way possible (338d 3–4). His statement was meant to remove the temptation to think of justice as indicating a moral excellence; we need to learn to evaluate justice properly by looking at the way justice relates to power, to 'the stronger'.

Thrasymachus' first speech (338d 7–339a 4) tries to bring this point home: in all city-states, whatever their political arrangements, the ruling element is the powerful element. They have power who are *in* power; and it is they who set down as laws what is to the advantage of the constitution in which they rule— democracies set down 'democratic' laws, tyrannies 'tyrannical' laws, and so on. Thrasymachus is clearly implying here (338e 1–3) that the ruling element institutes laws that promote its political advantage as a ruling element. Though it is not yet clear precisely how Thrasymachus intends to link the personal advantage of the powerful to their political advantage as defined by the constitution within which they operate, his speech in this section identifies power ('the stronger') with political power ('the ruler'). In setting down laws, the ruling element declares this (its own advantage) to be what is just for the ruled: those who transgress it are punished and are called 'lawless and unjust'. Thrasymachus concludes that justice is the same in all *poleis*, the advantage of the established rule. And, since the established rule is *the* power in a *polis*, we must infer that justice is everwhere the same: to act in a way that promotes the advantage of the 'stronger'.

The rhetorical message of the speech is clear, yet its conceptual structure is far from simple.[18] More importantly, unravelling this structure is essential to understanding Thrasymachus' later remarks about the supreme value of injustice, and his claim that justice is 'another's good' while injustice is one's own good (343c). Commentators are divided on the question whether overall Thrasymachus holds a consistent position.[19] Those who think that he does find that Thrasymachus' first formula about justice, that it is the advantage of the stronger, does not give us what he thinks justice is.[20] By 'justice' he really understands 'obedience to laws' (Hourani), or 'another's good' (Kerferd). Those who think that Thrasymachus is inconsistent (or, that Plato makes him so for his own purposes) take Thrasymachus' first formula as his definition of justice, but claim that he later introduces a different criterion of justice.[21] To avoid undue complexity of presentation in the interpretation set out below I will refrain from discussing directly the views of other commentators. Comments on points raised in their work will be confined to the notes.

We begin with a puzzling feature of Thrasymachus' initial formula: as a *definition* of justice it seems excessively narrow. How can Thrasymachus see justice only as a political relationship between rulers and subjects?[22] The range of conduct covered by rulers' enactments is too limited to confine the application of 'just' and 'unjust' to it. However much we stretch 'rule' (*archē*) and 'law' (*nomos*) to cover social regulation through custom, it would not include all moral conduct.[23] In any case, it is clear from Thrasymachus' examples later on (343d,e) that he is himself prepared to apply 'just' and 'unjust' to behaviour involved in social relations other than political ones. Moreover, it has seemed to some that Thrasymachus is 'espousing a version of the traditional values of the ordinary Greek'.[24] Since the traditional Greek conception of *dikaiosyne* does not confine it to political obedience, it is odd that Thrasymachus would so confine it in an effort to support his paradoxical claim that justice is the advantage of the stronger. It would be a mistake, then, to take Thrasymachus as defining justice in political terms, or as holding a 'legalist' or 'conventionalist' view of justice—the view that justice is nothing but obedience to laws.[25]

But Thrasymachus' formula need not be taken as *defining* justice in political terms, or as confining it to obedience to laws. As we saw earlier, the formula is introduced in the first instance as a 'different and better way' of talking about justice. It makes explicit a 'resistance' to the assumption that had governed the discussion so far, namely, that justice should be seen as a purely moral value. Thrasymachus believes, I claimed, that justice cannot properly be understood outside relations of power. But relations of power are not confined to political relations between rulers and subjects, even if the latter provide an especially perspicuous illustration of the former.[26] What, then, does Thrasymachus take political relations between subject and ruler to illustrate about the connection between justice and power? We approach a plausible answer if, once again, we reflect on what is *excluded* in Thrasymachus' understanding of political relations. As we shall see, in the next chapter, it is the implicit exclusions which Plato incorporates into Thrasymachus' speeches which reveal the structure of the latter's position, and lend coherence to his view.

Thrasymachus is claiming that it is the ruling element (*to archon*) in all cities which dominates (*krattei*—338d 10). It is because they are *the* powerful that rulers can present their advantage as 'the political will'; they can declare what is 'just and lawful' for citizens to do. They institute laws appropriate to the dominant political ideology which maintains them as rulers. The crucial point to note here is that for Thrasymachus it is the *fact* of power which 'converts' the advantage of the ruler into the conduct and policies that will count as desirable and beneficial in a *polis*. For, it is by virtue of their hegemonic position that rulers can declare what will be permitted as 'just and lawful' in the *polis*. In other words, the determination of what is worthwhile and beneficial in a *polis* has to go through the dominant political ideology whose authoritative spokesmen are the rulers. In deciding which conduct they will permit or forbid, reward or punish, in their *polis*, the rulers 'convert' what is advantageous to their established rule into a declaration of what is lawful. Thrasymachus' equation of 'the advantage of the established rule' with 'the advantage of the stronger' (339a 1–2) contains the following thesis: that what counts as advantageous in a *polis* is relative to the decrees of the rulers which, in turn, reflect the ideological interests of the politically dominant in that *polis*. In this case justice—the way in which a social organisation conceives of conduct that is good and proper—is reflected in the norms and regulations which govern life in that organisation. But the character of these norms and regulations, of 'justice' so understood, will vary in accordance with the ideological interests of those in power; that is, with whether a tyranny, an aristocratic oligarchy or a democracy is in power. Thrasymachus does not mean by power the imposition by force of the will of the powerful on unwilling and resistant subjects, on 'the weaker'.[27] Though law-enforcement is a feature of all political organisation, the power of 'the strong' is their capacity to formulate authoritatively what counts as being beneficial and advantageous to the community. The 'subjects' are those who accept that the rulers have that capacity. But while the rulers have that capacity *because* they are the powerful, the subjects believe that the political power of the rulers is made legitimate by virtue of their possessing the capacity to formulate authoritatively what is advantageous to the *polis*. Justice from the point of view of the rulers is an instrument of power, while for their subjects it is the determination of the good and proper ways to behave in the *polis*—a determination entrusted to the rulers to make authoritatively.

It would seem that Thrasymachus is excluding a possible separation of the aims and considerations proper to legislative and administrative activities from the ideological interests of those with a grip on political power. Thrasymachus cannot see ruling as anything other than the implementation of the ideas favoured by a political faction in the *polis*. Ruling is an *expression* of power, as well as being the standard outcome or effect of a successful bid to satisfy the desire to be in power. The latter desire can, of course, be satisfied without its being the case that those who come to occupy positions of power rule in a way which expresses *their* power. There can be 'incompetent' or 'misguided' rulers whose policies and legislation fail to adhere steadfastly to the advantage of the powerful interests in their *polis*. In doing so they are not rulers 'in the strict sense', for the aims they 'look to' in legislating will not be those which make them powerful in the constitution in question, even if they are in power.

That this is Thrasymachus' view is confirmed by his reactions to Socrates' questioning (Cf., for example, 339c–e and 341c–342e). It is also reinforced by the way Plato, in *Laws* IV (714b–c), associates the Thrasymachean formula 'justice is the advantage of the stronger' ('the best way to define justice "according to nature"') with the view (whose authorship is not mentioned) that legislation in all states is tied to the advantage of the politically dominant faction in the state.[28] In characterising this view the 'Athenian' indicates that what is at issue is of great importance; it concerns, he says, the standard of right and wrong, for the view holds that there are as many types of law as there are political arrangements.[29] In other words, the thesis mentioned in *Laws* IV holds with Thrasymachus that standards of legislation cannot be separated from the political advantage of those who rule; in each constitution the law should look to the interests of that constitution, and should not allow 'concern for what happens in war or what pertains to excellence as a whole' to guide legislation (714c). The standard of legislation for a constitution should be its own advantage, that which permanently secures it against dissolution. The view characterised in this passage · of the *Laws*, and contained in Thrasymachus' explication of his formula for justice, excludes a conception of ruling and legislation which regards as their aim the pursuit of what is *actually* the common good of the citizens.[30]

Thrasymachus' formula, then, does not attempt to define justice as a moral quality, since it does not set out to explain the criteria according to which certain types of conduct are good in themselves. As we saw, Thrasymachus wants to exclude this possibility. And he does so by claiming that 'defining' what is just in any community is part of the process by means of which those politically dominant there establish and maintain their power. This being so, it is wrongheaded to ask what is beneficial or advantageous about just conduct in itself. Since it is those who dominate and rule who determine what counts as just, the advantageousness of justice of necessity must refer to the interests of the powerful. It is these interests which 'convert' political advantage ('the advantage of the ruler') into justice; so that 'lawful' and 'just' conduct is nothing but the means whereby the power of 'the stronger' is expressed in a community. Justice is the advantage of the stronger because it is that advantage which determines the content of justice in each case.

Though Thrasymachus' words make it sound as if he is propounding a sociological theory of justice—what justice *in fact* is in every state—he is excluding the possibility, as we saw earlier, that justice could, or should, be cut off from dominant ideology.[31] For, if he were prepared to allow that, though contrary to fact, it is possible for legislators to 'look to' the common interests of all rather than to their own sectional interests, he could not have proposed his formula. Only someone who believes that what is just cannot but be defined by the dominant political interests could *recommend* that the formula 'justice is the advantage of the stronger' is 'a different and better' way of talking about justice.

Thrasymachus' explication of his initial formula, then, reveals it as an account (a *logos*) of how justice *should* be thought about. In support of this account he enlists the view that the aims of legislation and social regulation are, rightly, tied to the advantage of each political constitution and, therefore, promote the interests of those in power in every case. If Thrasymachus is 'defining' anything in this first speech it is not justice itself but the way in which one should define justice without assuming it to be a form of excellence. He is 'defining' a non-moral manner of defining justice. His formula sounds paradoxical because it seems to dispense with the traditional moral overtones of *dikaiosyne*. But it is not at all clear in any case that these overtones contained a purely moral understanding of justice. There was enough slack in the traditional notion to make it unclear how just conduct was to be separated from the requirements of social status.[32] Thrasymachus' dictum, by making explicit this unwillingness or inability to separate morality and status, serves admirably to convey a prevailing mood.

Whether that mood was prevalent in fact, and to what extent, is of course a question for the historians. But it may well have been *Plato's* judgement that it was. He may have thought that the social, cultural and political evolution of a city like Athens had made it exceedingly difficult for people to understand how there could be a purely ethical inquiry into justice as a personal or as a social excellence. In a climate where discussion of what benefits citizens and promotes the well-being of the *polis* is caught up in the ideological trappings of the political rhetoric of opposed factions there is little hope of isolating a moral conception of justice from the vicissitudes of the exercise of political power. Plato is capturing in Thrasymachus a rationale behind the *practice* of justice in city-states, whether or not that rationale was being articulated at the time. Behind the practice, Plato hints, we find a Thrasymachean exclusion of a moral perception of justice—an exclusion grounded on the view that justice is nothing other than the way ruling political interests establish themselves in a *polis*.

Commentators disagree not only about the force of Thrasymachus' original speech but also about how it relates to his second long speech (343a–344c). Problems seem to arise because Thrasymachus in response to Socrates' questioning appears to introduce a different criterion of justice (at 343c–d). 'Justice', he says,

is really the good of another, the advantage of the more powerful and the ruler, but the personal harm of those who obey and render service. Injustice is the opposite, and rules over those who are truly simple and just, and those over whom it rules do what is of advantage to him who is more powerful, and by rendering him service they make him happier, but themselves not at all.

The passage was worth quoting in full because there is a tendency to take Thrasymachus' main assertion to be that justice is the good of another (*allotrion agathon*). Nevertheless, both this passage and other things he says in this long speech create difficulties. It will be convenient to start with a brief characterisation of what they are.

The first problem concerns Thrasymachus' gloss in 'justice is the good of another, the advantage of the more powerful and the ruler'. Plato clearly presents

Thrasymachus as thinking that 'the good of another' is continuous with 'the advantage of the stronger'. Even if we allow that 'the good of another' is a broadening of 'the advantage of the stronger' to enable the latter formula for justice to apply to the just actions of both rulers and subjects, two difficulties remain.[33] We found that the explication of 'justice is the advantage of the stronger' which Thrasymachus gave earlier relativises just conduct to the legislation each constitution introduces for its own advantage. But if this is so, then either justice is restricted to the *subjects* of a state, and the ruler-legislator is removed from the sphere of justice and injustice, or both ruler and subject are equally under the dominion of law and can, thus, act justly or unjustly. But a ruler acting in accordance with the laws of the *polis* in which he holds sway will be promoting his *own* advantage—this being the point of the legislation he has introduced—and, hence, cannot be said to be doing 'another's good'. Equally, if the ruler contravenes these laws, his injustice will not be to his *own* advantage, but, perhaps, to no one's advantage. Consequently, the contrast between the personal harm of justice (doing another's good) and the personal advantage of injustice (serving one's own interests) in Thrasymachus' second speech is lost. It is only of the *ruled* that one can say that their just actions accord with or promote 'the advantage of the stronger [= ruler]' and, so, 'the good of another'. This requires that 'the ruled' be confined to those who are not in a ruling position. However, this leads to another difficulty. As Thrasymachus' own examples (344d,e) indicate, just and unjust conduct is manifested in the context of relationships where the contrast ruler/ruled is not applicable.[34] The obligations towards a business partner, or towards a tax-collecting agency, or towards recipients of administrative services are not relations between ruler and ruled; it is even dubious whether they are relations between the more and the less powerful. How, then, can justice in these contexts, understood as 'doing another's good', be glossed as doing 'the advantage of the more powerful', where by 'more powerful' we are thinking of those in ruling positions?

The second problem concerns what some have seen as a shift from a political/legal understanding of justice in the earlier speech to a moral one in the second speech.[35] The introduction of justice as 'another's good' leads Thrasymachus eventually (343d 2ff.) to talk of injustice as the violation of moral rules in general, not merely the specific legislation of particular constitutions. It can certainly seem that Thrasymachus' statements from this point on 'leave the political sphere for the moral, and identify justice, not with a relation between the individual and the law, but with a quality regulating the relation between individuals'.[36] Nevertheless, Thrasymachus at the end of his speech (344c 6–8) still maintains that he is saying what he said at the beginning: justice is the advantage of the stronger, whereas injustice is what is profitable and advantageous to oneself. It seems to be Thrasymachus' strong conviction that the powerful and those in a ruling position cannot, it they are to rule in the strict sense (341b; 343b), be interested in justice, in doing the good of their subjects. They must always look to their advantage as rulers within the constitution within which they are the powerful. In this respect the behaviour and motivational structure of the powerful is that of the unjust: they must seek what is advantageous to themselves and disregard the good of others. Injustice in this sense is not, of course, confined to the powerful who rule. Nevertheless, it is only they who have a full appreciation of its supreme value (344 a−c). Unfortunately, this claim raises problems about his earlier conception of injustice—acting contrary to the laws of the established rule. The injustice of the powerful as Thrasymachus presents it in the later speech cannot simply be equated with contravention of the laws of their *polis*; rather, it is the injustice of someone fired by great aquisitiveness (*ton megala dunamenon pleonektei*, 344a 1), and totally contemptuous of any principle of 'fairness' or fair-dealing.

Thrasymachus seems to have radically shifted the meanings of all the crucial terms in his speech, of 'stronger', of 'justice' and of 'advantage'. Where earlier 'the stronger' meant 'the ruler-legislator' it now refers to 'whoever gets the better of another' in any transaction, public or private. Where 'justice' meant 'obeying the laws of the stronger' ('faction government' as Plato calls it in *Laws* IV, 715b 5) it now means acting in conformity to 'fairness' and moral obligations. Finally, where 'advantage' meant the self-maintenance of the ruling power in a *polis*, it now means 'coming out ahead' in any transaction. Is, then, Thrasymachus confused, or is Plato deliberately creating the inconsistencies by juxtaposing the two speeches?[37] If the latter, what is Plato's purpose? If the former, why is Socrates not made to concentrate on sorting out this confusion, rather than (as he is made to do from 347e to the end of Book I) busying himself with refuting the view that the life of injustice is more powerful and better than the life of justice? In short, why does Plato present Socrates as disregarding Thrasymachus' initial formula (Socrates' disagreement with it is postponed 'till later' [see 347e])? Why does Socrates concentrate on the claim that injustice is stronger, freer and more masterful than justice?

The third problem is perhaps the most intractable of all three. It concerns the order and structure of Thrasymachus' overall position. Should we take him as presenting his case in *reverse*, that it is the long speech (his *macrologia* of 343b−344c) which contains his main thesis about justice, his opening formula following as a consequence?[38] Or, should we take the order of his position to be as the text presents it? Sticking to the superficial order of the text, we have Thrasymachus offering a definition of justice as the advantage of the stronger, explaining what he means by this, and subsequently recommending that doing the just thing is a low value worthy only of those in subordinate positions.[39] For the powerful it is injustice that should be the supreme value, not only because the unjust come off best in numerous relationships but because the truly powerful and dominant are made happy by systematic injustice on a grand scale. To be just, then, has little to recommend it, whether we look at ordinary relationships in a . *polis* where one of the parties in these relationships acts unjustly, or whether we consider what people really admire in the tyrant. In both cases it is obvious that only he who single-mindedly tramples moral rules underfoot in the pursuit of personal aggrandisement is genuinely happy.

However, if we take Thrasymachus' long speech to be a recommendation of the life of injustice, it is difficult to see why he thinks it follows from his 'definition' of justice as the advantage of the stronger. The rhetorical force of the long speech seems to be that *injustice* is what advantages a person and makes him stronger. Admittedly, he does see justice as advantaging someone other than the agent. So, Thrasymachus can claim that his recommendation of injustice and his definition of justice are not at loggerheads. But from the fact that my justice advantages someone else it does not follow that it damages me—perhaps it advantages both of us. Moreover, from the alleged fact that injustice advantages oneself, it does not follow that the powerful should pursue injustice—perhaps greater advantage to oneself may accrue from just actions because they increase the benefit of all. In any case, even granting that injustice advantages oneself and that justice advantages another (but not oneself), why should the recommendation to be unjust follow from the alleged fact that justice is the advantage of the stronger? Recommending injustice would be in order even if we defined justice as the benefiting or advantaging of the *weak*. This recommendation may not appeal to the weak, but it would appeal to the strong—the latter have no particular reason to advantage the weak. By parity of reasoning, if justice is the advantaging of the weak, the weak will have reason to praise and recommend justice when they are the beneficiaries, but would have no overwhelming reason for practising it themselves. Whichever way we look at it, if Thrasymachus holds his recommendation of injustice to follow from his definition, the result is a very muddled one indeed, and his doctrine is incoherent.[40]

Clearly, those who think, as I do, that Thrasymachus' position is not only consistent but coherent will have to deny that the surface order of the text represents the logical order of his view. They will have to deny that Thrasymachus' initial formula about justice gives what he regards as his definition of justice. Nevertheless, one can agree with this interpretation without also thinking that Thrasymachus' real view of justice is contained in the formula 'doing the good of another'.[41] In concluding this chapter I will give what seems to be the most plausible version of this approach. In the next chapter I suggest a somewhat different way of interpreting Plato's text. According to those who reverse the order of the text, Thrasymachus in his second speech presents his initial paradoxical statement as a special case of 'doing the good of another'. Acting justly is the advantage of the stronger because to be just is always to act in another's advantage, and to your own disadvantage. People who consistently pursue their own advantage, who are 'completely and perfectly' unjust, are the strong and happy. Therefore, to be just in relation to such people is, inevitably, to act to their advantage. But the consistently unjust, whose injustice makes them strong, are also those who know how to use the just person to their own ends. They are, thus, in control, 'the rulers', of the just person. The unjust are 'stronger' than the just both because they control them and because they know how the latter's actions promote their own advantage. Rulers are a paradigm case of those in control. So, if strength goes with injustice in general, it would be extraordinary if actual rulers of a community were just; their strength would then be difficult to explain. The essence of ruling is, therefore, to be unjust, and this is why the tyrant is the perfect ruler. He exemplifies in a perspicuous manner successful injustice; he always knows what is to his advantage and how to get it. The order of Thrasymachus' position is contained in the way the essential characteristic of just acts, 'to do the good or advantage of another', becomes 'the advantage of the stronger' when the just act is used by unjust persons for their own advantage. It becomes 'the advantage of the ruler' when the unjust person who uses the just person's act is the ruler. One can move from the essential characteristic of justice to its being the advantage of the ruler, but one cannot move from the latter, Thrasymachus' initial formula, to the essential characteristic of justice.[42]

One can thus reconstruct from what Thrasymachus says in his two speeches a consistent and coherent position on justice. But Plato is doing more in his presentation of Thrasymachus than merely putting forcefully a point of view; he is also delineating the 'inner' structure, as it were, of the standard discourse about justice. The 'paradoxes' of Thrasymachus, as we shall see in the next chapter, are the real puzzles inherent in how Plato's contemporaries thought about justice.

4

The Function of 'Thrasymachus' in Plato's Text

While the interpretation which concluded the last chapter contains important insights it needs to be supplemented with an analysis of the reasons why the order of Plato's text is as it is. We need to know, in other words, why Thrasymachus' views about how injustice relates to strength, happiness, and ruling in the second speech should be seen as grounding his earlier claim that in all political arrangements the determination of what counts as just in a society is tied to the advantage of the ruler. The link Thrasymachus sees between the essential injustice of the strong and the *ability* of rulers to rule needs explanation. How does a body of citizens remain more or less orderly within the bounds of particular policies and regulations when these represent and foster what is advantageous to rulers who, being 'the strong', must necessarily be unjust? If those who are strong and rulers are necessarily unjust, must those who are weak and subject be necessarily just? Granting that the driving motive of the strong is personal aggrandisement (*pleonexia*), must we postulate an opposite drive which keeps the just in a weak and subject position? Even so, how can people motivated by the 'anti-pleonectic' motive which confines them to the role of subjects not only allow themselves to be ruled by the powerful, but actually admire the driving force and tenacity which allows the latter's injustice to get them to the top? If, on Thrasymachus' view, admiration of strength is incompatible with admiration of justice, how is it nevertheless that some sort of 'justice' prevails in all *poleis*? Why is just conduct praised and unjust conduct reviled and punished?

The interpretation given in the last chapter explains how the motivation of the strong, being a motivation to injustice, enables them to rule over and have control over the just. But it does not make clear how Thrasymachus thinks of the *desire* to be just. Does Thrasymachus believe that the just are simply those not fired by *pleonexia*, or does he think that those who act justly do so *faute de mieux*—that they do not know how to estimate and pursue their own advantage without paying an exorbitant price for it? The idea in the second alternative is that those who are weak and subject, being ignorant of how to achieve their own advantage without loss, have to rely on what the strong allow them to gain—so long, of course, as they are prepared to be the 'subjects' of the strong. If this is

Thrasymachus' view, it explains why he believes that wanting to be just cannot be a desire for anything unqualifiedly good. The essential characteristic of just actions, which Thrasymachus identifies as 'doing the good of another', will not define a motive to achieve the good; it will simply refer to a common characteristic of just actions *as seen from the perspective of power*. In other words, Thrasymachus is suggesting that from the perspective of those who know how successfully to pursue *pleonexia*, just actions will appear as nothing but 'doing the good of another'. From such a perspective there is nothing *more* to behaving justly, whatever the just themselves may think about their actions.

It is along these lines that we should understand the link between the second speech and Thrasymachus' earlier remarks about justice, as well as his refusal to allow Socrates to speak of justice as advantageous or beneficial without qualification. It was pointed out earlier, in connection with Thrasymachus' first speech, that what structures his exclusion of an account of justice as in itself an excellence was the further exclusion of the idea that the ruler-legislator in framing his legislation, 'looks to' a common good independent of the dominant political ideology. The second speech is structured around yet a further exclusion—one which provides the rationale for the second exclusion, just as the second provided the rationale for the first. The reason why the ruler-legislator cannot 'look to' a common good, the good of the subjects, is because he must be powerful, the controller. As such he must of necessity be unjust: it is only the single-minded wish to pursue his own advantage, and his capacity to perceive what it is, which gives him power and control over others. And it is precisely because those who lack this capacity must latch on to the powerful if their own advantage is to be furthered that they are 'the weak' and 'subject'. Unlike the powerful, they have to behave 'justly'; that is, they have to obey what the strong lay down as rules. Their benefit is, thus, necessarily dependent on what secures the advantage of the ruler; it depends on justice being defined by the ruler in the process of securing his own advantage.

Thrasymachus further excludes in the long speech the idea that the 'good reasons' people have for praising justice and condemning injustice have anything to do with their believing that the ends of justice are desirable in themselves. As he says (344c 3–4), those who revile injustice do so because they fear to suffer from it, not because they are afraid to commit it. He who is capable of aggrandisement on a large scale, the perfect embodiment of this capacity being the tyrant, 'plunders by fraud and force alike the goods of others, sacred and holy things, private and public possessions, and never pettily but all at once' (344a 7–344b 1). Petty instances of such acts are punished on detection, and their perpetrators reviled with such names as 'temple-breakers', 'kidnappers', 'burglars', 'swindlers', and 'thieves'. But such conventional condemnations of unjust acts are not applied to the absolute ruler, 'who despoils citizens of their money, and captures and enslaves their persons. He is called blessed and happy, not only by those over whom he rules but by all who hear of his complete injustice' (344b 7–344c 2).

The important point being made here is that ordinary condemnations of injustice are not based on an admiration of justice as an excellence. For if they were, not only unjust actions, but the motive (*pleonexia*) which underlies petty and grand injustices alike would be equally condemned. But it is not. Because the motive is seen as a necessary condition for the achievement of power and control—and these ends are universally admired—people tend not to see it as evil when they are faced with the grand achievement of those single-mindedly fired by it. They only look down on it when those acting from it fail. It follows that admiration for power and control excludes an admiration for justice because, properly speaking, the motives that inspire the just must make them reject *pleonexia*, one of the mainsprings of the drive to power and success.

It may still seem that Thrasymachus has shifted his ground between the two speeches. Earlier, injustice meant acting in contravention of the laws of the established rule, whereas now it seems to mean acting out of *pleonexia*. Such a shift will, of course, bring with it corresponding shifts in the meaning of the other key terms he employs: 'the just', 'the stronger' and 'the ruler'. To see that no such shifts are involved we need to attend to certain crucial conceptual connections which flow from Thrasymachus' last and most important exclusion. As we have just seen, this is the claim that a desire for justice cannot be a desire for excellence in the way in which the desire for injustice *is* such a desire. In Thrasymachus' view it is the successful pursuit of the latter desire, successful *pleonexia*, which leads to the universally admired values of power, control and freedom (344c 4–6).

The central feature of the long speech is to assert a necessary connection between power, ruling, and injustice. It is not merely a matter of empirical fact that the strong and those in power are unjust.[1] On Thrasymachus' view they must be so if his main contention that justice is the advantage of the stronger and the ruler is to be defended. What enables Thrasymachus to support this strong connection between power, control and injustice is his implicit denial that wanting to be just can be a desire for excellence. To see this we must reflect on the logical force of his claim that 'justice and the just is really the good of another, the advantage of the stronger and those who rule, but the personal harm of those who obey and serve, whereas injustice is the opposite, and rules over those truly simple and just . . . ' (343c3–7).

Thrasymachus clearly has in mind the essential exploitability of just actions by those who are unjust.[2] There are transactions (business deals, taxation, distribution of social goods, and so on) where fairness or fair-dealing is expected of the participants. In these transactions the unjust, motivated as they are to have and to be more than others, will be advantaged by the just actions of others. What has not been noticed by those who have seen this point is that the description 'doing the good of another' does not necessarily imply that the good the just act is *aimed* at is the advantage of another.[3] It may well be the case, as Aristotle points out, that of all virtues only justice is thought to be another's good because it is directed to someone else (*pros heteron estin*).[4] But this does not mean that the exclusive aim of the just person is to serve another's interest or advantage. Being fair in the cases Thrasymachus mentions (343d,e), as well as in others, may mean that the just person desires the overall, the 'common', good of all concerned. If, as Thrasymachus claims, doing the good of another is doing what is advantageous to the strong and those who rule, he must be employing the notion of 'conversion' we found him using in his first speech. Thrasymachus' point there was that the power of the ruler in a *polis* with a particular constitution 'converts' his advantage into what counts as right and proper in the *polis*. The policies and laws the ruler wants may not *in fact* be right for the *polis*, but they become the criteria of what is right there precisely because the ruler has the power to enforce them. A similar 'conversion' is involved in how Thrasymachus understands 'justice is the good of another'. It is the fact that there are people who seek that which makes them strong, and which puts them in a controlling position, that 'converts' the acts of those who act justly into acts which serve another's advantage. So, Thrasymachus understands 'the good of another' (as a description of a just act) in a way which makes it *already* equivalent to 'the advantage of another'.[5] But he can do this only if he believes that the benefit just persons attribute to their actions is *illusory*: the good the just aim at or intend is irrelevant to the true character of what they do. From the perspective of the drive for power, then, the only true and important characterisation of just acts is that they advantage the strong and put them in control, while they disadvantage those who perform them.

It is this exclusion of the idea that justice has a good that is 'its own', a benefit that only acting justly brings, which unifies all that Thrasymachus says. By consistently adhering to the perspective of the drive for power, which he believes excludes viewing justice as an excellence, Thrasymachus can coherently maintain both that justice is the advantage of the stronger *and* that injustice is essential to being powerful and in control. It is the adoption of this perspective which also explains why he does not allow Socrates to define justice as 'the obligatory', 'the beneficial', 'the advantageous', and so on, without qualification.

This interpretation accounts for all the aspects of Thrasymachus' view as it unfolds from 336b to 344c, as well as remarks he makes later. In the first place, it explains why he thinks the formula 'justice is nothing but the advantage of the stronger' is a 'different and better' way of talking about justice. It is 'different' because unlike traditional conceptions it looks at just conduct from the perspective of the drive for power. It is 'better' because it reveals in 'a clear and precise' way how, in a world which places a high priority on power, control and freedom, the correct assessment of those who act justly must be that they will always and necessarily be 'the weaker'. The just are those always destined to obey and serve the powerful.

In the second place, the interpretation explains why Thrasymachus associates his formula for justice with the view that legislation in each state is tailored to the advantage of those in political control within the constitution of that state. From the perspective of the drive for power, political control of the citizenry excludes concern for 'a common good', since such concern would limit the power of the rulers to achieve their own aim. Accordingly, the laws and policies they declare as 'right and just' for the citizens are presented as advantageous and appropriate to the political arrangement which gives them control over others. In punishing those who do not obey or conform as unlawful and unjust, the rulers justify this punishment not on the grounds that 'unlawful' behaviour damages a common or universal good, but on the grounds that it damages the good of the *polis* as interpreted by the dominant ideology enshrined in the political arrangement. Being just in each state is obeying and serving the advantage of the established rule. This is why Thrasymachus will not allow that rulers, in the strict sense, can make mistakes in their edicts (340d,e; 341a), or that rulers can 'look to' the advantage of their subjects, or that they can be just (343b). From the point of view of the drive for power, no one who *is* strong can be ignorant or mistaken about what is to their advantage, and about how to pursue it. Such ignorance or error signifies a 'weakening', a check on that drive. It is precisely the capacity to identify correctly, and pursue successfully, their advantage which enables people to be strong and in control. Similarly, any concern for what benefits and advantages others, unless subordinated to a correct perception of their own advantage (see his remarks about shepherds, herd-owners and sheep at 343b), would 'weaken' the capacity of the powerful to rule and control. Exclusive attention to the benefit of others undermines the *cognitive* capacity needed to be strong. It cannot, therefore, be entertained either by those in power, or by those aspiring to power.

In the third place, the interpretation explains why Thrasymachus speaks of the just as truly 'simple-minded' or 'good-hearted' (*hōs alethōs euēthikōn*, 343c 6; *genaian euētheian*, 348c 12), and of injustice as not malignity (*Kakoētheia*, 348d 1) but 'good counsel' (*euboulia*, 348d 2). From the point of view of the drive for power there is nothing unadmirable about injustice. Injustice is 'wise and good' (348d 3−5) because it aims at power and control. It is always profitable, as is exemplified by those 'who can bring cities and nations under their dominion' (348d 5−9). The consistently unjust, capable of *pleonexia* on a grand scale, are, as Thrasymachus says, universally admired (344b,c). The condemnation of unjust acts is conventional; it is not genuine moral disapprobation. The institutional punishment imposed on such acts does not signify a contempt for the character of those who perform them; it only expresses the fact that *exposed* violations of social rules must be punished by those in power and control. Otherwise, that power and control will be undermined, and with it the capacity which makes the rulers powerful. It is essential to the power-perspective that it severs the connection between the description of just conduct and the description of the just character. For, within that perspective just actions always turn out to be to the advantage of the unjust; they make them strong and put them in control both of the situation and of the just person. Consequently, Thrasymachus has *two* sets of descriptions for those who act justly. They are 'simple-minded' when he talks of their character, and there is nothing good or admirable about this. But they are 'obedient' and 'servants' when he talks of the true nature of their *acts*. In the latter respect the just are always worse off than the unjust (343d,e).

Yet, there is no corresponding isolation of act from character in how Thrasymachus thinks of the unjust. The driving force to act unjustly is the same in both petty criminals and those capable of grand *pleonexia*: it is to assert oneself against one's fellows, to do better and to have more than them. To do this successfully one needs to be in power and control over others. If one is not, then one's acts of injustice, when detected, are likely to be punished by the powerful. Nevertheless, both the character and the acts of the unjust are 'profitable', and they are a mark of wisdom and virtue (348e 1–4). From the power-perspective they cannot fail to be such since they have as their aim the achievement of universally admired ends. The failure of unjust persons who are caught and punished is not to be attributed to anything bad or base (*aischron*) about their character or their actions. Their only failure is that they are not sufficiently sagacious to determine correctly their real advantage in the situation. In all cases the unjust character and action gives a person power and control over the just. But the unqualified excellence of the unjust character is only perfectly realised in the benefit it bestows on those who approach absolute power and mastery over others—the tyrants.

The model of the perfect tyrant is Thrasymachus' picture of the 'power' of injustice. It enables a person to be strong, in control, and free from the limitations others have to operate under—others, who by dint of character or circumstance find themselves compelled to 'toe the line'. They are not capable of attending single-mindedly to their own advantage. But the tyrant also exemplifies, indirectly, the *epistemic* advantage of the power-perspective. Only those capable of fully adopting that perspective in their lives can see clearly how justice serves the advantage of the powerful, for it is only they who can assess precisely how the actions of people 'justly' motivated turns them into obedient servants—that is, into people who can be relied upon to do the advantage of the stronger because they consistently neglect to consider their own advantage. From the power-perspective the just are simply blind to what their actions really promote.

We are now in a position to explain why the order of presentation of Thrasymachus' ideas on justice is as it is in Plato's text, while the logical order of the connections between the ideas reverses the surface order. Plato constructs his characterisation of 'Thrasymachus' around three implicit *exclusions*, the denial of three ideas, all of which form part of conventional ways of talking about justice. These ideas are, in the order in which they appear in the text,

(1)   that justice is part of excellence, a quality valuable in itself;
(2)   that justice as exemplified in a state consists in the ruler, through legislation and its implementation, attempting to ensure what is beneficial to all;
(3)   that injustice, whether exemplified in individuals or rulers, is a contemptible and shameful thing, never an object of admiration.

Since Plato is writing a dialectical examination of views—a dialogue—he presents Thrasymachus' implicit denials of these three ideas as 'paradoxes'. The assertion of each 'naturally' leads Thrasymachus to the next one. The fact is, of course, that each of the propositions could be denied or disputed on grounds that were independent of each other. But this is not Plato's purpose. He wants to articulate a single, coherent perspective from which the rejection of these three pieces of conventional wisdom can be seen to be equally mandatory, and for the same fundamental reason. Why Plato may want to do this we shall consider presently. *That* he does so is evident from the key position the notion of power— the 'strong'—occupies throughout what Thrasymachus says. What I have called the 'power-perspective' is precisely that which provides the unifying outlook Thrasymachus adopts. The unity of the perspective, we may say, gives coherence to the dramatic presentation of the character. It is its adoption which enables Thrasymachus to regard his exclusion of the ideas in (1) to (3) as interconnected, as part of a coherent stance on justice.

It is also this fact which explains why the logic of the interconnection between the ideas goes in the opposite direction from that which the rhetoric of his speeches follows. The reason for this is that though each of the speeches is grounded on an implicit exclusion, the speech itself appears as the assertion of something *positive*. The speeches do not appear to be, yet they are in fact, 'resistances'—resistances logically entailed by the adoption of the power-perspective. Thus, in the speech corresponding to the exclusion of (1) we have the positive assertion that there is a 'different and better' way of talking about justice. As we saw, the real intent of Thrasymachus' claim is to block any assumption that an inquiry into justice must take it as given that it is a form of excellence. But his real reason for this does not fully emerge until the speech in which he rejects (3). It is not because he thinks that justice *sometimes* diminishes the well-being of the agent that he rejects (1). Rather, it is because, from the perspective of achieving power and supremacy, justice is a source of weakness, something unadmirable, that it must not be allowed to be defined as something good in itself.

But if justice is to be thought of as a source of weakness, another idea, concerning the central exemplification of political justice in the laws and constitution of a *polis*, must be resisted. This is the idea, expressed in (2), that rulers aim at the 'common good' of all citizens. However, the speech corresponding to the exclusion of (2) takes the form of a positive assertion: that justice is nothing but the promoting of the advantage of the strong who are everywhere the rulers. But Thrasymachus' real intent here is not to argue that for all their ideological claptrap about the 'good of all', or 'the good of the *polis*', rulers, as a matter of fact, only pursue their own interest. This is a possible view. But it allows the person who holds it to claim that this is not how things *ought* to be, and that good rulers should attend to the common good. This is precisely what Thrasymachus wants to reject. Once again, his reasons do not fully emerge until his long speech, the central thrust of which is to undermine (3). From the power-perspective those in power cannot afford to be just, or to attend to the good of their subjects, because to want to do someone else's good is, logically, to make yourself servant of the other's interest. You thus *create* the possibility of being taken advantage of. But no ruler, to the extent that he exemplifies what it is to want power, can want to be the servant of others. To want to act justly is, conceptually speaking, a potential source of weakness. Therefore, no one who wants to be strong, who adopts the perspective of power, *can* want to be just and do the good of another. Rulers are paradigms of a (successful) desire for power. Consequently, they must, logically speaking, ensure that their subjects are inclined to act justly, while they themselves resolutely guard against any inclination they may have to act justly.

How are they to do this? By constantly preserving in their mind's eye both what makes (3) utterly false, and the fact that those who give voice to the sentiments expressed in (3) are really motivated by a fear of being the victims of injustice in the hands of others rather than by contempt for those who profit by it. The best safeguard of the desire for power from contamination by inclinations to act justly is furnished by the ideal of the totally successful tyrant and the high regard everyone accords to his success. The speech which corresponds to Thrasymachus' rejection of (3) appears as the positive assertion that the life of injustice is better and more beneficial to the agent than the life of justice as evidenced by the splendid things it yields to the tyrant. However, as Socrates points out later and Thrasymachus agrees (348d 5 – 349a 2), to hold that there is a sense in which the unjust are better off than the just is not necessarily to deny (3). The conventional view of injustice can allow that it is profitable, while declaring it to be an evil and a disgrace (*kakian* . . . *ē aischron*). Thrasymachus' real intent is not merely to extol the social and material advantages of injustice but to deny that there is any real foundation to its being regarded as an object unworthy of admiration. From the perspective of power, injustice not only comes out as an object of admiration, it emerges as its highest form. 'Injustice', Thrasymachus concludes, 'is mightier and freer and more masterly than justice.'

Thrasymachus' rhetoric in his last speech manages to bring off an interesting conceptual reversal of the traditional discourse about justice without, in any important sense, upsetting the *values* held most dear by those employing it. These are the values in terms of which he compares justice and injustice: power, freedom and mastery. He achieves this conceptual reversal in how to talk about justice by insisting that since these are the primary or highest values, justice can only be understood in relation to what leads to their realisation. His view is that grand *pleonexia*, the desire to have more and to be more than anyone else, if pursued unchecked, cannot fail to achieve these values. Its single-mindedness protects those who are, or desire to be, powerful from what are truly sources of weakness. Now, the *terminology* of traditional and conventional morality implies that *pleonexia* is a (perhaps the main) source of 'unjust' conduct, while it regards acting 'justly' as doing the good of another. But such terminology does not by itself tell us how the people using it really think, or should think about aggrandisement, for it leaves vague the rational grounds of the beliefs expressed by means of the terminology.

One can remove this vagueness by looking at matters from the perspective of power—a perspective which clearly and unambiguously takes power, freedom and mastery to be the highest human values. From such a perspective things begin to look the reverse of what the traditional terminology suggests: the more thoroughgoing one's *pleonexia* and, hence, on the traditional terminology, the likelihood of acting 'unjustly', the nearer one gets to realising these supreme values. Likewise, the stronger one's inclination to do the good of another and, hence, on the traditional terminology, to act 'justly', the weaker one becomes *vis-à-vis* the strong if one acts on these inclinations. Therefore, if one wants to be powerful, free and masterful, one must be completely 'unjust'; for, this entails that one will be stronger than, and in control of, those who act 'justly'. In the political context this means that the strong, the rulers, can lay down the norms of how people are to behave in the *polis*—the rulers can determine the *content* of 'justice', even if its form in the abstract is contained in the vague expression 'doing the good of another'. It follows from all this that one cannot say *unqualifiedly* that 'justice' refers to something good in itself. Just conduct is good, profitable, obligatory, and so on, only to the extent that it promotes the interests of power, freedom and mastery. But these are precisely the values exemplified by 'the strong', those who adopt the power-perspective on life. Therefore, the benefits of justice must be determined by reference to the advantage of the stronger. Only so will the conceptual priority of power, freedom and mastery over that of justice, a priority that reflects the actual ranking of values among people, emerge clearly. The reasons Thrasymachus has for rejecting (3) entail that he rejects (2). Both of these rejections, in turn, entail the rejection of (1), which was, after all, what brought him into the discussion in the first place.

What is the significance of Plato's highly complex characterisation of Thrasymachus? Given our meagre information about the real Thrasymachus our attention must perforce turn to the function this character has in the overall plan of Book I. This chapter ends with some general and speculative remarks about the type of moral and political attitude Plato incorporates in the character. The philosophical worth of the views, and of Socrates' criticism of them, is discussed below.

Is Plato presenting a view of morality which was critical of traditional values and which had become fashionable in Athens?[6] Or, does this part of the dialogue contain Plato's diagnosis of the ethical underpinnings of much current political and social thinking, especially within Athenian democracy? Why is Thrasymachus' emphasis on injustice presented as a ground for the view that the excellence of a ruler consists in the issuing of decrees that promote the interests of a particular political faction, the faction whose ideology is prominent in a *polis*? After all, in most Greek city-states, particularly in Athens, there was the idea of an 'ancestral constitution', a set of somewhat statically conceived laws, in terms of which proposed decrees and changes in law were fairly rigorously judged.[7] Even if we assume, as seems reasonable, that being no special friend of democracy Plato is addressing himself to sympathetic oligarchs and aristocrats, the view he associates with Thrasymachus does not differentiate democracy from other types of rule. In all cases, the latter says, the ruler and the strong legislate the advantage of their political faction. Is Plato suggesting that whatever the type of rule, and in spite of the lip-service paid to 'the rule of law'—an especially democratic slogan—the *ethics* of political practice are as Thrasymachus presents them?[8] Is Plato hinting that those who aspire to political leadership are inevitably ruled by the values the pursuit of power brings? And are these values those Thrasymachus takes to be exemplified by the absolute tyrant?

Adopting this last suggestion would explain why the disillusioned tone, which some have detected in Thrasymachus' speech, is really Plato's own; a disillusionment directed at those who had led Athenian democracy through the disasters of the Peloponnesian War and its aftermath.[9] But even if it is true that Plato harboured such sentiments towards democratic leadership, he and his audience would have been fully aware that it was the pro-Spartan oligarchs of 411 BC and, again, of 403 BC, among whom were some of Plato's relatives, who had acted more like Thrasymachus' tyrant. Plato himself admits that the leaders of the restored democracy after 403 BC had dealt with their opponents in a generous and law-abiding way.[10] Thus, though Plato's sympathies may have been on the oligarchic side in the previous century's debate about the right constitution, it is more likely that his concern in the *Republic* is with fourth-century anxieties about the nature of political power and of how to avoid its corruption by unstable political arrangements.[11] It may well have been Plato's view that none of the accepted political arrangements, and especially a democracy, contained the requisite capacity to produce genuine unity in the *polis*. As things had developed, leaders could generate a shallow and unstable unity through their demagogic ability to hold an Assembly together.[12]

Speculations about the connections between Plato's political views and his portrait of Thrasymachus would be idle if the portrait was exclusively a characterisation of an ethical doctrine. But is it? Many have taken it to be such, attributing to Thrasymachus a 'nihilist' view of morality, or a 'conventionalist' outlook on justice.[13] But Thrasymachus associates 'grand injustice' with excellence, good counsel and nobility of action—all key notions in Greek ways of thinking about virtue. He cannot, therefore, have been a 'nihilist'. Nor is Thrasymachus claiming, as Callicles is made to do in the *Gorgias*, that it is 'natural' *justice* for the strong to prevail over the weak, in contrast to 'conventional' justice, the product of enactments or agreements among people to keep the strong in check.[14] What Thrasymachus does say is that everyone publicly denounces injustice when in danger of suffering it, but praises it when doing it is not threatened with retaliation. Also, though he thinks that the aims of '*pleonexia* on the grand scale' provide one with better values than wanting to act fairly, it is more than doubtful that he is propounding the doctrine of Natural Right—the view that morality has an independent existence which arises from the nature of man, and that according to that 'nature' one has a moral obligation to act unjustly.[15] It seems difficult to extract a clear-cut moral theory from Thrasymachus' speeches. He does not even argue that pursuing one's own interest is a criterion of right action (ethical egoism), or the view that everyone acts with a view to his own private interest (psychological egoism). He merely says that injustice is sound, good, judgement (*euboulia*), whereas justice is simplicity. His use of 'good person' (*agathos*) and 'advantage' (*sumpheron*) are tied to prudence, efficiency, success—the effective production of desired results.[16] There seems to be no clear evidence that Plato introduces Thrasymachus in order to contrast his own view of morality to one opposed to it, or to an amoralist one.[17]

But from the fact that Thrasymachus is not meant to represent a rival moral theory to Plato's, it does not follow that he does not present an attitude to life in society which has its own moral implications. If our interpretation is right, Thrasymachus seeks to subordinate justice, the moral precepts governing relations between people in a community, to the phenomenon of power. He holds that the drive to power provides the only clear perspective from which to apprehend the true character of justice and injustice; only from that perspective can one effectively judge which of them leads to a better and nobler life. He does not theorise the connection between power as he understands it and goodness; he simply takes it that the life of those in a dominant position is manifestly better. If Thrasymachus' view is a rival to Plato's, it is primarily over how best to *investigate* the question of justice and its value.[18] A further test for this suggestion is provided by the type of arguments Socrates uses against Thrasymachus. They are all concerned with the relation between justice and power, of the ways in which one can construe the 'strengths' of justice. The result of these arguments is not a demonstration (no such demonstration is offered) that justice is a moral good and injustice a moral evil; what they attempt to show is that justice is *more powerful*, more effective, at achieving the excellences Thrasymachus sees as the 'strengths' of injustice. If these arguments are successful, then Thrasymachus' proposal that justice be investigated from the power-perspective understood in terms of *pleonexia* is effectively blocked. Thrasymachus is shown progressively to lose interest in the discussion precisely because he feels that the perspective he takes as the only sound one is being systematically supplanted by another; one which attempts to link 'power' with rationality, and which regards justice as a manifestation of reason.

The bearing of these remarks on Plato's characterisation of Thrasymachus is that he is 'making use' of the character to bring out a type of sophisticated resistance to treating justice as a central feature of moral excellence. He does, therefore, have indirectly in mind the line of inquiry he will pursue later in the *Republic*.[19] But it is essential, if this is his purpose, to present Thrasymachus' alternative account of the nature of justice in as coherent a fashion as possible. It is no advantage to someone who believes, as Plato evidently does, that he has a novel suggestion about how the nature of justice is to be understood to counterpose it to an obviously confused and muddled alternative. Thrasymachus' proposal has to be vigorously and coherently put, and its plausibility must be firmly anchored in attitudes which could plausibly be identified as widely spread. Only so would Plato's counterproposal be a genuine philosophic intervention in the state of thinking of his contemporaries. But to whom were Thrasymachus' proposals likely to appeal? Even if we accept the real Thrasymachus as a 'disillusioned moralist', Plato builds much more into his characterisation than this simple attitude.[20] The question is, does Plato build into 'Thrasymachus' his *own* assessment of how his contemporaries really thought about life and conduct in the *polis*?

One cannot be sure, of course —any more than one can be certain that Thucydides, in order to point a moral about the evils of imperial Athens, put into the mouths of Athenian spokesmen what he considered to be their real sentiments stripped of rhetorical claptrap. However, the suggestion in Thucydides' case is far from implausible. As one scholar put it, 'if these speeches are intended to reproduce the actual tenor of Athenian public utterances, it must be admitted that the Athenians of the fifth century . . . were a very remarkable, if not unique, people in openly admitting that their policy was guided by purely selfish considerations and that they had no regard for political morality'.[21] If Thucydides—another oligarchic sympathiser—uses this device to point a moral, it is not far-fetched to see Plato's use of the character of Thrasymachus in the dialogue as having an analogous purpose. Accepting this parallel we can interpret Thrasymachus' subordination of justice to considerations of personal success, effectiveness and aggrandisement, as reflecting Plato's judgement that the link between *pleonexia* and the drive to power accurately expressed the perspective from which political and social conduct in democratic Athens was to be understood. Not only did all known political arrangements fail in his view to eradicate *pleonexia* in the hearts of people, the ways evolved in his own city to administer justice and combat injustice were *structurally* dependent on the processes by which people could secure political supremacy there. The outcome had been the gradual emergence of a dangerous habit of thought—to regard appeals to justice as inseparable from the way the leading political faction determined what benefited the *polis*. Under these conditions the success of the social policies proposed by leaders of the dominant faction could gradually erode the belief that the precepts recorded in 'the ancient constitution' were a repository of impartial wisdom—a safeguard of justice and fair-dealing. Appeal to the decrees of rulers could gradually take over from appeal to the laws.

We are dealing with an analysis of the connection Plato *may* have drawn between *pleonexia*, the drive to achieve supremacy, and an inability to keep separate the grounds of moral authority from the sources of political success and dominance in the *polis*. We are not assessing whether Plato's diagnosis was correct. We are exploring a possible insight Plato built into his characterisation of Thrasymachus. The formula about justice Thrasymachus offers initially makes explicit this refusal to accept that moral authority is anything other than a function of political power. Though it is highly unlikely that any Greek or Athenian would have been as blatant, Thrasymachus' shocking pronouncement is not meant merely to elicit wise nods of sad regret on the part of oligarchic or aristocratic sympathisers; it articulates the attitudes really at play in the very soul, as it were, of democratic Athens. It is with the ethos of the democracy, with what character it fostered in its people, that Plato was concerned—not with whether democracy was an effective political arrangement. If our speculation is correct, then Plato's characterisation of Thrasymachus gives us an image of the democratic character: arrogant, ambitious, competitive and preoccupied with power. More importantly, the message contained in the image is, firstly, one of underlying arbitrariness about expected standards of conduct. Secondly, there is an essential haziness about how one knows what is good or advantageous—the opportunity that is made to *seem* good at any time is judged to be the right one to follow. And, thirdly, there is a fundamental lack of direction in how to conceive what generates order and stability in communities and individuals.

Though Thrasymachus denies the separateness of moral authority from political hegemony in any existing constitution, one can construct a case why such denial would have been seen by Plato as more likely to seem attractive to those imbued in the democratic ethos. A full account of such a case, let alone the assessment of its validity, would involve a detailed examination of the history, character and growth of Athenian democracy—a project well beyond the limits of this book. Nevertheless, since we are speculating about Plato and his characterisation of Thrasymachus, it is worth reconstructing reasons Plato may have had for thinking that the failure to separate moral authority from political supremacy was the essence of tyranny—not so much the ordinary tyranny of actual states but the 'paradigmatic' tyranny of a type of personality. A 'tyranny', moreover, not unwelcome to democrats.

The dependence for justice on the strong (*the kreittones*) by the weak and less influential in a community is a well-attested feature of archaic Greek societies.[22] It was expected of heads of households, of tribal chiefs, or of members of rich and influential aristocratic families to show concern for the welfare of those dependent on them, and to intervene to redress injustices. But the taking up of the cause of the poor and less powerful by an influential aristocrat against mistreatment by other aristocrats in positions of power could not, in the nature of the case, be sharply distinguished from the political ambitions and rise to power of the 'protectors'.[23] The key aspect of the traditional scene is that the demand for justice occurs within an essentially paternalistic class structure. The powerful in their dealings with each other do not need justice, though they may demand it. It is not essential that they possess a code of conduct which limits their will and interests not by force but by a disinterested consideration of what is best for everyone. The confrontations among the strong are contests for supremacy of one set of interests over others. The powerful use any means to increase their power. When the strong speak of 'justice', however genuine their sympathy for the plight of the weak, such talk cannot escape being part of their bid for power. There is therefore, an essential asymmetry between the way the 'weak' see justice, being dependent on 'the strong' for its implementation, and the way the strong assess its value for their own activities. The powerful aristocrat who secures justice for those he intends to 'protect' by assuming power in a state is *eo ipso* made the powerful ruler in that state. He gets the support of the weaker whose cause he is championing. But though the lot of the weak may thus

improve, their improvement is not an increase in *their* power; they are still
dependent on the power of their 'protector'. It is his power, not theirs, that
obedience to his decrees maintains. The main objection to paternalism, whether
that of governments, influential groups or individuals, is not that the strong
proclaim worthwhile values hypocritically, that they use them as a cover for their
self-interested desire to maintain themselves in power. Rather, the objection is
that the pursuit of justice by means of a paternalistic structure is liable to confuse
adherence to certain values with conformity or obedience to the decrees and
decisions of the powerful. The 'paternal' ruler is liable to see disagreement as
disobedience, to regard non-conformity as evidence that the non-conformist is
trying to undermine authority. The point is, of course, that inherent in the
paternalistic structure is the impossibility of equating 'what we all want' with
'what we all *can* have'—the acceptance by the weak of what the strong lays
down as 'good' and 'right' is *thereby* a confirmation of the latter's position of
dominance and authority. In contrast, the pursuit by the strong of what they
judge 'good' and 'right' for all is in no way an acknowledgement of anything
authoritative about the judgement of the 'subjects' who agree with them. The
subjects' agreement with the rulers' values confirms the rulers' power, while the
rulers' support for these values, at best, only marks their current desire—a thing
subject to caprice and the vicissitudes of changing circumstances.

The idea of a code of law arrived at by a wise legislator (say, a Solon) is the idea
of someone lifted for a time above the conflict of sectional interests to determine
what may achieve order, harmony and peace within a community. This idea
represents a rejection of the paternalistic framework. It recognises that justice
requires the creation of a distinctive moral 'space' within a society—a space, as it
were, within which an authoritative perception of the communal good can be
disentangled from the distorting perspectives of conflicting political factions.
The Solonian idea had certainly been preserved as an ideal in Athens. But to what
extent the subsequent history of the development of democracy had kept alive
that ideal is a moot point. Pericles, Cleon and others thought that it did. They
thought that the involvement of all citizens in the political and judicial processes
of the *polis* ensured that leadership by the able and the well-born was not
premised on the view that the poorest and most insignificant of citizens lacked
the moral authority to judge what is best and fairest for the city as a whole.[24]
Others, like Socrates and Plato, had severe reservations about the capacity of the
democratic structure to preserve the Solonian ideal—to keep the 'space' for
justice free from sectional interests and the scramble for political power. Indeed,
they thought that the functional dependence of the democracy on demagogues
had the reverse effect: it confused moral authority with majority opinion.[25] This
meant that discovering what is good could not be submitted to the processes of
rational inquiry and knowledge but was, rather, subordinated to the techniques of
rhetoric and political manipulation.[26]

Irrespective of which side was right about this, one thing is certain: Thrasymachus does not think much of those who are ready to be just, who do not have the power to declare what is just. Democrats who had become conscious of their political power would share Thrasymachus' contempt for people whose 'just' behaviour was decreed not by themselves but by the powerful and influential. To an aggressive democrat, conscious that the *demos* in legislating for itself sees justice as its own creation, not as a gift from the socially superior, Thrasymachus' view is appealing. To brand as servile the old-fashioned attitude that saw justice as dependent on another's will, that, say, of a Peisistratus or even of a Cleisthenes, would have been most welcome to democrats. Plato's ingenious association of this attitude with *pleonexia* brilliantly articulates his own grim assessment of the moral danger he took to be inherent in the character likely to flourish in a democracy. It is a character committed to equal participation in the political process and, consequently, one which values majority decision.[27] However, decisions in 'participant' democracies can be as beneficial or harmful, fair or ruthless, as they can be in less 'participant' constitutions. But in no other constitution does being in power come to appear as a value which every citizen is encouraged to make their own.

Therein lies the moral danger, Plato thought. For, the citizen body as a whole can grow accustomed to think and behave like a tyrant; to value its 'being strong, free and masterlike' above the wisdom, goodness and nobility of how it lived. In short, the danger for citizens in a democracy is that they may come to subordinate justice as a moral value to the interest of maintaining their grip on power. It is this investment in power which renders citizens in a democracy susceptible to the influence of ambitious leaders, whether these leaders are competent, misguided, or unscrupulous.

Democracy, then, like other traditional political arrangements, can be 'sold' on power in a way that reduces morality and the value of justice to a low, pragmatic, and dependent status in the culture. Plato's construction of Thrasymachus' speeches brings this out most forcefully. But Plato hints at something else which is of greater importance. The concept of power Thrasymachus employs is, of course, the one prevalent in traditional political arrangements. But it is not part of the *ideological* expression of these arrangements to devalue justice. So, the devaluation of justice which Plato incorporates in 'Thrasymachus' contains a critical message for traditional political arrangements. Made explicit the message may be something like this. Traditional political arrangements are both the outcome and an expression of the bid for power on the part of individuals or factional groups. Thus, though the ideological defence of these arrangements recognises justice as an important value, the conception of political power engendered in them treats such power as the object of a desire which is not primarily but, at best, only derivatively concerned with justice. As things are, this desire is basically *pleonexia*, the urge to better, to outdo, others. But in itself such a desire is inimical to justice, since it is likely to lead to acts of injustice. Therefore, even when some sort of 'justice' results from the successful attempt to satisfy this desire in the political context, the value of justice is always at the mercy of, and dependent upon, the desire for political control being satisfied. It follows that any conception of the good life that places pre-eminent value on justice as a virtue will have to admit that no existing political arrangement and, hence, no conventional conception of power, can have the virtue of justice as its chief aim. Alternatively, a view which places justice at the centre of the good life will have to show that power, suitably reinterpreted, *can* be the object of a desire whose nature is the reverse of *pleonexia*. The *Republic* as a whole tries to show that only when power is seen as essentially flowing from knowledge (as Plato understands it) will the desire for it incorporate the desire for virtue and justice. This is because it is only under this condition that it would be rational to entrust the fulfilment of the desire for virtue and justice to the desire for power. Under ordinary political arrangements such trust is foolhardy and dangerous.

We are not, of course, concerned in this study with Plato's larger claims about justice, power and knowledge. Nevertheless, in an interesting and important way the character and significance of 'Thrasymachus' prepares the way for what becomes the main theme of the *Republic*. The preliminary task of Socrates' confrontation with Thrasymachus in Book I is to show that Thrasymachus is mistaken in confining the desire for power to *pleonexia*. As a consequence, the latter's belief that the value of mastery, control and freedom is yielded by the successful pursuit of that desire is shown to be an illusion. As we shall see later, Socrates' arguments acquire a special significance when seen against this background. They are meant to remove some of the foundations of Thrasymachus' confidence that he is right about the nature of power and its relation to justice; they are definitely not aimed at proving that, *contra* Thrasymachus, justice is an unqualified good.

Part Two
The Argument

5

Defining Justice

SOCRATES

Socrates' life, his character, and his intellectual activity in Athens have been the subject of comment from antiquity until the present day.[1] Among philosophers and intellectuals in the West he has become the symbol of philosophic activity—of a lifelong commitment to the search for truth and of an uncompromising critical stance to accepted beliefs and attitudes. His trial and execution in 399 BC for impiety and for engaging in activities liable to corrupt the Athenian youth, has also made Socrates a kind of cultural hero: a good and just man, a sharp wit, and an outstanding intelligence, who stands up to the uncritical attitudes of his contemporaries. Out of this confrontation with his fellow Athenians, Socrates emerges as the reflective individual, resolutely refusing to compromise his search for the rational foundations of morality and human excellence. The resulting image, partly due to the manner Plato presents Socrates in the 'early' dialogues, is that of the exemplary courage, wisdom and self-control required by those who will pit an 'intellectualist' conception of morality to one bound by custom and tradition—a lesson, and a warning, to all those who find the Socratic ideal seductive.[2]

No doubt this portrait is somewhat romantic. It is highly unlikely that even the band of admirers around Socrates, let alone the rest of his fellow Athenians, would recognise in it the Socrates they knew.[3] It is even dubious whether they would have fully understood the terms in which this image of Socrates is articulated. For, it is an image shaped by the development, in the intervening centuries, of what has established itself as the Western philosophical tradition—a tradition in which the search for Truth through reasoned argument came to occupy a central place. But Socrates and Plato were at the beginning of that tradition. Indeed, they formed a crucial moment in the movement that sought the separation of philosophy from the activity of poets, dramatists, orators, itinerant teachers and intellectuals bent on persuading people how it is best to live and to arrange the affairs of one's *polis*. It is highly probable, therefore, that at this early stage philosophic activity would have seemed to be part of the general art of persuasion—an art that perhaps reached its highest point in the democratic Athens of the fifth and fourth centuries BC. Plato in the dialogues is at pains to distinguish Socrates' method of cross-examination by question and answer (the *elenchos*) from other techniques of public persuasion that were enjoying a vogue in Athenian political circles. But Plato's almost obsessive concern throughout his life to draw demarcation lines between 'dialectic' (the skill of philosophic discourse) and rhetoric, suggests that it was not at all easy, even for him, to get clear the difference between philosophy and the art of persuasion.[4] To his, and Socrates', contemporaries the Socratic 'method' of dealing with current opinions and attitudes may have appeared to differ not in substance but only in style from other techniques of persuasion.[5]

It does not fall within the scope of this book to deal with the general aspects of Socrates' method, nor is it my purpose to discuss whether the views and practices of the historical Socrates matched those given to him by Plato. The fact that Plato wrote dialogues whose major character is Socrates unavoidably raises the question of the relation between the two. There is reasonable consensus among scholars that the dialogues of the 'early' period give us a reasonably faithful account of Socrates' thought, while it is generally recognised that in the *Phaedo* and the *Republic* Plato is introducing ideas that are not Socratic.[6] But even if we confine our attention to the 'Socratic' dialogues, we cannot avoid the almost overwhelming impression that what Nietzsche called Socrates' 'despotic logic' is aimed at persuading people to adopt a new ethical outlook. Socrates' *elenchos* is not, as on the surface it appears to be, merely a negative, critical, discussion of views and opinions. His logic is, precisely, despotic because beneath its formal structure there lurks a constant and relentless effort to get interlocutors to abandon their customary ways of talking and thinking about moral excellence in favour of a new way. Whether or not this was the purpose of the historical Socrates, it is certainly the intent of the character 'Socrates' in Plato's 'Socratic' dialogues. To the extent that Book I of the *Republic* has all the attributes of such a dialogue, that intent is present in it.

The second part of this study deals with Socrates' contribution to the discussion in Book I of the *Republic*. My main purpose is to analyse the nature and significance of the ways 'Socrates' in this particular Platonic text attempts to bring about a 'replacement' of the ordinary discourse about justice. The main thrust of the argument earlier was to suggest that Socrates' interlocutors represent 'resistances' to Socrates' new discourse about morality—resistances embedded in the discursive practices of his contemporaries. My aim is to explore how Socrates attempts to overcome these resistances. My concern, therefore, is not primarily to assess the formal validity or invalidity of Socrates' arguments, but to investigate Socrates' tactics, his strategy as it were. The main result of this investigation, as we shall see, is that Socrates (or Plato through 'Socrates') wants to convince his interlocutors that there must be an 'internal' relation between justice and power if the ordinary belief that justice is part of human excellence is to be *rationally* grounded. The chief stumbling block to accepting this, he feels, is located in the very habits of thought and action which shaped the views about justice and power exemplified in the discourse of Cephalus, Polemarchus and Thrasymachus. For, though their views are different, and even opposed, the way all three discourse about justice and power reveals, under Socratic examination, that they assume the relation between the two to be 'external'; that it is one thing to be just and act justly, and quite another thing to be powerful or to act powerfully. Though they think that the one can be subordinated to the other (the subordination can go in either direction), they find it impossible to understand the idea that being just *is* an exercise of power, and that a true conception of human power must include the ability to act justly.

This was a new idea, as paradoxical and radical now as it must have been then. I believe it is important to consider again its meaning, and the consequences that flow from it. The view that justice is something external to power still forms the backdrop to discussions about justice. It is the foundations of what one may call the liberal conception of justice, exemplified not only among its philosophical defenders but, also, in the views and attitudes of the people who live in, and accept the assumptions of, the social structures of Western capitalist democracies.[7] I shall postpone discussion of the substantive issues that arise from a confrontation of these two conceptions of justice till the concluding chapter. The task of the following chapters is to trace the way Socrates tries to make room for this new idea by a two-pronged attack on ordinary discourse about justice: while he stresses aspects of the use of the concept acknowledged in common opinion, he tries to expose weaknesses in how this opinion conceives of justice. These weaknesses become apparent only when the ordinary conception is juxtaposed to how the people who have that conception also think about human excellence.

Socrates' insistence on a definition of moral qualities, on discovering the 'essence' of what 'virtue' words refer to, as well as his negative criticism of the answer he gets, are part of a strategy to change the discourse of his contemporaries. He wanted to persuade them that how they acted and lived was based on an understanding of justice, and of morality in general, which did not square with what they were prepared to admit constituted living and acting successfully. But given that they also regarded (or said they did) the morally good person as admirable and fine, there ought to be a conception of justice which tied it logically to living well and successfully. At least, it should be possible to construct a view of justice and human well-being which, though intelligible to everyone, required a radical shift in how the relation between justice and excellence in human activity was understood. Socrates is a conceptual reformist because he is a moral reformist. But he is a moral reformist of a very special kind; he believes that ways of speaking and thinking about virtue reflect or correspond to forms of living, to the social structures, the practices and customs, prevalent in a kind of community.

To make people truly convinced that their discourse is deficient is, therefore, to reveal to them faults in how they lived. In Socrates' hands the critique of beliefs is a critique of culture. It would seem that those Athenians who were suspicious of Socrates, who regarded his activities as undermining the ethos of democratic Athens, were not far wrong. Why else would the man so stubbornly persist in showing up people's inability to reason consistently instead of, like any decent citizen, publicly attempting to sway his fellow citizens towards the policies he favoured?[8]

This total faith in the power of discussion will certainly strike us as strange today. Even taking into account the special economic and socio-political structures which enabled Athenian citizens to spend considerable time conversing and politicking, it may still seem odd that one could think of discursive critique as an instrument of moral and political transformation.[9] Faced with the *atmosphere* of the dialogues one is tempted to wonder how Socrates and Plato could neglect the power of wealth and position to influence public and private conduct. If they really cared about their city and its people, if they were disturbed by its conduct and wanted to reform it, why did they choose such an aloof way of intervening?[10] Yet, this 'intellectualist' approach to moral and political life is precisely the one Socrates and Plato wanted to urge was necessary. Whether it contains any important insights I shall consider at the end of this study. Nevertheless, it explains some of Socrates' strange convictions, as well as certain general principles which govern his method of investigation into 'virtue' in general, and justice, in particular, in Book I of the *Republic*. As a preliminary to the discussion it will help to note how these Socratic beliefs and procedural assumptions relate to his aim to change the discourse of his contemporaries.

Among Socrates' convictions about virtue and justice which we have no reason to think Plato abandoned, are the following: that justice should be valued for itself, that it cannot be the 'work' of justice to harm anyone, that virtue is self-sufficient and ensures happiness, and that virtue is knowledge of the good.[11] None of these beliefs are sustainable on an ordinary or traditional conception of justice. For, to the extent that one views justice as having to do with how one treats others, or with the treatment one receives in the hands of others, the value of just conduct will always depend on how the interests of those involved are affected. It may well turn out, as it often does, that acting fairly, or in consideration of what is due to someone else, entails a loss or a sacrifice on the part of the agent. Now, while such a loss may be justifiable on the grounds that so acting secures a greater, overall, benefit, this still does not justify the belief that justice should be valued for itself. For if, in some circumstances, it appears obvious that the just act will not increase what is beneficial to all, what sense is there in acting justly? To value justice for itself means that there is a good 'internal' to acting justly which no circumstances, no matter how adverse, can affect. But what sort of notion of justice is it that makes this sort of benefit clear? Certainly not the traditional one. Similar considerations make it difficult to see how the traditional conception could account for the belief that virtue is self-sufficient and ensures happiness.

From the traditional point of view the idea that it is not the 'work' of justice to harm anyone is positively paradoxical, if not downright false. Among other things, justice means redressing wrongs committed, bringing criminals to account for their misdeeds, removing opportunities for unfair practices, and so on. All these involve the exercise of power and coercion which standardly result in culprits being punished or disadvantaged in some way. How, then, can being just avoid injuring others, especially when one considers that such injury is required by the overall benefit allegedly secured by justice? As to the belief that justice is knowledge of the good, implying that there is a skilful or rational *procedure* for determining what is objectively good, the traditional view of virtue and justice would have found it difficult to comprehend. Assessing what constitutes a fair treatment, a malpractice, or a wrong, ultimately relies on the norms, the judgements, and decisions enshrined in the laws and customs—the ways—of a community. Other than degrees in depth of acquaintance with these ways, there is no expertise whose field is the determination of the good.[12] All people are capable of forming an opinion on these matters, even if not all opinions are equally worthy. The beliefs that justice does not harm and that it is knowledge of the good, require a conception of justice radically different from the traditional one. The latter certainly cannot explain why one should hold these beliefs about justice.

Socrates' method of inquiry into 'virtue' is guided by a strong sense of this need to transform the common or traditional ways of understanding what the terms signifying recognised virtues, moral excellences, must refer to. It has been well said that the therapeutic, negative, and critical function of the *elenchos* is seen by Socrates as preceding positive progress towards discovering the truth about the virtue under discussion.[13] His aim is not merely to produce a healthy moral scepticism in place of the thoughtless dogma of tradition, but also to improve moral convictions. A central assumption in his procedure is that knowledge of a particular virtue, or virtue in general, is prior to knowledge of anything else about it.[14] This implies that the truth of statements attributing certain characteristics to a virtue, such as that it benefits its possessor, or that it can be taught, and so on, depends on the truth of statements asserting what is the nature or 'essence' of the virtue in question. This is directly contrary to traditional ways of speaking about virtue. Everyone readily agrees that courage is a good and admirable thing while there may be divergences of opinion as to how exactly to define what courage is. Socrates thinks that the inability to have a clear idea about the nature of a virtue entails that agreement about its attributes does not bespeak anything stable and reliable. Such agreement is compatible with holding different and, even, incompatible, forms of conduct to be courageous. Consequently, Socrates always begins his questioning by asking for a definition of the virtue under discussion. This is the way he chooses to press upon his interlocutors the need to revise their conception of virtue.

As a recent commentator has pointed out, Socrates' demand for a definition in relation to the virtues is implicitly a request for an understanding of virtue which is at once theoretical and 'reformist'—and 'reformist' because it is theoretical.[15] This comes about because in asking for a definition Socrates is not seeking an analysis of the *meaning* of the terms of denoting virtues. He is asking for an account of the virtue which (a) fits ordinary intuitions about the type of conduct that counts as an example of the virtue; (b) incorporates people's judgements about what is good and beneficial; and (c) explains what the virtue is in the sense that it sets out a standard or a general criterion for deciding what makes virtuous an act or a state of character considered to be an exemplification of a virtue. The reasoning behind Socrates' assumption seems to be something like this: people have intuitions about what are examples of virtue and they also have beliefs about what is good and beneficial. But these beliefs often conflict with the intuitions, and this leads to confusion not only in thought but in action. The way out of this confusion is to hit on a characterisation of virtue which is not only true of it, but which *justifies* the beliefs and intuitions one has, and harmonises the one with the other. To justify acting justly, for instance, one must show that the person performing the action, or who possesses the character, benefits *in the way* justice benefits. But we cannot show this unless we have an account of justice and of how it relates to what is genuinely good. There is nothing to say in advance that achieving the latter account will leave undisturbed the ordinary or traditional criteria for determining what counts as an instance of justice. Achieving a theoretical understanding of the connection between justice and goodness may require a revision of our intuitive ways of determining what are cases of justice. Socrates is a reformist about virtue because he has an 'intellectualist' approach to it: what is perceived as virtuous is subject to how one thinks about virtue in general, and how one thinks about virtue should be (it often is not) under the control of reason. If what controls thought about virtue is left to factors other than reason, widely divergent judgements as to what counts as virtuous conduct, and of its worth, become unavoidable.

Socrates' procedure in conducting the *elenchos* incorporates these central assumptions. He almost invariably brings into interaction three kinds of belief: beliefs about general moral rules and definitions of virtues, beliefs about what conduct exemplifies the virtues, and theoretical beliefs about the necessary connections between virtue and value—for example, that virtuous action is necessarily good (*agathon*), admirable (*kalon*) and beneficial (*ōphelimon*).[16] What most often happens in a 'Socratic' dialogue is that Socrates is dubious about those of his interlocutor's beliefs which belong to the first kind. He relies on agreement between himself and them about the second and third kind of belief to force the interlocutor to revise in a certain direction his belief about a moral rule or the definition of virtue he proposed. This is the case, as we shall presently see, with how Socrates deals with Cephalus and Polemarchus. In other instances there is disagreement about whether a type of conduct is an example of virtue. Socrates relies on the belief that whatever is held to be virtuous must be worthwhile and beneficial to the agent to reject the disputed example. This is illustrated in the discussion with Thrasymachus, though, as we saw earlier, the latter's challenge raises some important questions about power and excellence.

One may say, then, that in general Socrates asumes that whatever the moral beliefs about virtue, whether traditional or critical of tradition, they are corrigible 'from within' as it were. This is because he thinks that whether the holders of these beliefs realise it or not, their beliefs contain an incipient image of virtue, or of some particular virtue; an 'outline', so to speak, of what a moral term really refers to. If, for example, an interlocutor is prepared to admit (that is, it is reasonable for him to admit) that some type of action commonly thought of as an exemplification of a virtue cannot properly be described by using the name of the virtue because it harms the agent, this must indicate that the interlocutor recognises, however dimly, that the type of action does not fit the 'outline' of what the virtue really is. Since a correct account of what the virtue-name genuinely refers to must explain how and why what the word refers to is necessarily beneficial, one can use this principle as a test to decide whether a given virtue-word should be applied to a type of conduct. The adoption of this principle is essentially revisionary: however haphazard and unreflective the *learning* of virtue-words in a community, and in spite of the fact that moral beliefs are frequently held without rational grounds, both the beliefs and how people use moral language are revisable through discussion.

Socrates' view is based on what he takes to be an important fact. People may be misguided in their conception of goodness and excellence. Nevertheless, they possess a fundamental desire to achieve goodness and excellence which must involve the desire to understand them correctly. Therefore, an intellectual examination of virtue and excellence is one that can appeal to people's general desire to achieve excellence. If you can demonstrate to them that how they understand virtue will frustrate their efforts to achieve genuine well-being, they will be strongly motivated to re-think their ways of conceiving virtue, and to be critical of the social and cultural factors which shape their inadequate conceptions. Discoursing on virtue unavoidably has socio-political implications precisely because people can be made aware that some of the central limitations in their moral thought are due to the social structures within which they live. And given that no one desires to live miserably, people have an overwhelmingly powerful motivation to reject critically not only the aspects of their thinking which prevent them from achieving a satisfactory life, but also the social practices which give rise to and maintain these ways of thinking. Socrates' *elenchos* is not merely a preliminary to moral reform; it is an instrument of cultural transformation through the critical revision of moral discourse. Socrates does indeed have a mission, and it is a revolutionary one; his search for a definition of the virtues is no mere 'academic' exercise.[17]

SOCRATES AND CEPHALUS

From Socrates' point of view, then, the stakes of engaging people in the *elenchos* are very high indeed. This explains 'the personal character of the elenchos'.[18] It also explains Socrates' assumption that those reputed to possess some virtue ought to be able to tell us what that virtue is, if they genuinely have it.[19] This assumption governs Socrates' hope that Cephalus, having reached the condition of old age, would be able to tell what is good or bad about that condition (328e 5–7). As we saw earlier, Cephalus' response is that finding old age a good thing depends on whether you have the disposition of those who have 'order and peace within themselves' (329d 4–6). He subsequently identifies this disposition with the inclination not to tell lies or deceive, and the willingness to fulfil obligations to gods and men. He believes that a life which manifests these dispositions is the life of a just person, of a person conscious of having lived free from injustice (331a,b). Cephalus leaves unsaid how he thinks of the relation between having order and peace within oneself and having the dispositions he specifies. It is also unclear whether Cephalus takes it that being conscious of having lived free from injustice is merely to be aware that one has not cheated or told lies, and that one has fulfilled one's obligations to gods and men. For, if the consciousness of living justly is the knowledge that one has performed certain types of action, it is not clear why the disposition to perform these actions should be attributed to a particular kind of personality. Perhaps the disposition to act in the relevant ways is acquired by habit, and can be so acquired by people who differ widely in character. If to be just is *simply* to manifest a disposition to act in certain ways, there is no reason to think that the disposition must be the effect of an orderly and peaceful character. If there is no reason to think this, Cephalus will not be justified in linking without argument this awareness of living justly with the possession of a certain character. Moreover, given that Cephalus also believes that living justly is a good thing, and that it contributes to a man's happiness (*eudaimonia*), he ought to be able to say whether the excellence and benefit of just conduct ought to be attributed to the nature of the character which, in his view, generates the conduct. Otherwise, it could turn out that the benefits of just conduct are 'external' to the possession of a particular sort of character.

Socrates' remark that telling the truth and returning what one has received cannot be the definition of justice (*horos dikaiosynēs*, 331d 2−3) is a conclusion based on Cephalus' agreement (331d 1) that, in view of Socrates' counter-example of returning borrowed weapons to a man gone mad, we cannot simply (*haplōs*) identify justice with certain types of action. What does Socrates' counter-example show? He claims that instances of the types of action Cephalus thinks of as just can, in different circumstances, be identified as cases of 'acting unjustly'. The latter is a true description of the act of giving a borrowed weapon back to a friend who, while being out of his senses, reclaims it. Everyone would acknowledge, says Socrates, that under the circumstances one should not return the weapon, that it would be unjust to do so. One could certainly agree with Socrates that returning the weapon to the friend would be wrong because of the damage the friend might inflict on himself or others. But why should that render the borrower's action *unjust*? One could grant that a just person, being a person whose conduct is directed at good and laudable ends, will refrain from acting in a way likely to bring about harm. But this does not tell us what is distinctive about acting justly. How does it relate to acting wisely, judiciously or even bravely? It may be, for example, that the 'friend' is a personage of great power, capable of inflicting severe penalties on the borrower.[20] To think that returning the weapon in the circumstances would be unjust, the borrower must be aware of something more than that the action is wrong. He must know that the wrongness of the action is of a kind which makes it *contrary* to the rightness that inheres in the way the just person standardly, or characteristically, estimates the worth of returning things borrowed, or of telling the truth. If this is so, we cannot derive the rightness of acting justly from the supposed rightness of the actions, for they may or may not manifest the virtue. The just action is not merely a good or beneficial action: it is an action whose goodness is that which specifically belongs to justice.

The borrower who refuses to give back the weapon will be just if, and only if, the way he assesses the alternatives in the situation is the *same* as the way he assesses the alternatives in other circumstances when he does return the weapon. If this 'epistemic' capacity is part of the virtue of justice we will want to know how it contributes to the just person's ability to lead a good and happy life. For if it does not, there will be no reason to think that living justly necessarily contributes to doing well in one's life. The borrower who refuses to return the weapon may suffer considerable disadvantages from the very fact that his action is responsible for averting harm coming to others. In what way, then, is one's justice of essential benefit to oneself? The just action can produce benefit or avert harm, but must it do so necessarily, and in a characteristic manner, for the just agent?

Some of the issues raised here are further explored by Socrates in his discussion with Polemarchus. But there is a point which specifically concerns Cephalus. He seems convinced that persons in whom there is 'order and peace' lead the life of justice and avoid injustices. One may assume that such a person would agree with

Socrates that it was wrong to return the weapon in the circumstances imagined. But would he do so *from* justice?[21] For all Cephalus says, such a person may so act because he is well-disposed towards the friend, or because he does not like to see any harm coming to people, or because he loathes disturbances and upheavals, or . . . because of a variety of motivations. The question is whether all, or any, of these are the motives operating when a person acts justly. It is not difficult to imagine that people who act from the above motives may not have the goals just persons are supposed to have. More importantly, if these are the motives in avoiding injustice there may be circumstances of external pressure (deprivation, intimidation by others, personal loss, and so on), in which 'the mild and orderly' person may be forced to act unjustly. However pleasant and desirable it is to live among people who are mild and orderly, and though it may be good for people to have this character, there is nothing to say that this must be the character of the just person. Nor is it obvious that even if just people do have gentle and orderly personalities, their justice is *due* to that personality, rather than the other way round. The crucial moral question is whether the psychic structure of the peaceful and orderly character is of the sort to prevent a person from committing injustice. Cephalus' conviction that persons with such a character live justly is insecure and ungrounded unless he can give an account of the type of connection he believes exists between this type of character and justice.

Socrates' probing of Cephalus effectively exposes the weaknesses and inadequacies of the views and attitudes Plato incorporates in the character. As we saw earlier (see above, Chapter 2), the main thrust of that characterisation was to signal that the traditional conception of the life of goodness cannot explain why it regards certain ingredients (character and good fortune) as being essential to it. Socrates takes this to mean that living in accordance with the traditional interpretation of the life of virtue may not be good, since it does not enable those who live that way to explain what stops them from being vicious and unjust. Cephalus' account of what makes his life a good and just one does not show that he avoids injustice because he understands the harm 'internal' to being unjust. Thus, paradoxically, a life lived 'in accordance with justice' may not in fact be a life lived 'from justice'. If the reasons Cephalus has for not departing from the path of justice are not the reasons justice itself prescribes, then in an important sense the life 'in accordance with justice' will not be able to supply the right reasons in support of the claim that it *is* just. Under questioning the life reveals itself incapable of providing those who live it with a justification of why they attribute certain qualities to it.

It is important to understand this Socratic emphasis on 'self-examination'. There is nothing more natural than to interpret Socrates' counter-example as an effective way of blocking definitions of justice along behavioural lines. It certainly does that. But Socrates' move is not directed at a proposition put forward by Cephalus in the course of an abstract, 'academic' debate. The proposition (articulated by Socrates) is a summing up of the idea of acting justly that Cephalus' life itself affords or generates. Cephalus is a spokesman for the life, not a theorist *about* the life. Thus, Socrates' counter-example is not aimed at Cephalus' lack of argumentative ability, since the latter's failure in this regard may not show anything significant about his picture of the good life. Nevertheless, Cephalus' lack of a reflective capacity is linked to his failure to provide an adequate definition of justice. The failure shows that the-good-life-according-to-Cephalus does not generate an adequate understanding of justice, since, from the point of view of that life, one cannot explain that the benefits 'internal' to justice belong to it, even if the life appears good in other respects. The life regards itself as good and just, but it cannot explain that its goodness is the goodness of justice, since it is unclear about what the latter goodness consists in.

Socrates' counter-example, and especially the way he characterises it, effectively brings home the fact that the life led according to traditional values characterises justice in terms which do not account for its excellence. It is a mode of life which locates the capacity in people to conduct themselves justly in the fact that they possess a character which disposes them to avoid deceit and to fulfil obligations to gods and men. But people who share that mode of life are also capable of seeing that in some circumstances telling the truth or returning something borrowed is acting unjustly. Thus, the capacity to recognise what is just or unjust appears separate from, and unrelated to, the disposition to tell the truth and fulfil obligations. Perhaps the character which produces the latter disposition is also responsible for the former recognitional capacity. If it is, then just persons tell the truth and fulfil obligations only because they recognise that doing so in some cases is just while in other cases it is not. The just person does not perform these acts if circumstances render them unjust. But if life according to traditional values produces a character disposed to act in certain set ways, how can that life also produce the recognitional capacity that sometimes acting in these set ways is wrong? To be able to attribute to character a person's capacity to recognise justice means that we cannot define (= understand) the just character as merely the disposition to behave in these set ways. This is because any definition of the latter kind would cut off the possibility of using the terms 'just' or 'unjust' as part of a reflective vocabulary about one's conduct. It would mean, for example, that those who lived, like Cephalus, the life of 'traditional' justice could not use the concept of justice to *ask* whether that life was a just one. And if they cannot ask this question, on what grounds can they *assert* that the life of honesty and fulfilled obligations is the one just persons must lead?

SOCRATES AND POLEMARCHUS

Polemarchus does not see this problem because, unlike his father, he does not locate the capacity to recognise what is just in the character of a person. The criterion of just conduct for him is contained in Simonides' dictum that it is just to render to each what is his due. His father's idea of how the just person specifically behaves should be separated from any vague reference to a 'peaceful and orderly' character. Justice is conformity to a general (social) rule from which can be derived what is specifically required in any given case. Thus, the returning of a borrowed weapon is 'due' if the lender, who may have been a friend, is still friendly; withholding the borrowed weapon is 'due' if the lender has in the meantime become in some ways hostile (by going mad). We saw earlier some of the implications of this view of justice. Let us now examine how effectively Socrates deals with these implications. The argument proceeds in two stages. The first (331d–334b) appears as a negative attempt to show that Polemarchus' use of the Simonides dictum would make the knowledge of the just person relatively unimportant, and usable in morally dubious ways. The second stage (334b–336a) is more positive. It suggests that the way justice functions or 'works' in a person cannot lead that person to harm or damage anyone; the excellence of justice cannot be separated from a concern to promote and safeguard the goodness of that with which it deals.

The first stage of Socrates' argument follows a complex strategy. He establishes that, in Polemarchus' understanding, the 'due' action is the action appropriate or fitting (*prosēkon*) to a recipient under some description. If returning something borrowed is harmful then its being a just act depends on whether the lender is a friend or not (332a,b). Polemarchus' notion of rendering what is fitting to everyone implies that persons are engaged in just activity if, and only if, the benefit or harm their actions bring to others is *knowledgeably* produced. The just person not only must know that action A is beneficial to X and harmful to Y; he or she must also know to what end X is to be benefited or Y harmed. Only so can one say that in doing A to X or to Y the just person did what was appropriate or fitting. Socrates' analogy with craft-knowledge here (332c) is apt, since whether a craftsman does the 'right' or 'fitting' thing in the exercise of his skill is determined by reference to the product of that skill. The craftsman can give an explanation of the goodness or correctness of his productive activities by showing how they are undertaken for the sake of a given kind of product.[22] The destruction of tissue, for example, or the disturbance of a balance of substances through a change in diet, cannot be said to be a bad or good thing except by reference to the knowledgeable production of health which is what medicine *is*.

There are some important and difficult questions about Socrates' analogy which we shall consider at the end of the discussion of this phase of the argument. At the moment let us note how by means of it he forces Polemarchus to consider the implications of his view of justice. If just persons benefit friends and harm enemies because this is the 'fitting' thing to do, then there will be a 'field' or subject-matter of justice, and a 'product' or 'outcome' of it, with reference to which the excellence of just activity will be judged. The 'field' of medicine is the body (bodily conditions). By means of drugs or diets the craft renders what is fitting to the body (332c). But the aim and 'product' of medical skill is a healthy bodily condition, and it is knowledge of what bodily health consists in that makes the administration of a drug, or the recommendation of a certain kind of diet, the 'fitting' thing in each case.

Socrates' analogy forces Polemarchus to reflect about the implications of the view that being just consists in doing what is expected or required of a person to do in the context of a type of social relationship. For, *if* acting justly is acting excellently, then we should be able to specify, with respect to helping friends and harming enemies, the excellence of the goal that is being served by so acting. We do not know whether particular acts of helping friends and harming enemies are good things to do (and, hence, that acting justly is a good thing to do), unless we know that there is a specific kind of good that this type of conduct is aimed at. Is there a 'good of justice', in terms of which we can explain why helping a friend or harming an enemy is the 'fitting' thing to do? The trouble with Polemarchus' conception of justice is that it does not provide him with a clear answer to this question. He believes that acting justly is a good thing, and so he believes that doing what is 'due' to friends and enemies (his notion of justice), is a good thing. But are there rational grounds for this belief? Polemarchus' dictum about friends and enemies expresses an expectation and, perhaps, a permission recognised in a community. People are expected to behave co-operatively towards those well-disposed to them and to act aggressively towards those not so disposed. But why should the treatment any individual 'deserves' depend on his or her relationship to those in a position to dispense it, rather than, say, on the nature of that individual's conduct? Polemarchus' view does not distinguish acting justly from acting in accordance with what is socially expected. Consequently, he is unable to explain the belief that there is a specific kind of goodness or excellence of justice, one which, though related to goodness in general, marks a distinctive aspect of it. Are there any features 'internal' to acting justly which help explain how it contributes to goodness, and, hence, why it is desirable in itself? Polemarchus' idea of what people value when they value justice does not allow him to take this question seriously.

Socrates' craft-analogy, and his subsequent argument, bring out the features Polemarchus' notion of justice overlooks. The notion overlooks the 'powers' of justice—the capacity to achieve a certain type of excellence which the virtuous person, *qua* just, must of necessity possess. The ability to achieve certain good results is not a virtue unless that ability is grounded on a capacity the virtuous person, as such, possesses. Hence, the analogy of the just person with the craftsman. The relation between the craftsman's activities and the 'product' of his craft is 'internal': it is because various procedures are the best, or the most efficient, or the only, ways of achieving certain ends, and the craftsman knows this, that achieving these ends by means of these procedures constitutes a skill (a *technē*). A person's success in bringing off certain results bespeaks a skill only if the success is due to the exercise of a knowledgeable capacity. The exercise of that capacity does not, of course, guarantee the result (there could be interference). Nevertheless, it explains it when the result is brought about through the exercise of the skill. This is why the craftsman can explain himself: he can tell what his actions enable him to achieve within a certain 'field'.

Polemarchus believes that helping friends and harming enemies achieves some good. But he cannot show why one should think of such actions as achieving the good of justice, or how the capacity to achieve this good belongs to the just person as such. Polemarchus does not, of course, think of justice this way. Socrates forces this conceptual framework upon him, his justification being that Polemarchus' discourse about justice leaves it utterly obscure why, within that discourse, justice should be understood as a virtue. The craft-analogy is a powerful instrument for uncovering the fact that the Polemarchian discourse about justice neither explains nor justifies beliefs framed in its terms. Therefore, either his discursive practice or his belief that justice is a virtue must be given up. Socrates clearly wants to retain the belief. He must, consequently, press Polemarchus to jettison the way he talks and thinks about justice. The craft-analogy organises the overall strategy of this pressure; it enables Socrates to highlight, indirectly, the requirements of how one should characterise justice if one believes it to be an excellence.

To speak of justice as a virtue one must be able to nominate the type of action or the kind of 'function' (*ergon*) with respect to which the possessor of the virtue is most capable (*dunatotatos*). We have to specify the 'field' of justice, otherwise we shall not be able to say concerning any putatively just act that it *is* an exercise of the virtue. The weakness in the conventional view that justice consists in behaving in certain ways within a community—the idea of a *polis* or 'civic' justice—is that it takes the goal of the just person to be the securing of what is thought beneficial to different kinds of social relationship. Being in war, for instance, or entering business transactions, imposes certain requirements; how to select allies and enemies and how to behave towards them, how to decide on business partners and the conditions of partnership, and so on. We may call the right decisions on these matters those which secure the 'goods' of war relationships and business deals, respectively. By these 'goods' we mean not the benefits one may obtain as a result of engaging in war or business, but what is the 'good', the 'right' and 'proper', thing to do *qua* someone engaging in war or business. But why should the goal of the just person be the 'good' of war or business in this sense? If the just are virtuous one would expect that their aim would be to achieve the ends set by that virtue itself, irrespective of what is demanded of them by the social relationships in which they find themselves at any given time.

The craft-analogy helps to bring these points home. Conventionally we expect the physician to cure us of our ailments, advise us on how to preserve our health, to arrest the progress of a deteriorating bodily condition or, at least, to relieve us from the misery of an incurable illness. But while a physician may succeed or fail to meet these expectations, the criteria of the success or failure of the skill of medicine are not set by the fact that it meets the expectations of lay-people. These criteria are 'internal' to the complex set of bodily conditions that constitute health or disease which the skill of medicine aims to produce. It is with reference to these bodily conditions that the actions of physicians are judged to be *medical*. It is the knowledgeable manipulation of the bodily processes that constitute healthy or unhealthy states which makes someone a physician, and which provides a criterion of what it is to act medically. Medicine, then, has a 'field' by reference to which we can determine what are the goals of a physician *qua* physician, and the respects in which the physician is most capable to act well (*eu poiein*), irrespective of the benefits those who *use* the physician's skill may or may not obtain.

Polemarchus' 'helping friends and harming enemies', or 'rendering everyone their due', in relation to justice cannot distinguish the specific capacity to act well that the virtue of justice designates from the 'usefulness' of a just person in social relationships. It is because we know the 'field' of medicine and, so, the respects in which a physician is most capable of acting well, that the physician may be of use in benefiting friends or harming enemies (332d 10–332e 4): if that is what we want him or her for. But what we may want *of* a physician in no way settles what the physician, as such, wants. There may very well be a conflict between these two wants. Socrates is pressing Polemarchus to acknowledge that there is room for an analogous distinction between, on the one hand, the 'field' and goals that justice as a virtue sets, and on the other hand, the 'usefulness' of such a virtue to social relationships. To say that justice consists in helping friends and harming enemies cannot tell us what capacity to act well is specific to being just. Consequently, Polemarchus cannot say how the *way* the just help friends and harm enemies differs from non-just ways of doing so. Polemarchus' view of justice makes him incapable of entertaining the very real possibility that in some cases what the just desire and aim at will be in conflict with what others want or expect of him or her. If conformity to the latter expectations is the criterion of being just, no sense could be attached to the idea that it was *unjust*, for example, to help a friend or harm an enemy in some circumstances. This would be analogous to thinking that prescribing curative drugs or diets is what medicine consists of, thereby ruling out the possibility that in some cases to prescribe a drug or a diet may be *unmedical*; that there could be a conflict between what the physician, as such, should aim at, and what people want of him or her.

Polemarchus has difficulty in specifying a 'field' of justice—he first suggests wars and alliances (332a 5) and, later, commercial deals or financial agreements (*sumbolaia*, 333a 12)—precisely because he cannot distinguish the goals that the virtue of justice itself lays down from the 'usefulness' of certain types of conduct in social relationships. If justice consists in being useful in the latter sense, it will not have goals of its own. The goals just persons have will always depend on the expectations created by the social relationships in which they find themselves.

Equipped with the framework of the craft-analogy, Socrates can draw out how miniscule and ambiguous must be the moral value one attributes to justice if one thinks of it the way Polemarchus does. This sort of conception does not identify any important dimension of life with respect to which justice alone and by itself is useful in satisfying a need (*chroia*), or in procuring (*ktēsis*) benefits. Suppose, for example, we thought that a person's justice made them useful in circumstances where we had to decide whether to go to war with a city, or where we needed advice as to whom to ally ourselves with in a situation of inter-city conflict, or intra-city politics. Or suppose that the situation was one of peace. We may think that the just person is useful in helping us decide with whom to strike bargains or agreements, and in advising us about good and bad business partners. Thinking of justice this way suggests that we regard the co-operative and conflictual aspects of human life as the 'field' of justice (333a). The trouble with this is that though knowing how to co-operate, or how to fight and resist, may be necessary to the exercise of justice, they are not sufficient. To think that they are diminishes or obliterates any special moral value justice may have. It does so because it runs together knowing which situations call for the exercise of justice with knowing how to *be* just. To know, for example, that victory and defeat, honour and disgrace, are, respectively, the goods and evils of being in a situation of conflict, is not to know what makes either of them just or unjust. And similarly with the goods and evils of gain or loss in co-operative ventures.[23] It may be just to lose and unjust to gain; it may be unjust to assist friends or to harm an enemy. If there was no difference in these two types of knowledge, why would a just person be more useful than one who was merely a military or a financial expert? If anything, it should be the other way around (331b 1–9): the just person is less effective and less useful than such experts. Indeed, the 'usefulness' of justice in money-matters will not be in respect to the *use* of money, but when it lies idle. The just will be those most useful in guarding and safe-keeping it, while the financial expert advises best on how to use it (333b 10). One can rely on the just when money, and everything else, is not in use. When things are used, it is various experts that are most useful (333c–e). But no expert, military or financial, need be just. It follows, Socrates concludes (333e 1–2), that justice cannot be a very important thing.

The analogy of virtue with skill strikingly conveys the force of this point. For, suppose we (mistakenly) think that knowing what situations call for medical treatment constitutes the medical skill. This would mean that there were persons who could tell you what drugs or diets were most (or least) successful in dealing with certain conditions. But such knowledge would not be the most useful one could have in matters of health and disease. A knowledge of how and why a drug or diet was effective would be more useful because more reliable. Therefore, if we thought that the skill of medicine consisted in the former sort of knowledge, such 'medicine' would be relatively unimportant and, in crucial cases, useless compared with the latter knowledge. It would not really constitute a skill. Analogously, the 'field' of the virtue of justice dwindles in scope and importance the more we fail to discover any determinate goods or evils that constitute its province.

Polemarchus' failure to identify any specific aims of justice has the further consequence that he cannot justifiably declare to be unjust acts commonly thought to be such: theft or perjury, for example (334a 10–336b 3). Again the analogy with skill helps us to see the force of Socrates' point. Suppose we thought of bodily conditions as the 'field' of medicine without, however, having any clear conception of the sense in which health is *the* aim of medicine. Thus, observing correctly that the ability to reduce or increase weight falls within the range of the doctor's 'capacity for opposites', we think that the medical practitioner is most useful if we want to gain or lose weight. Given that we do not reflect on whether, in any given occasion, a medical good is being served by the use of slimming or fattening techniques, we shall determine the usefulness of the doctor's capacity for opposites by reference to aims external to the goal of health. Analogously, if we think of the 'field' of justice without acknowledging that there is any specific good that constitutes its goal, we shall judge the usefulness of a 'just' person's 'capacity for opposites' in terms 'external' to the goals of justice. Thus, the capacity to defend and attack in battle, to avoid or inflict disease, to guard something or to get around the guard of others, to keep money safe or to remove it from the safe-keeping of others—all these are abilities possession of which makes one advantageous to one's friends and dangerous to one's enemies. To think that to be just is to help friends and harm enemies means that we cannot reject any instances of the exercise of these abilities on the grounds of injustice—the way, for instance, we can declare cases of reducing or fattening procedures unmedical from the standpoint of regarding health as the aim of medicine. If, failing to grasp the goal of justice, we cannot distinguish the benefit of just acts *as* just from their advantageousness to friends or harmfulness to enemies, why should we morally condemn all theft or perjury as unjust (334a, b)? Some instances of these acts may be quite 'just'—the very thing we might expect from someone who thought of justice like Polemarchus.

Polemarchus is thoroughly perplexed, but he does not want to give up his belief that the goal of justice is to benefit friends and harm enemies. The second stage of Socrates' argument (334b 7–336a 10) examines this conception of the goal of justice, having shown that such a goal is not grounded on attributing any important 'field' to justice, or on an 'internal' criterion for assessing the benefit of just actions. Before we look, in the next chapter, at this second stage of Socrates' critique of Polemarchus, it is worth reflecting on the issues raised by Socrates' negative argument so far.

The analogy between the knowledge involved in virtue and craft-knowledge is a central feature of the 'Socratic' dialogues. Though there is some doubt among scholars how far Plato was aware of the difficulties in this analogy, one can reasonably assume that it played an important dialectic role in Socrates' examination of the moral beliefs and attitudes of his contemporaries.[24] We need to distinguish between the use of this analogy for the negative purposes of the *elenchos* and the suggestion that virtue *is* a moral craft. The reason for distinguishing these two aspects of the analogy is that the negative use may reveal important insights which are not affected by the problems besetting the idea of virtue as a craft.[25]

A common reaction to Socrates' assimilation of justice to a skill is that it confuses moral rules with 'technical' or prudential rules. Impressed by the Kantian claim that moral rules and maxims have a radically different status from those of skill and prudence, some think that moral rules apply unconditionally to a person, whether that person wants to achieve a given end or not. 'Technical' rules only apply when a given end is wanted; a skill is dependent on its end and if one does not want to achieve that end, one no longer has any reason for exercising or using that skill.[26] Polemarchus, therefore, should not have agreed with the analogy. However, even though he thinks of justice as observing certain rules and maxims as they apply to conduct within different kinds of social relationship, he implies that there is something like a point or end to being just—to benefit friends and harm enemies. Socrates' whole critique of Polemarchus is based on this implication. Though Polemarchus could have suggested that justice had a much more general end—happiness or a satisfactory life, as Cephalus thought—he could not easily do so since for him the rules of justice are a form of *regulation* of social interaction within a *polis* and, perhaps, between *poleis*.[27] However necessary and useful just conduct is to life in society, there is no overwhelming reason why Polemarchus should think of justice as *per se* contributing to a person's happiness or well-being (*eudaimonia*). Thus, though he could admit that just conduct made for an orderly and undisturbed social life, he need not have seen the 'work' of justice as anything more than securing the social conditions within which people flourished and pursued activities which led to or constituted their well-being. On this view it is dubious whether justice is a component part of personal flourishing, and, therefore, whether such flourishing can be thought as the goal of just actions.

Polemarchus' reference to benefiting friends and harming enemies suggests that he thinks of justice as a virtue fundamentally circumscribed by social aims. Being a virtue, justice must be thought of as an aspect of a person or an act which is of benefit to the agent. But given, also, that justice concerns how people act in relation to each other, the benefits of justice, those that accrue to the just agent, must be understood by reference to what the just act effects upon others. Putatively 'just' acts which harm friends or benefit enemies are not ultimately beneficial to the agent and, thus, cannot be virtuous. If follows that the benefits of justice for Polemarchus are 'reciprocal' benefits; that is, they are benefits which accrue to an agent as a result of doing good 'turns' to people friendly and well-disposed towards the agent, and bad 'turns' to those who are hostile and ill-disposed. This means that one cannot require that people act justly for the sake of benefits just conduct directly or *of itself* brings to the agent. Polemarchus' view, therefore, allows the possibility that the things one does *in* being just may not be particularly excellent or important. Justice may be a 'virtue' for Polemarchus, but its relation to a life of excellence is extremely vague and hazy.

Socrates' dialectic in this 'negative' stage of the argument has one main aim: to undermine Polemarchus' belief that the goodness of justice is to be understood in terms of its social effects. This belief needs to be undermined because if virtue is a human quality, and justice is part of virtue, we would be seriously wrong to think of justice as an attribute of relationships, or of a system of social relations, irrespective of what sort of human beings entered into these relations. For, to think of justice as an attribute of social relations does not impose any restrictions on the type of persons such relations require, or on the type of character which results from engaging in such relations. Socrates' negative use of the craft-analogy is forcing upon Polemarchus the realisation that he cannot explain why the people he regards as just exemplify a quality excellent in itself, one which enables them to lead excellent lives. Interestingly, though Polemarchus is prepared to allow that the just person is useful, he does not grasp what such a person is specifically good for. This is precisely what we can specify in the case of craftsmen; we can explain how the knowledge they possess is good *for*, makes them capable of, achieving results that are the aim of their skill. The important point about a craft and its 'product' is that the goodness of the activities the skill involves is not judged by reference to values external to the product, but to the nature of the product itself. It is not because we think, for other reasons, that health is a good thing that we judge medical activities to be good. The activities of the physician are good because they are *medical*; they are medical because they are good for producing health. The relation between the 'product' of a skill and the goodness of the activities constituting it is 'internal'. If justice is a virtue, and its goal is something essentially good, we should be able to specify a similarly 'internal' relation between the acts that constitute its exercise and its goal. Otherwise the 'goodness' of just acts and the good justice aims at will fly apart.

It is this flying apart of the benefits socially expected of just conduct from a good essential to justice itself which Polemarchus' view of justice is powerless to prevent. This powerlessness characterises not only the *view* but also a life led on Polemarchian lines.

6

Limits on the Just

The parallel Socrates employs between virtue and craft aims to show that if virtue is a human quality productive of excellence, then the relation between the ends virtue aims at and the excellence of the actions that constitute its exercise must be 'internal'. The goal of justice relates to just conduct the way that the 'product' of craft relates to the excellence of the activities that constitute the skill. The goodness of just actions must reside in the fact that they bring about what justice aims at, not in the fact that justice is thought desirable or useful on other grounds. This leaves Socrates with the large problem of explaining not only what are the specific aims of justice, but also, why they are necessarily good and beneficial in themselves. This problem does not arise with 'products' of ordinary skills. The value of such products can be determined by reference to our needs, to our wants and desires, and even by reference to their usefulness in helping produce the 'products' of further skills. Is Socrates prepared to accept that the value of the goals of justice is to be similarly determined? It would seem that such a view would render justice an instrumental good—a good in the service of other goods.

However difficult the positive task Socrates sets himself, there is an important insight contained in the analogy. Like a craftsman's knowledge, one's justice must enable one to explain that one's actions are good because of the way they contribute to the ends of justice. The just must be aware of the 'internal' connection between these ends and the goodness of their acts. As we saw, Polemarchus' account cannot accommodate this point because what he takes as the ends of justice—to benefit friends and harm enemies—do not determine anything morally distinctive as their component or constituent. The action which benefits friends in one kind of situation may harm them in another situation, or may benefit an enemy in yet another situation. The knowledge, therefore, of what benefits friends and harms enemies in any given instance is not one which the just possess *by* being just—there is no neccessary link between the knowledge productive of harm or benefit (to friends and enemies) and the knowledge productive of justice. This is because, unlike for example health and disease, 'benefiting friends' and 'harming enemies' do not indicate a unified or coherent 'field' within which the goodness or badness of different types of action can be assessed. Polemarchus' attempts to specify such a 'field' are conventional—war, alliances, commercial dealings. But though these may be traditionally important areas of the exercise of justice, he gives no clear idea as to the reasons why he wants to confine the 'field' of justice this way, or why it should be so confined.

Socrates' critique of Polemarchus brings out the moral and conceptual inadequacies in the idea of justice which accompanied the social and political developments in Athens. We saw earlier that they had to do with the emergence of 'civic' justice, the justice that is the 'business' of every citizen in the *polis*. But while this promoted an ethos preoccupied with the idea of receiving and administering justice, it had led to an atrophy of reflection about the human capacity inherent in *being* just. The effect of this atrophy was that the demand for certain 'values'—justice, for example—had come adrift from thinking of these values as the outcome of the exercise of specific human capacities. The 'goods' demanded had come to be seen as 'delivered' by institutions, as 'goods' which people receive or consume.

The phenomenon is not confined to Socrates' and Plato's Athens. Some contemporary thought-patterns are subject to a similar Socratic critique. For instance, the social and political transformations brought about by the 'Industrial Age' have led to the development of institutions which 'deliver' educational and health 'services'. The demand to expand these 'services' and to make them more widely available is steady and relentless. We think that everyone has a 'right' to them. But emphasis on this demand can bring a deep shift in how people evaluate education and health-care. While at an earlier stage being healthy and educated could have been seen as part of what it was to be an excellent person, that achieving these ends required certain qualities of character, the 'value' of health-care and education may not be judged this way in a context where people regard them as 'goods' distributed by the social system. Though it is true that in the earlier period these values were class-bound, that being uneducated and unhealthy was a mark of social inferiority, it was possible to regard failure to concern oneself with the improvement of one's mind and body as a moral failing—one that diminished one's excellence as a human being. Providing education and health-care as a social service to which everyone has a right can transform how the recipients of such service come to think of becoming educated and healthy, or of failing to do so. Success or failure in achieving these ends tends to be attributed to the capacity or incapacity of the social system to provide and distribute these 'goods' equitably. They are not seen as aims indicative of a person's moral frame of mind.

Though there are signs at present of a wish to return to this latter conception, it is uncertain whether one can reconcile regarding being healthy and educated as necessary for the morally good person, with the fact that health and education are considered 'consumable goods' provided by the social system. For, the latter mentality, while it may ensure that the opportunity to these 'goods' is not denied to anyone, may, nevertheless, foster the wrong conception of what makes health and education desirable. Similarly, Polemarchus' idea of justice as providing benefit to friends and harm to enemies does not show how acts of 'delivering' justice will promote in the 'receivers' the right conception of the good of being just, or, indeed, that there *is* such a good.

The pursuit of excellence in any field presupposes a context in which persons are able to judge what they can and cannot do, what disciplinary practices they must submit themselves to if they are to reach certain levels and achieve certain skills. The danger with regarding health or education as things provided as a 'social service' is that it may cause atrophy of the desire to acquire the relevant sort of judgement about limits required in one who is to consider being healthy or becoming educated as part of achieving excellence in how they live. If health and education are 'goods', I naturally will want more and more of them. But as a consequence I may lose sight of what it means to want to be good at them. In recent years Ivan Illich has forcibly urged that viewing health and education as 'services' is potentially destructive of our ability to perceive the quality of our minds and bodies as personal achievements.[1] Such an ability, he claims, can only survive in a clear recognition by each of us of what are proper human limits to a desire for educational and medical facilities.

We turn now to the second stage of Socrates' argument. It explores in a more 'positive' fashion the sources of inadequacy in Polemarchus' definition of justice. The chief defect is its failure to recognise that justice cannot signify a 'power' within the soul capable of yielding anything other than good. A social or 'civic' conception of justice, Socrates is suggesting, cannot give us a true characterisation of the nature of justice if it allows that a person *in* being just can bring about harm to anyone. Polemarchus, in spite of his inability to assign any significant 'field' to justice, does not want to abandon the intuition that the harming of enemies and the benefiting of friends is the true aim of justice (334b 7–9). Socrates' argument attempts to show that this intuition is morally mistaken. He does this in two steps. He argues, first, that unless those designated 'friends' are just and good, and those designated 'enemies' are evil and unjust, benefiting friends and harming enemies, which on Polemarchus' definition is just, could turn out to harm the good and just and to benefit the evil and unjust. Justice, in other words, could turn out to be a 'power' to harm the good and to benefit the evil (334c–335e). Socrates argues then that harming a human being at all cannot be the 'natural' effect of the 'power' of justice in the soul; rather, it must be the 'natural' effect of the 'power' of injustice (335b–d). It follows that benefiting friends and harming enemies is not a 'power' essential to justice.

Both of Socrates' arguments here raise important issues, even if their reasoning is less than decisive. They depend on the implicit assumption that justice, having

as its essential aim to improve, to 'render' good, is the human virtue *par excellence*.
In other words, it is the virtue in terms of which the other qualities of character,
such as wisdom, temperance and courage, commonly regarded as virtues can be
made intelligible as specifically human virtues. The assumption is not, of course,
explained by Socrates at this stage; it is simply made.[2] It is explicitly mentioned in
the course of the second argument (335c 1-4), but it seems to guide the spirit of
Socrates' remarks throughout this section. He is, after all, trying to get
Polemarchus to see that he is morally, nor merely conceptually, mistaken about
justice.

To see the force of Socrates' first argument we need to appreciate what may
seem plausible about Polemarchus' view of the aim of justice. It is not uncommon
to think, like him, that a neccessary condition of an *action* being just is that the
'recipients' of the act possess characteristics which make them such as to deserve
(be entitled) to . . . . The empty space is meant to be filled by the description of
what the act intends to bring about. So, for example, those who are criminal, who
by virtue of damaging or disrupting in some way the 'social order' are thought of
as 'enemies of society', behave in ways that puts them in the class 'deserving to be
punished'. Putting criminals in gaol, say, is just because imprisoning is a way of
punishing, and the criminals are such as to deserve punishment. To put non-
criminals in prison is unjust because the way such people behave does not make
them such as 'to deserve to be punished'. The punishing of innocents, on this
view, is not only a bad but an unjust thing to do precisely because punishing is,
conceptually, what only the guilty deserve.

One may believe this independently of whether or not in any given case what
is regarded as punishment *in fact* benefits or harms the recipient. A person may
welcome the death penalty as a benefit. This does not make it any the less a
punishment, or its guilty recipient any the less deserving. The same point holds
where possession of certain characteristics make people of the kind 'deserves (is
entitled to) rewards'. It is unjust to reward the 'undeserving' precisely because
rewarding is what *only* the 'deserving' deserve. This stricture applies just as much
to those in society who are in need (the poor, the sick, the underprivileged, and so
on) as to those whose activities are thought to make positive social contributions.
Justice demands that 'rewards' given to either group are 'deserved'. This remains
so, whether or not in a particular case the deserved 'reward' *in fact* benefits or
harms its recipient. A person may not in fact welcome a 'social benefit'—for
example, a grant or an honour—as a good. This does not make it any the less a
'reward', or its 'deserving' recipient any the less deserving. One could add that on
this view a sufficient condition of an action's being just is that the characteristics
which make people of the relevant kinds are in fact those to which the 'just'
person responds. To do something good to another person merely because out of
kindness, benevolence, or friendship one is inclined to do so, is not, as such, to
perform an act of justice.

Admittedly Polemarchus confines the 'deserving' categories pertinent to justice to those that satisfy the descriptions 'friend' and 'enemy'. But the conceptual structure of his view—the structure of 'reciprocity' or 'fairness'—is not altered if, as above, we interpret these categories more expansively. Alternatively, we may understand 'friend' and 'enemy' broadly enough to cover a number of more specific categories: 'friend' may be shorthand for all the different characteristics which render anyone of the kind 'deserving a reward', and, correspondingly, 'enemy' a shorthand for the characteristics which make anyone of the kind 'deserving punishment'. The thesis that justice is to benefit friends and harm enemies is not made trivial by this broadening of 'friend' and 'enemy'. It is not trivial to claim that it is just to benefit or harm *only* those who deserve it. Socrates, for one, believes it to be false. His reasons seem to be that, on the view outlined above, the conditions necessary or sufficient for an action's being just do not rule out an action from actually doing something bad. This is unacceptable if we think justice to be a virtue, and, as such, a quality in persons productive only of good.

Socrates' argument is deceptively simple. These are its steps:

(1) A friend is a person one *believes* to be worthwhile (*chrēstos*) (334c 1–5).

(2) People can be mistaken in such beliefs: they take to be worthwhile those who are not, and take to be worthless those who are in fact worthwhile (334c 6–9).

(3) So, to such mistaken people, the good will be enemies and the bad friends (334c 10–11).

(4) But, on Polemarchus' definition, it will be just in these cases to benefit bad people and to harm good people (334c 12–334d 1).

(5) Yet, the good are just and such as not to act unjustly (334d 3). It follows that:

(6) It is just to do ill to those who do no injustice (334d 5–6).

Polemarchus is shocked. It is the argument that is evil (*ponēros*) if it makes out that the just person is capable of doing evil to someone innocent of injustice. To avoid the conclusion he can do any of three things: change the definition of 'friend' in (1); drop his definition of justice (implied in (4)); or, question (5). It is worth noting that (4) is not as outrageous as (6). One may be prepared to accept that as a result of the exercise of justice some unworthy people may profit and some worthy people suffer. The overall goodness of justice may compensate for such unforeseen, unwelcome effects. But it is quite another thing to think that the just can treat those innocent of injustice as enemies, as deserving harm! Socrates derives this conclusion by getting Polemarchus to agree to (5). But why should Polemarchus, or anyone else for that matter, accept this premise? One may grant that the just are good without also agreeing that no one is good who is not just and who avoids injustice. Similarly, Socrates seems to shift from 'worthwhile' to 'good' in the transition from (2) to (3).

Greek usage allows the inference from *chrēstos* (worthy) to *agathos* (good) in the sense, for example, that to have a brave soldier on your side is to have someone worthwhile on your side—someone who is good, because he is reliable.[3] But it is not clear that the usage would support the judgement that someone good *as* a human being is *eo ipso* a worthwhile person, a *chrēstos* in this sense. The latter notion is much too tied to context, function, role, purpose, use, and so on. Thus, if we thought that a good person was necessarily just (as (5) says), and, like Polemarchus, we had no clear idea what the just was *good for* (*chrēsimos*; cf. Socrates' previous argument at 333b–e), we may hesitate to assert that the just were good (*agathoi*) because they were worthwhile (*chrēstoi*). At least, in saying so we would not be sure why we thought this. However, given the 'reciprocal' or 'fairness' structure of Polemarchus' view of justice he may well think that since the just respond to the 'deserving' they will benefit those they think worthwhile. Friends are worthwhile because one can expect them to act beneficially to their friends. Friends are worthwhile to each other; their being good to each other, therefore, requires that they be just to each other, that they reciprocate benefits. This is why Polemarchus accepts (5). But (5) could bear quite a different interpretation of goodness; one that went along with a radically different conception of justice. The just may not be good because they are worthwhile; they may be worthwhile because they are good, in the sense that they do not harm anyone. This raises a question as to what their worthwhileness consists in.

Polemarchus wants to say that it is just to harm the unjust and to benefit the just (334d 9–11). He opts, therefore, for an amendment of his definition of 'friend' and 'enemy', since it could well happen that one's friends were unjust people and one's enemies just—thus, contradicting Simonides' formula about justice as benefiting friends and harming enemies (334d 12–334e 4). Polemarchus now claims that a friend is one who not only seems but is worthwhile. He who only seems worthwhile is not really a friend. And so with enemies (334e 5–335a 2). This, Socrates points out (335a 3–5), makes being good a condition of being a friend, and being evil a condition of being an enemy. Once again we have the shift from 'worthwhile' to 'good' which is allowable given a restricted understanding of 'good'. But Polemarchus makes an important concession in accepting this point. For, it will no longer be the case that a person is of the kind 'deserves to be rewarded (or punished)' because he is a friend; rather, it will be his being good in some as yet unspecified sense. It is this which makes him a real friend.

Socrates' critique applies to the general structure of Polemarchus' position, not merely to the particular version to which the latter gives voice. As we saw above, the general structure involved is that of regarding justice as a matter of 'reciprocity' or 'fairness' in relations between people. If Socrates is right, this view of justice entails that no one is treated justly who, in receiving a benefit or a harm, does not possess characteristics which make him or her 'deserving'. These will be characteristics which make him or her *worthy*, in some respect, of the benefit or the harm.

It does not matter how widely we cast our net of what makes people worthy of different types of treatment—being a person might, for example, be the most general criterion of worthiness, though there will be argument about conditions of personhood. All the same, the point remains that the justice of an act (and of the person performing it) will depend on the worthiness in some respect of its 'recipient', and on the fact that the agent is responding to that worthiness. This, in turn, implies that we can only be sure that acting justly is acting well if we *know* that the characteristics which make people 'worthy' or 'deserving' are, indeed, such as to make our acts of responding to them instances of doing something unqualifiedly good. If the characteristics which make people 'worthy' are such that in responding to them we do something bad, our belief that justice is a virtue will contradict what we think of as acting justly. But this means that justice cannot consist in merely 'responding to what makes people worthy'. For, if justice *is* a virtue, acting justly must be acting well in an unqualified sense. It follows that responding to what makes people worthy is genuinely just if, and only if, so responding is acting well in an unqualified way. Acting 'fairly' or 'reciprocally' does not by itself yield such an unqualified sense of acting well. Therefore, a notion of acting justly based on 'fairness' cannot explain why acting justly is, necessarily, acting virtuously. The argument does depend, of course, on the proposition that the only moral sense we can give to 'acting well' is acting virtuously. It would be open to someone who believed that justice was a supremely good thing but not a personal virtue to deny this proposition. Such a person would still have to explain not only what made justice a good thing, but also why it was a *moral* good.[4]

Socrates' next argument explores the idea that if the essential aim of justice is to achieve something unqualifiedly good it cannot, contrary to Polemarchus' interpretation of Simonides, bring it about that the person acting justly harms anyone. The 'power' of justice in the soul must necessarily exclude such actions. We need to look carefully at this argument not only because it articulates a significant moral claim, but also because it has struck many as less than satisfactory, and as exploiting an ambiguity in the notion of 'harming' (*blaptein*).[5] Once again the argument is deceptively simple in its compression of a number of important points. Socrates argues that it does not 'belong' to the just man to harm anyone because:

(a)

(i)   for anything to be harmed is to be made worse in respect of its specific
      excellence or virtue (to harm a horse or a dog is to make it worse *as* a horse or
      dog)—335b 6–12.
      Therefore,

(ii) harming human beings is making them worse in respect of their specific
      virtue as human beings—335c 1–3.
      But,

(iii) justice is human excellence—335c 4–5.
      Therefore,

(iv) being harmed neccessarily makes human beings more unjust—335c 6–7.
      Further:

(b)

(i)   It is impossible that those who practice a craft (musicianship, horsemanship,
      and so on) are enabled (*dunantai*) by (knowledge incorporated in) the craft to
      produce in others the characteristic opposite to that they themselves
      exemplify (being a bad rider, and so on)—335c 9–13.

(ii) How, then, can the just be enabled by justice to produce in others a
      characteristic opposite to the one they exemplify? In general, how can the
      good be enabled by their virtue to produce badness in people?—
      335c 14–335d 2.
      And further,

(c)

(i)   The characteristic action or effect (*ergon*) of a 'power' is to produce in things
      its own essential feature (the *ergon* of heat is the opposite of making cold, and
      of dryness the opposite of moistening)—335d 3–6.

(ii) It cannot, therefore, be the characteristic action or effect of the good to harm;
      rather, of their opposite—335d 7–8.
      But,

(iii) the just are good—335d 9–10.
      Therefore,

(iv) it cannot be the 'work' (*ergon*) of the just to harm, neither a friend nor anyone,
      rather it is the 'work' of their opposite, the unjust—335d 11–13.

At face value this argument appears to trade on an ambiguity in (a), and to make
the unwarranted assumptions, in (b) and (c) respectively, that justice is like a craft
in what it enables its practitioners to produce, and that it is like a 'natural' power in
what it effects on its 'recipients'. Even if we allow that Polemarchus had

previously committed himself to justice being like a craft, Socrates is here clearly prepared to press that analogy further. The argument cannot be merely *ad hominem* against Polemarchus if Socrates wants to adhere to its premises. Let us, therefore, examine whether the charges brought against the argument affect its real force.

It might be thought that when Polemarchus talked of harming enemies he meant damaging their interests, not making them worse men.[6] The word Socrates uses, *blaptein*, thus covers both 'hurt' and 'harm' and Socrates' inference is valid only if Polemarchus meant that it is just to make enemies worse as men. But this move of separating damage to interests from harming people is not open to Polemarchus, or to anyone who accepts 'reciprocity' or 'fairness' as the structure of justice. For, as we saw above, it is essential to this view that the harm meted out to enemies is 'deserved' by them as people who are bad and unjust (cf. 334d). Their ill-treatment, therefore, is directed at whatever characteristics make them enemies; that is, at whatever it is that makes them 'worthy' of punishment. But what makes someone a real enemy is not the fact that their interests are opposed to mine but, plainly, their capacity to pursue successfully activities antithetical to my well-being. My act of harming them, therefore, is just only if it succeeds in diminishing or destroying that capacity. It could be the case, for example, that the burning of crops and the razing of the enemy's territory, though hurtful, did not in fact incapacitate the enemy as an enemy. Perhaps, by arousing the indignation of the population and of (so far) neutral parties it strengthened their capacity to inflict adversity on me. In that case, my action would not be 'just': it would not be what the enemy 'deserved' as an enemy since it would not be an appropriate response to what empowered him to be an enemy. Justice, on the model entertained, requires that an act of harm incapacitates a person with respect to capacities which make him or her 'deserving' of the act. The just act, one could say, may or may not be hurtful, but it must be punishing (or rewarding) if that is what is 'deserved'.

Socrates relies on this point to secure Polemarchus' acceptance of (a) (i): to harm X is to make X worse in respect of the 'virtue' or excellence which they possess *qua* X. To harm the enemy is to make someone worse in respect of the excellences they possess *qua* enemy. It is, therefore, to make them worse in respect of some capacity they possess—be it physical strength, material or mental attributes, social standing or reputation, and so on. Much more problematic is Socrates' application of this point to the specific virtue of human beings, and the equation of that virtue with justice (cf. (a) (ii) and (iii)). The inference to (a) (iv) clearly requires that justice is not merely *a* human virtue among others, and independent of them, but that it is a virtue characteristic of human beings—that it *distinguishes* humans from all other animals, the way, for example, excellence in certain functions distinguishes a horse from a dog. Later in

Book I, and in the *Republic* as a whole, Socrates will try to explain why justice is *the* human excellence, why someone who lacks that virtue cannot live well. But the assertion of the view (unexplained here) as an obvious point seems unjustified. Why should Polemarchus accept the proposition?[7]

It is not necessary to import Socrates' later elaborate explanation to understand Polemarchus' acceptance of the point. The very reasons which I suggested prompted his acceptance of (a) (i) should also incline him to accept (a) (ii); his acceptance of (a) (iii) may be based on the fact that it was a widely held belief.[8] This does not mean, of course, that what he understands by these propositions is what Socrates makes of them later on. Thus, Polemarchus' and Socrates' agreement about the premises of this argument need not imply concurrence about their significance. For the purposes of this argument (a) (ii) is more crucial than (a) (iii), even though the latter is a much more important, and more controversial moral doctrine. We shall, accordingly, postpone discussion of the full implications of (a) (iii) until later (see Chapter 10 below), and concentrate here on the combined effect of (a) (ii) and (a) (iii).

It was argued that, given the way he understands justice, Polemarchus must regard harming an enemy as incapacitating him or her with respect to the capacities or abilities which enable him or her to be hostile and do hostile things. Socrates plausibly thinks that anyone prepared to contemplate that it is just to inflict such incapacitation under some circumstances will not flinch from admitting that diminishing someone *qua* a human being may in fact be a good thing; it is only thus (let us suppose) that the just action could be a really punishing action. There is nothing in the principle of 'reciprocity' or 'fairness' to exclude the possibility that the thing someone 'deserves' involves diminishing them with respect to capacities they possess *qua* human beings. And this means that justice on this model may require making human beings worse with respect to their specific excellence(s) as human beings.

Many people—perhaps a majority both then and now—have not found this consequence objectionable. Justice, which is a good thing, may require that people of certain kinds be harmed or incapacitated. It is likely that Socrates found this view morally unacceptable.[9] But his tactic with Polemarchus does not rely on a piece of controversial moralism which, in any case, would have to be justified. Instead, he avails himself of beliefs that Polemarchus could regard as plausible, and which show the latter's model for justice, by allowing that one could harm human beings justly, does not rule out the possibility that acting justly is responsible for making unjust the 'recipients' of justice. This consequence, unlike the previous one about harming human beings in their specific virtue, cannot be welcomed by Polemarchus. For, even on *his* view of justice there is something paradoxical in the claim that the effect of acting justly towards enemies—harming or incapacitating them—is to make them incapable of acting justly, or actively to promote the opposite capacity in them.

This would be the case, for example, if the effect of the punitive action upon the enemy was to make him or her incapable of benefiting friends *or* of harming enemies. The question is not whether rendering an enemy incapable is a good thing in the sense that it is useful, profitable or convenient. The question is whether incapacitating an enemy is a *just* thing to do if it makes the enemy unjust, or makes him or her incapable of being just. There is nothing in Polemarchus' model of justice which compels a negative answer. The possibility of making someone unjust by acting justly is inherent in the model, and it generates a dilemma. If we answer the above question in the affirmative we have to face the consequence that acting justly may not be advantageous to the person so acting; the outcome of the action may be to bring suffering to himself. In that event, one could not affirm that being just was always and necessarily a good thing. We would have very good self-regarding reasons at times for refraining from acting towards our enemies as justice requires. But if we answer the question in the negative, if we say that it is not just to make someone unjust in our pursuit of what justice demands, our reasons for doing or for refraining from doing 'the just thing' in a given case, will be other than that we are doing what justice demands. In other words, if doing the 'just thing' *could* generate injustice in someone else, and we avoided doing it for that reason, doing 'the just thing' in any given case would not unambiguously indicate a love of justice or a hatred of injustice. Our reasons for acting justly could not be taken to reflect the conviction that being just was an excellent thing to be adhered to at all costs. On either count, therefore, Polemarchus' model of justice cannot explain why he, or anyone, should take justice to be an unqualified excellence.

The role of (a) (iii), that justice is human excellence, is to bring home to Polemarchus that his model of justice cannot explain why anyone who accepted the model would *believe* (a) (iii). It does not matter for the purpose of showing this how one interprets (a) (iii). It is sufficient that Polemarchus (or anyone else) believes that acting 'reciprocally' or 'fairly' is a fine thing to do. Given that acting so does not rule out harming human beings in their specific excellence, there is nothing to prevent acting justly from generating injustice in others. The crucial question Socrates is raising here is whether just persons can be unconcerned about the effect their actions have, about the possibility of producing justice or injustice *in* others. Polemarchus' model leaves it unclear in what way a concern with doing the just thing *is* a concern to secure excellence overall.[10]

The analogies in (b) and (c), though limited and based on ancient models of 'power', are meant to suggest that a concern for excellence must be 'internal' to acting justly; that no account of justice can be correct which does not show it to be a 'power' bent on reproducing its character, as it were, on those it acts upon. As we saw earlier, a central function of the craft-analogy is to convey the 'internality' of relations between skilful acts and their 'product' or outcome. Socrates singles out two important respects in which the relation between acting justly and excellence must be 'internal'. In the first place, as the analogy in (b) suggests, the effect of acting justly upon 'recipients' should be 'internally' related to the capacity in the agents to 'infect' those they act upon with the quality their act exemplifies. The good effect of a just act on others cannot be contingently related to the good aimed at by the just agent. Acting justly must be a 'communicator' of goodness in this sense. For if it is not, and the goodness of the just agent is quite distinct in type from the benefit the 'recipient' may or may not receive, it becomes unclear why the manner the 'recipients' of a just act are benefited, if they are benefited at all, should be of any concern to the just person. If the benefit to the 'recipient' is unrelated to the goodness *in* the agent, how the 'recipient' benefits is unrelated to the goodness *of* the agent. The 'recipient' becomes merely the occasion for the just to exercise their own kind of goodness.

But if we allow this, then the view the just have of their own justice as a personal quality will not be that of a capacity to *make* just, whether themselves or others. In other words, the just will not be able to tell how the quality they possess is responsible for their excellence, if they cannot see justice as an excellence-producing quality in general. In this respect they would be unlike craftsmen. The latter's skilful activities 'communicate' the type of excellence of which their knowledge makes them capable. This is so because the knowledge involved in a craft is an excellence-producing quality of a specific kind, whether the excellence is in the craftsman or in those who come under his influence. It is impossible that the effect of musicianship or horsemanship is to make something less musical, or someone a lesser horseman. It is not something the musician or the expert horseman could bring about through the exercise of their craft. If such a thing was possible, the craftsmen would not *know* that it was their craft-knowledge which was responsible for anything excellent they achieved. Similarly, if the just could make others unjust, they would not know, when acting justly, that it was their justice which produced the good they achieved.

Socrates' second analogy, (c), reinforces this point. If justice is to be thought of as having an invariant effect on those upon, or in whom, it acts, its characteristic 'work', its *ergon*, must be conceived as analogous to 'powers' in nature such as heat or dryness. The 'natural', that is, the uninterfered with, operation of justice in anything or anyone is 'to make just', the way the action of heat on anything is to heat not to cool. If we think of heat and dryness as the tendencies of certain substances to have specific and invariable effects, then we have a general pattern of explaining what it is for something to have an invariant effect. The belief that goodness is an essential feature of justice (cf. (c) (iii)) cannot be divorced from the question whether justice has invariably good effects. For if the two could be divorced, we would not be able to tell whether the effects of justice were fortuitously beneficial rather than the invariable outcome of its nature.[11] Thus, taking justice to be essentially good requires that we view it as a 'power', an invariant tendency, to bring to things its own essential character—to benefit them by making them good. The general pattern, therefore, of explaining invariant effects must prevent us from thinking of justice as a tendency to bring harm *at all*—given, of course, that we think of justice as a good thing, and that it is a quality capable of producing invariant effects. It cannot be the 'work' of justice, but of injustice, to bring harm to things.

The serious fault with conceiving justice as conduct appropriate to types of social relationship is that it cannot account for the conviction that just conduct is of itself a source of goodness. But it is precisely this conviction which underlies the view that justice is (a) human excellence, a virtue. Therefore, a 'civic' conception of justice, like Polemarchus', does not contain an explanation of why we should regard it as a virtue. Nevertheless, it must be admitted that the positive effect of Socrates' argumentation is to suggest an idea of justice and of virtue whose 'power' is such as to make it difficult to conceive what in human 'nature' could lead us to regard it as possible of human achievement. I do not mean that human nature is too 'weak' for Socrates' implicit conception of virtue. Rather, the difficulty lies in anchoring that conception to the *strengths* of human capacities as we know them, whether these are taken singly or collectively. Plato's suggestion in the *Republic* is that the 'power' of virtue and justice does not reside in human capacities themselves but in how they are ordered or structured. We shall consider later (Chapter 9 below) some implications of this idea.

7

Power, Skill and Ruling

But what if there is nothing unqualifiedly excellent about being just? To look for its 'power' to effect invariably good things would, in that case, be to mistake the sort of thing it is. As we saw in Chapter 4, Thrasymachus believes he has grounds for thinking that the qualities of character which make men act justly have the effect of keeping them in subservient, unfree and non-autonomous relations to those in power. On the assumption that the life of excellence, the life of material, political and social success, presupposes being in a position to master, control, and determine the processes by which one achieves personal well-being, no excellent person can be interested in being just. Excellence requires being in power, while to be just is to be condemned to a condition of powerlessness. The powerful, therefore, according to Thrasymachus, owe their success and well-being to the quality within them which makes for a disregard of justice. It is that quality alone which is 'productive' of personal benefit and advantage.

Socrates' examination of Thrasymachus can be usefully divided into two stages: in the first (339b–350d) he attempts to undermine the links Thrasymachus seeks to forge between power and being unjust, and between injustice and excellence; in the second (350d–354a) Socrates tries to explain why he thinks the life of justice is better and more 'enabling' than the life of injustice. The dividing point between these two stages corresponds to the stage in the discussion when Thrasymachus ceases to be an active participant (350e). What comes after that point is Socrates' characterisation of the effects in people and communities of the 'power' of justice. This chapter and the next deal with the first stage, while Chapter 9 discusses the second.

Plato shows perspicacity in having Thrasymachus follow the discussion with Polemarchus. For if, as we saw, a 'civic' conception of justice cannot explain why one should view it as a personal excellence, then an understandable reaction is to deny that justice, so conceived, is an unqualifiedly good thing. Indeed, we found elements in Polemarchus' view which already make it doubtful whether it is always wise and advantageous to do what justice requires (cf. above, p. 103). If, like Thrasymachus, we regard the abilities which put people into positions of power and sustain them there as those which enable them to pursue skilfully their own good, we have good reason to regard the value of 'civic' justice as nothing but of benefit to the powerful. The latter exploit the justice of others in order to achieve what is advantageous to themselves. In the context of political power and the control of a *polis* this means that being just, observing established rules of conduct, is the political *measure* of how intelligently and skilfully the ruler promotes his own advantage.

The connection between knowledge, skill or expertise, and virtue came up in the discussion with Polemarchus. The issue there concerned whether we should think of justice as a kind of skill. Thrasymachus' view of the link between power and excellence raises a parallel question about the relation between injustice and knowledge or expertise. Socrates must agree with Thrasymachus that a conception of justice which severs its ties with human abilities, such as intelligence and wisdom, which enable one to do well in life, cannot sustain a belief in justice as human excellence. But if the view that justice is an excellence is to be defended at all, the idea that intelligence and wisdom are essentially tied to acting unjustly must be defeated. The use of intelligence and wisdom to achieve unjust though personally advantageous ends cannot be allowed to appear as what is most distinctive of human excellence. Socrates must show that Thrasymachus *misrecognises* how knowledge and skill relate, first, to being in power or control and, secondly, to that use of sagacity and intelligence which generates something good. Under the first heading Socrates needs to argue that the knowledge which makes someone skilful as a ruler does not have as its 'object' the promotion of the ruler's own benefit or advantage but, instead, the well-being of those subject to his rule. Under the second heading Socrates needs to argue that the use of sagacity and intelligence in the service of graspingness (*pleonexia*) is antithetical to a use of these abilities to achieve what is good. In both instances, in the proper exercise of ruling and in the proper use of sagacity and intelligence, Socrates must show that the excellent person is more like the just than the unjust. In this and the next chapter we look at the arguments Socrates uses to accomplish these two tasks. The first task relates to what Socrates argues at 339b–342e and, again, at 345b–347e. The second task concerns Socrates' argument at 348a–350d.

The argument with Thrasymachus brings forth aspects of how Socrates thinks about *technē* which did not emerge in his discussion with Polemarchus. In the earlier context the important thing about a skill was that it involved an intellectual or theoretical grasp of how operations on certain 'material' in a given field were 'internally' related to the production of certain desirable products or outcomes.[1] In the present context Socrates is concerned to identify the aspects of craft-knowledge that make the expert necessarily 'stronger', more capable and effective, than the non-expert. This theme is announced in the line of questioning Socrates pursues in response to Thrasymachus' political explanation of his formula that justice is nothing but the advantage of the stronger. If Thrasymachus is right the real source of the ruler's power cannot be the fact that he declares what counts as just conduct in the *polis*. It must be his ability to identify correctly the rules which the subjects have to obey so as to give him the power to promote his own advantage. If the ruler is wrong about these rules, the 'justice' of his subjects will not benefit him; it would be more to his advantage if they disobeyed these rules. If the ruler's edicts are antithetical to what, within the framwork of his political ideology, he identifies as his advantage, obedience to the rules will 'fail' that advantage, while disobedience will promote it (339c−e).

The pattern of Socrates' argument is interesting in that it resembles the pattern of thought one may plausibly entertain in relation to conduct which 'fails' or promotes the aims of a craft. Thus, suppose it to be the case that the diet or drug a physician recommends is the wrong one for my condition. Then, the best and 'right' thing for me to do in the sense of co-operating with the good of medicine (health), an aim which the doctor has *qua* practitioner of the craft, is to disobey the recommendation. Thrasymachus has two options: either to dissociate the (political) power of the ruler from a *skilled* capacity to achieve a personal good, or to treat the achievement of such good as 'internally' related to the skill of ruling. The first option—one suggested by Cleitophon (cf. 340a−c)—is not one Thrasymachus can entertain seriously. For it would make the ruler's power depend on securing his subjects' obedience to the rules he promulgates by means other than the subjects' rational acceptance of the ruler's ability to rule. If the ruler has to rely on force rather than intelligence to maintain power, then in an important sense the source of his political power will be external to the exercise of any abilities on his part reflective of his excellence. The ruler may do well out of exercising power, but the benefits obtained would, at best, be only contingently related to his personal capacities. It is far more reliably effective, as well as more admirable and excellent, to elicit the obedience of the subjects by having them recognise that the ruler knows what he is doing. The subjects will obey because the power of their ruler is the power his skill gives him. Why, after all, should anyone admire a ruler for the conformist tendencies of his subjects?

If Thrasymachus' admiration for power is to be rationally grounded he must embrace something like the second option. One admires the tyrant because he *knows* how to put his own good above everyone else's. The real source of his power is that he knowledgeably pursues injustice. These are the considerations which lead Thrasymachus to claim that since no craftsman's activities, *qua* skilful activities, can in the strict sense be said to fail to produce the relevant product, so the ruler's activities, taken in the same strict sense, cannot fail to achieve what is best for himself (340d−341a, especially 340e 4−341d 2). But how is the ruler's knowledge or skill to be construed? The crucial point to bear in mind about Socrates' next argument is that it is the ruler's knowledge which makes him truly powerful. This is required by Thrasymachus' view that what makes the ruler 'stronger' is that he knows how to be unjust, that what renders his injustice effective is his skill.

Socrates' argument makes an important point about the reasons why (craft) knowledge can be seen as a manifestation of power: it is not so much the craftsman's ability to produce certain results that makes him 'powerful'; but the fact that the craft itself is a way of overcoming, of bringing under rational control, circumstances in a given field which are 'natural' sources of resistance, recalcitrance, deficiency, inadequacy, or unsatisfactoriness. *Technai* are reasoned and knowledgeable responses to that in things which *needs* to be controlled. The 'objects' of *technai* are things considered under the description of having such needs.[2] The 'power' a craft gives to its practitioner is that which it has over its 'objects'; more precisely, over those features of its 'objects' which need or require its exercise. The 'power' a craft yields to its practitioner, therefore, derives from its ability to meet the 'needs' or requirements of what it deals with. The specific benefits it yields are, consequently, logically tied to its meeting these needs or requirements. There may be other and further benefits one can obtain from the exercise of a craft, but they are not benefits specific to the 'power' of the craft; they depend on other, contingent, factors which are 'external' to the craft *qua* craft.

Here is Socrates' argument, somewhat abbreviated:

(a)

(i) Things true of craftsmen by virtue of circumstances necessary for them to practise their craft are not essential to the description of the type of relation they have to the 'object' of their craft *qua* craftsmen. (Doctors make money, and sea-captains are sailors because they sail. But the *medical* relation to the sick is healing, and the 'captaining' relation to a crew is ruling or commanding them.)—341c 4–341d 3

(ii) Correspondingly, there is the essential benefit of the 'object' of a craft. That is, there is the benefit to the recipient of the activities of a craft *qua* 'object' of that craft in the strict sense. (Being healed is the advantage of the sick *qua* 'object' of the medical craft; being given orders about what to do is the advantage of the sailor *qua* 'object' of the craft of commanding a vessel at sea.)—341d 5

(iii) The natural goal (*pephuken*) of a craft is to seek and provide the essential benefit of its 'object' (people benefiting, for example, *qua* sick and *qua* sailors)—341d 7–8.

(iv) What is advantageous to a craft *qua* craft is not determined by reference to anything other than its being the particular perfection it is—341d 10–11.

(v) A craft in the strict sense is not subject to defects or mistakes, and, thus, it is not 'fitting' (*prosēkei*) for it to seek the benefit of anything other than the 'object' of its concern—342b 3–5.

(vi) Therefore, a craft, not itself being 'needy', does not seek its own advantage but that of its 'object'—342c 4–6.

(b)

(i)   The crafts rule and master over that which is their 'object'—342c 8 – 9.

[(ii) In respect of the strict relation between a craft and its 'object', the practitioner is the 'stronger' and the 'object' of the craft the 'weaker', since the 'power' of the craft consists in making good the deficiencies in the 'object' which it is itself incapable of remedying.]—this is an understood premise.

Therefore:

(iii) knowledge neither seeks nor prescribes the advantage of the stronger but the advantage of the weaker, and of that over which it rules— 342c 11–342d 1.

(iv) Craftsmen are, strictly, rulers over their 'object', and seek its advantage rather than their own—342d 3 – 342e 5.

It follows that:

(v)   no one standing in the strict relation of governing will seek or prescribe his own advantage; all that he says and does will have in view what is suitable and advantageous to the subjects of his rule since they are the 'object' of his craft—342e 6 – 10.

Some commentators think that the argument 'overstates its case', and that it is 'absurdly optimistic' about the practitioners of skills.[3] It has also been thought that the argument exploits different senses of 'ruling' in assimilating the way a craftsman has control over his 'object' with the way a ruler controls his political subjects.[4] But the question Socrates is addressing is whether the power rulers have over their subjects has as its source the knowledge they possess; that is, whether the power of rulers over subjects is like the 'power' of a skill over its 'object'. If Thrasymachus thinks of ruling as a skill, then the seeking of their own advantage by the politically powerful cannot be an essential, an 'internal', aspect of *that* skill.

The argument is important because it looks forward to some central ideas about ruling in the 'ideal' *polis* later in the *Republic*—the notion that such a *polis* is constructed on a consideration of *needs*, and the idea that knowledge should be the only source of political authority.[5] But the argument also raises issues, important in themselves, about the relation between knowledge, need, and benefit or advantage. Socrates is not, of course, arguing that the only thing which *motivates* practitioners of a craft is to benefit the 'object' of their craft. He is concerned to establish whether, and how, the knowledge which constitutes a craft introduces the idea of an *interest* that is specific to the craft. If there is such an interest no ruler can fail to have it if ruling is a craft. The question is whether any such 'knowledge-interest' can be a *self*-interest. Socrates, in a somewhat compressed explanatory passage (341e 1–342b 2), puts forward a view which is central to the argument as a whole: the capacity to improve things, inherent in all craft-knowledge, is the capacity to meet a 'need' created by the sources of insufficiency in its 'object'. Craft can only manifest that capacity if its exercise is not aimed at meeting a 'need' of its own; that is, if the exercise of a craft has not as its aim to meet an insufficiency in itself. If this is so, a 'knowledge-interest' is always other-orientated, towards its 'object', and cannot be self-orientated. 'Self-interest', in this sense, is excluded by, or antithetical to, 'knowledge-interest'. Socrates' contention here has not been sufficiently appreciated, though it must be admitted that it is not straightforwardly obvious how to construe its force. If correct, its implications are far-reaching.

Suppose that like Thrasymachus we think of the ruler's power as due to his skilful pursuit of his personal advantage. He is a great strategist, supremely clever at determining the sort of legislation which will curb the graft and greed of other citizens without affecting his own ability to benefit enormously (from taxation, from rules governing commercial ventures, and so on). The point is that the legislation which the ruler who is an unjust man sets down may not differ at all, or very little, from that set down by a ruler who is a just person.[6] Nevertheless, the *aim* of the unjust ruler would be radically different from that of the just ruler. In the former case the exercise of reason and intelligence is directed at securing the ruler's self-interest, while in the latter case the aim is to secure the benefit and well-being of the governed. Now, to think this way about the skill of the unjust ruler is to think of the knowledge embedded in a skill as a set of rational recipes for bringing about results in a given field; results which the possessor of the skill (or the person using them) considers desirable on some grounds. The interest of the craftsman *qua* craftsman, on this view, is to achieve certain results whose desirability or otherwise is 'externally' determined. The 'knowledge-interest' of the craftsman, therefore, is subordinate to the interest one has in the 'products' of the craft. When Thrasymachus agrees that no craftsman who makes mistakes can be one in the strict sense, he has in mind that to the extent, for example, that a doctor misdiagnoses an illness, or an accountant makes a miscalculation, they are ineffective as a means of achieving the 'products' which are, *by definition*, achievable by the crafts in question.

Socrates suggests a different conception of the benefits of skills—one which locates them not in the fact that people *deem* the products of these crafts to be desirable, but in the impersonal or objective fact that the crafts meet 'needs' which arise out of 'natural' weaknessess, deficiencies and insufficiencies in various areas. In an important sense, therefore, the value of a craft for Socrates resides in achieving the good of whatever it is the craft deals with; its value does not spring from its being useful in bringing about what anyone *thinks he wants*. The benefits of a craft can be objectively, rather than subjectively, determined only if the criteria of such determination are existing 'needs' in the field of the craft.

The most important consequence of this view—from which Socrates obtains all the other consequences in the argument—is that the infallibility of a craftsman is not the avoidance of mistakes in bringing off certain results, but the capacity inherent in the knowledge of the craft to cope with the 'needs' of its object. A surgeon, for example, who removes organs and tissues he knows are healthy in order to gain an undeserved fee, or to enhance his reputation, 'fails' the medical craft, even though he is not guilty of any technical errors. This is because such operations fail to meet the 'need' to which the medical craft is in itself a rational response. But then, the actions of the inexperienced physician who misdiagnoses an illness or misprescribes a diet or a drug also fail to meet such a 'need'. In both cases, it is the *activity*, not their overall intentions or their motives and desires, which makes the practitioners a repository of 'ignorance'; their activity ignores the 'need' which medical knowledge evolved to meet. This 'ignorance' remains even if their activity achieves other benefits for themselves or for others.[7]

Socrates' reasons for thinking that knowledge is necessarily non-self-orientated rely on the idea that the benefits of a craft are derivable 'internally'; from the very nature of the craft. The 'good' of medical knowledge is not that it achieves health and we happen to believe health to be an ultimately desirable end (some may not believe this). The 'good' specific to medicine comes from the fact that the body is not 'perfect', and that medicine is the activity which is good at dealing with the needs arising from this imperfection. This implies, according to Socrates, that assessing the value of a craft by reference to ends other than those constitutive of the craft is to treat the craft as if it were itself imperfect and 'in need'.

Socrates' thought at 342a is highly compressed. He cannot mean that medicine, for example, is not capable of improvement and development. After all, the discovery of further ways of dealing with the body's imperfections is an indefinitely extendable process. What Socrates says is that medicine is 'perfect' and that it cannot be said to be 'in need' in the sense in which a bodily organ can be said to be 'in need'. An eye or an ear is defective to the extent that its sight or hearing is impaired. These organs can, therefore, become 'in need' of the 'excellence' (*aretē*) of sight and hearing which the craft of the eye-doctor or the ear-doctor can provide. If medicine was 'in need' in this same sense it would mean that it depended on some other craft to restore or maintain its characteristic excellence (what it was good at)—the way the eye-doctor maintains or restores the excellence of the eye, of its being good at seeing. But this supposition leads to a vicious infinite regress: that which made medicine effective as an *activity* would be provided by the exercise of some further craft, and that which made this second craft thus effective would be provided by a third craft, and so on *ad infinitum*—leaving it a mystery why we thought the first craft to *be* a craft. Unless the excellence of activity incorporated in a craft was its own 'perfection' at dealing with a type of imperfection, we could not decide what made it an instance of excellence in the first place. If, like Thrasymachus, we value a craft as a means of achieving what we want, the excellence of the craft would not consist in its own specific 'perfection', but in its achieving the end prescribed by some other kind of knowledge. This entails, however, that the exercise of a craft is subject to 'correction' not by reference to its own goals but by reference to how effective it is in achieving goals 'external' to itself. Its excellence, therefore, would reside in something other than itself. This way of viewing the excellence of a craft would make what the craft was good *at* depend on what, in any given instance, its products were deemed to be good *for*.

Thrasymachus is not convinced. Some crafts are practised for the benefit of the practitioners, or of those who employ them. Shepherds and herdsmen have their own good, or that of their masters, in view when they fatten and tend their sheep or cattle. Thus, rulers regard their subjects as a man regards his sheep—they tend them with nothing other than their own benefit in view (343b). It is not immediately obvious what Thrasymachus' counter-example achieves. If he means that a craft can be used for ends other than those which inhere in its practice, this is no objection to Socrates. Clearly, the shepherd is good at producing fat and healthy sheep which can then be sold for profit. But profit-making is not what the shepherd is good at. The excellent shepherd is useful to the owner of the sheep without its being the case that the excellence of shepherding consists in this usefulness. To be an objection to Socrates, Thrasymachus' point must be that self-benefit is a goal *inherent* in the exercise of some crafts. This implies, in the light of the points made earlier by Socrates, that crafts like shepherding, cattle-raising, and, perhaps, the skills involved in food-production in general, are responses to 'needs' which arise not out of imperfections in sheep, cattle, crops, and so on, but out of insufficiencies which have to do with the relation of human beings to their environment. Thinking this way we may look upon agriculture and animal husbandry as responses to scarce food resources. In an abundant environment the need which gives rise to these crafts would not exist, even though it is possible that the imperfections in plants and animals did give rise to horticultural and veterinary skills.[8]

The question, then, is not whether some of the shepherd's or the cattleman's activities benefit sheep and cattle, but whether sheep and cattle are the 'object' of crafts. If they are not, the 'skill-benefit' in these cases cannot be identified with the benefit of sheep and cattle. Thrasymachus' point requires that it is not. The 'object' of shepherding, we might say on his behalf, is not tending sheep *tout court*—it is tending sheep as food, as 'consumables'. A shepherd who does things which benefit his flock will not be a good shepherd if the sheep turn out to be inedible, or if their fleece becomes unsuitable for various human uses. A shepherd is not a veterinarian. Analogously, Thrasymachus could argue, the 'object' of the skill of ruling is not simply ministering to subjects, but doing so with an eye to what maintains and strengthens the type of political arrangement which is to the ruler's benefit and advantage. In assimilating the ruler to the shepherd Thrasymachus clearly intends ruling to be one of the crafts which have self-benefit as a goal inherent in them. He must think that government as a craft does not arise to meet imperfections in the 'body politic'; rather, it issues from a 'need' to control other people. This 'need' arises because competition for limited resources means that the satisfaction of any one person's ambitions and desires requires them to be able to manipulate and control what others want to achieve. The ruler is not a 'healer' of the body politic; he is a controller of interests and aspirations on the part of others that might be antithetical to his own.[9] The craft of ruling 'deals' with other people *as* subjects; the ruler's self-interest and well-being require that the *will* of people, the way people in a community think and behave, be brought under his control. In a similar fashion the craft of shepherding deals with sheep as 'usables'; the shepherd's or the sheep-owner's interest and well-being require that the way sheep grow and develop be brought under their control. Some crafts are constituted by such skills of control for the interest and well-being of those on whose behalf they are wielded. Such is the craft of ruling; it is a *managerial* skill.

Socrates thinks that this way of looking at ruling confuses the aims of the person who is the manager, or of those who use managers, with the goals inherent in the managing skill. He claims (345c 1–345e 2) that Thrasymachus is not observing the same strict criteria when he thinks of the shepherd as he did when talking of the physician. The shepherd is not like the gourmand who fattens sheep with an eye to good eating, or like the money-maker with an eye to profit. Shepherding in the strict sense only looks to what it can best achieve for that which is under its care; its own interests *qua* craft are already provided for in sticking to its nature. The same should apply to the craft of government, whether exercised in public or private affairs: it considers what is best for that over which it rules and tends. Is Socrates overstating his case?[10] After all, even if profit-making is only contingently, or historically, an aim of the skills involved in the production of food and other 'usables', nevertheless breeding and looking after sheep and cattle aims at producing things fit to satisfy human needs. Why else would such skills have developed? The 'needs' which call forth shepherding, agriculture, and so on, are not the 'needs' of animals and plants, but *human* needs—so one might argue on Thrasymachus' behalf.

Socrates' reply is that to think of shepherding and other such skills in this way is not to think of them as skills in the strict sense. As we may put it, one should distinguish the aims of *production* ('use-value', 'exchange-value', and so on), from the various ends of the different skills involved in production.[11] The interests production of sheep serves may vary widely, while the 'interest' of shepherding does not; it remains invariant with respect to the goals of production. The interest of shepherding is satisfied by the proper exercise of the craft; to provide what is best for the flock under its care. The end of shepherding is not to produce meat for the table or profit for the sheep-owner, even though these may be the ends of 'meat-or sheep-production'. Analogously, the end of medicine is to do what is best for the body, which is to be distinguished from the goals of 'health-production', if there is such a thing. The latter may be concerned with profit, or with the production of bodies fit for war, or for labouring activities of certain kinds.[12]

Socrates does not, of course, talk of 'production' in the modern sense. But he does refer to the specific 'power' of each craft to give us a distinctive benefit, in contrast to 'common' benefits. He uses this point to argue that no craft of ruling provides for the practitioner's benefit, only for the benefit of its 'object'. Here is the argument:

(c)

(i)　The test for distinguishing different crafts is that each possesses a different 'power' (*dunamis*)—346a 1–3.

(ii)　Each such 'power' yields a specific, not a common benefit—medicine yields health, navigation safety, and so on—346a 6–8.

(iii)　The specific benefit of the craft of wages are wages. Even if a person earns wages in practising medicine, the benefit (wages) is not due to the 'power' of medicine, any more than the health produced in the captain by being at sea leads us to call his craft medicine—346b 1–6.
Therefore:

(iv)　if there is any benefit which all craftsmen enjoy in common, that will come through their use of a further craft—346c 5–7.

(v)　Craftsmen who earn wages derive that benefit from their use of the additional craft of wage-earning—346c 9–11.
Therefore:

(vi)　the receiving of wages in the case of each craft does not come from that craft. Each craft fulfils its own 'function' (*ergon*) and benefits that over which it presides—346d 1–6.

(vii)　Without the addition of pay the craftsman is not benefited by the voluntary performance of his craft—346d 6–346e 1.
Therefore:

(viii)　no craft provides for its own benefit, only for that over which it presides. In the case of ruling, it provides for the benefit of the subjects and the weaker, not for the advantage of the stronger, the rulers—346e 3–7.

Socrates' argument is somewhat confusing. The use he wants to make of it is to show that genuine rulers do not rule willingly; that they demand recompense for their office (cf. 345e 2–346a 1). No one, says Socrates, willingly becomes a ruler and undertakes to set straight the ills of others without requiring pay, whether it be money, honour, or the avoidance of the penalty which a refusal to rule involves (346e 8–347a 6). There is some lack of clarity, however, about the relation between the principle that the specific benefits of a craft are always those of its 'object', and the idea that wages, or earning pay, is a *common* benefit of craftsmen yielded to them by the use of the craft of wages. Clearly, Socrates wants to say that though doctors and sea-captains get paid for providing, respectively, health and safety, the capacity to earn pay which they also possess is not due to their medical or navigational capacity, but to a distinct wage-earning capacity. This latter capacity is common to many craftsmen, a capacity not merely additional but *external* to the special capacity they possess as the craftsmen they are. But premise (v) attributes the wage-earning capacity to the *further* craft of wages (*misthōtikē*), which the craftsmen are said to make use of (*proschrēsthai*). But it is not clear why the wage-earning capacity is due to the exercise of a craft. True enough, the doctor or the captain must know how to work out proper remuneration for their services since the exercise of medicine or navigation by themselves do not determine a wage. Nevertheless, what *earns* them wages is not the craft of wages, but the medical or navigational services they provide. Propositions (vi)–(viii) only follow if we grant (v). But (v) (and (iv)) do not necessarily follow from (i)–(iii). Even if there is a special craft of wages, a skill in working out benefits appropriate to work, it does not follow that the remuneration which is the common benefit of craftsmen, the pay which craftsmen in fact receive, is yielded by the craft of wages. The pay could be the result of any number of factors: gratitude on the part of those receiving medical or navigational services, a system of patronage exercised by the wealthy, the fact that the craftsman is a slave and compelled to work, and so on.

Socrates seems to shift from 'wage-earning' (*mistharnētikē*) to 'making use of the craft of wages' (*tou proschrēsthai tē misthōtikē technē*). Thus, while it is quite true that the craft of wages is concerned with fixing a wage for a certain type of work, and that craftsmen can use this craft for their own benefit, it is far from obvious that in *receiving* pay the craftsmen are, necessarily, the recipients of the specific benefit of a craft of wages. The only way Socrates' point could be defended would be to argue that if there is such a thing as wage-benefit—as distinct from other types of benefit a craftsman may receive—then it will be the specific benefit of a particular skill. Thus, if doctors, sea-captains, and so on, are *also* wage-earners (= recipients of wage-benefits), the benefits they receive *qua* wages will be the 'product' of the wages-craft (*misthōtikē technē*), even it it is true that the wages they receive are for work they do.

The point is that since there is nothing in the principles of a craft which prescribes a specific type of benefit to its practitioner (for example, wages), wage-earning must be a benefit craftsmen receive as 'objects' of the craft of wages. The *capacity* to earn wages, therefore, is, paradoxically, not generated by the specific work a craftsman performs, but is 'internal' to a wage-fixing craft. The interesting point Socrates is making here is that the capacity to receive wages—the 'entitlement' to pay—is not generated by the work of a craftsman but by the existence of a further branch of knowledge. This leaves it open that in a possible (social) world the practice of various crafts is not attached to a wage-fixing skill. Such a world would be a social system in which the various needs of its members were mutually and co-operatively satisfied without their having to make use of a craft of wages. Socrates' view is contrary to modern liberal views of the 'value-creating' function of labour.[13] It is not productive activity as such but such activity in the context of a certain kind of social system which leads to the idea that all work has a 'price'.[14]

The argument enables Socrates to separate benefits that a ruler might expect for his services from the benefits which the craft of ruling yields to those upon whom it is exercised. Glaucon is intrigued to hear Socrates refer to a benefit the ruler who agrees to govern may rightly expect which is neither money nor honour; the benefit, namely, of avoiding the damage of refusing to rule and of becoming the subject of someone less competent than oneself. This passage (346c–347e) seems to anticipate the claim Plato makes later in the *Republic* (cf., especially, 519d–521b) that the rulers of the good city he describes in Books II–VII will rule unwillingly, through a kind of compulsion, and in spite of a more fulfilling activity they desire to pursue. It is odd to encounter this anticipation of the later doctrine here, before anything has been said about what a city of good men would be like, and about the nature of justice in it. Even if we allow Socrates that ambition and love of money are, and are thought to be, shameful incentives for ruling, the claim that good people accept ruling as a compulsory task because they are afraid to be ruled by worse people introduces a consideration that goes beyond what the argument has shown so far.[15] The contentions that no craft taken by itself aims at the benefit of its practitioner, and that a monetary benefit, apparently caused by the practice of a skill, is in fact a product of the 'accompanying' skill, wage-earning, do not have a bearing on what *incentives* a craftsman may have for exercising his skill; nor on what makes some incentives good and others bad. One could grant Socrates the point that the ruler in exercising his craft aims at benefiting his subjects as the strict 'object' of the craft, without agreeing with him about the sort of motives those who seek rule should have, or about the type of benefits they should expect for their services. For all Socrates has said so far, both the motives for, and the benefits of, rule *for the rulers* may come quite close to those Thrasymachus had in mind. Socrates' argument merely undermines the necessary link Thrasymachus sought to establish between ruling and self-advantage; it in no way establishes that rulers will be good and just persons, any more than the fact that medicine benefits patients makes doctors good and just people.

Plato clearly sees that a different type of argument is needed to combat Thrasymachus' view of what leads people to contend for power. Socrates sketches here, in the barest outline, the type of incentive good persons in a good city would have in exercising their skill of ruling. His point is that good people will not merely feel compelled to consent to rule for fear of leaving the task to inferiors; 'in a city of good men they will contend to escape office as they now contend to gain it' (347d 2–4). Socrates' point needs elaboration. It does, of course, later receive considerable amplification in the main body of the *Republic*. At this stage Socrates contents himself with the reflection that in a 'city of good men' the virtue of the rulers is not merely something *additional* to their skill in ruling; a 'true' ruler is one who does not seek his own advantage but that of those he rules, so that all those who know or understand will prefer to be benefited by such a ruler rather than concern themselves with benefiting others (347d 4–8).

The claim is intriguing in that it suggests that in a good city one will know or understand that it is better to receive the benefits of an 'impersonal' excellence at ruling rather than relying on the altruistic motives, or the goodwill, of those in power. The thesis that a craft necessarily looks to the benefit of its 'object' introduces a notion of benefit which transcends altruism or good intentions precisely because it yields an impersonal good.[16] It is not an essential feature of the doctor or the sea-captain in the strict sense to want to do good to their patients or to their passengers, even though it is a necessary feature of the exercise of these crafts that they benefit their recipients by dealing with deficiencies, weaknesses, inadequacies, dangers, and so on. This is as true of crafts which deal with material objects as it is of crafts which have people, plants, or animals as their 'object'. There is nothing *per se* altruistic about a craft as Socrates understands it.[17] It concerns itself with bringing about, with creating and maintaining, in things a 'proper order and condition': a state which constitutes the peculiar excellence of the things the craft makes its 'object'.

A good city, therefore, will be a city whose rulers maintain its excellence the way other craftsmen do with the 'object' of their craft. In such a city the usual incentives to rule, even, perhaps, the 'wage' of avoiding misrule by inferiors, will be out of place. It becomes clear that in such a city the best thing to be is a recipient of the benefits the craft of ruling provides in keeping the city excellent. But *someone* has to exercise that craft. For, unless someone did, even if doing so was not the best thing *they* could be doing in such a city, it would not be true that the best thing for anyone in that city was to be a subject. Clearly, Socrates has to come up with some convincing account of what would induce people to rule in the good city. Paradoxically, not only money and honour, but even an altruistic motive would not be sufficient. For, those who recognise why it is best to be a subject in such a city, do so precisely because they know that their well-being as subjects does *not* derive from the altruism or goodwill of the rulers—it flows from the rulers doing what they are good at. But, then, what makes anyone good at ruling? And will possessing that ability be the sort of thing that prompted or compelled such a person to want to exercise their craft once they experienced the benefits of being a subject in the good city? It looks as if Socrates' way of undercutting Thrasymachus' association of ruling with the pursuit of self-interest has given rise to the notion of a craft of ruling which, if exercised, would generate a society in which people would prefer to be the beneficiaries rather than the practitioners of the craft.[18] Socrates undertakes to return to this question later (347e 2), and well he might!

8

Excellence and the Motivational Structure of the Just

Socrates turns his attention to the other major contention of Thrasymachus: that the life of injustice, which the powerful necessarily pursue, is what truly makes for their excellence and well-being. The general rubric under which Socrates examines this contention is that injustice is stronger and superior (*kreittōn*) to justice (347e 3–4). However, his first move—to be discussed in this chapter— consists in an attempt to undermine Thrasymachus' association of being unjust with possessing the sort of qualities in virtue of which people are thought to be wise, sagacious, and good. It goes without saying, of course, that the notion of 'good' employed here cannot have a conventional moral sense. However much Thrasymachus may be attempting to revive the old, 'heroic', values of autonomy, supremacy, and personal success in competition with others, the 'quieter' qualities of justice and co-operation had become too much part of what was expected of citizens (as Thrasymachus himself recognises about 'subjects') to allow these qualities to be simply dropped from the traditional conception of the good man (the *agathos*).[1]

Thrasymachus' praise of injustice is based on the fact that he regards it as the more profitable (*lusitelesteron bion*: 347e 7; 348b 9–348c 1). But his grounds for thinking so are that the qualities which make for successful injustice on a grand scale are themselves manifestations of excellence. The perfect tyrant does better for himself than the just, and he does so in a way which elicits admiration; he knows how to avoid or overcome curbs and limitations on his *pleonexia*. Thrasymachus must think that there is something excellent about the qualities which enable the powerful to pursue their kind of injustice, that they are qualities indicative of intelligence, practical wisdom, and a grasp of what is really worthwhile. Injustice is better than justice not merely because one profits materially by it, but because it is a form of excellence; it can lead to greatness, to great achievements. It is, therefore, more profitable than justice as a way of life (cf. 348d 5–9).

Socrates elicits these assumptions when he obtains from Thrasymachus the admission (cf. 348c,d) that he thinks of injustice not as ill nature (*kakoētheia*) but as good counsel (*euboulia*). Thrasymachus cannot quite bring himself to say that justice is a vice—it is 'good nature' (*euētheia*)—but it is certainly not a mark of sagacity (*phronēsis*), and of what makes someone a good (= effective) human being. He is prepared, therefore, to put injustice on the side of excellencce (*aretē*) and wisdom (*sophia*)—qualities no Greek could fail to admire—and justice on the opposite side (cf. 348e 1–4). This is like saying, 'the social "virtue" of justice is not a mark of personal excellence (real virtue); rather, the reverse is true, injustice, though a social "vice", is a mark of true human excellence'. As Socrates says (348e 5–349a 2) this is a tougher thesis to combat than the view that injustice, though more profitable, is a vicious and an ignoble (*aischron*) thing, as the conventional view holds it to be. Someone who thinks like Thrasymachus must regard injustice as something noble, beautiful (*kalon*), and as a strength (*ischuron*).[2] This is because, having classed injustice with wisdom and excellence, the attributes of nobility and strength, conventionally accorded to justice as a mark of wisdom and virtue, will transfer to injustice.

The argument that follows (349b–350c) has outraged some commentators, leaving others sceptical about the merit of its inferential steps.[3] It is certainly highly compressed, and its force depends on how we understand its premises. I believe that within its limited scope the argument is successful. More importantly, given the *context* of its employment (as distinct from questions of its validity), it raises some extremely important issues about the relation between the desire to be knowledgeable (to overcome ignorance), and the desire to be just (to overcome *pleonexia*). The philosophical value of the argument lies in what it suggests: that understanding various kinds of limits to be placed on human action is the kind of expertise involved in justice. Plato explores this idea with considerable insight later when he considers the well-ruled political community.[4]

Perhaps the most profitable way of approaching the argument is to reflect on what might lead one to cut off, as does Thrasymachus, justice from the standard concepts of human excellence, wisdom, intelligence and effectiveness. If we think of personal fulfilment as the outcome of a continuous effort to satisfy the desire to excel in life, we may well come to think of *pleonexia* (acquisitiveness, the desire for aggrandisement) as a fundamental expression of that desire. This will be particularly so in an environment which, being essentially competitive about material possessions and social and political esteem, generates a special kind of 'need'; namely, the need to protect people from the socially unwelcome consequences of unbridled efforts on the part of some to 'outdo', to 'better', to 'surpass', both themselves and others. In branding some forms of the desire to excel as '*pleonexia*', conventional morality, it may be thought, is not so much castigating the *desire*, as expressing its apprehension that things 'might go too far'. Perhaps the old fear that the gods will bring disaster upon those who overstep 'proper limits' (the *metron*) is but a projection on the supernatural plane of what is basically a secular fear; a 'quietistic' resentment aimed at the ambitious by the timid members of the social group. Viewed this way, the limits to action implied by the social demand that people curb their *pleonexia* and avoid injustice will appear only as a 'social' value; not as a condition of personal excellence. Indeed, without much conceptual stress, the unjust can think that pushing boldly and resolutely beyond these conventional limits of 'proper conduct' is precisely what human excellence requires. There being no 'natural' but only 'conventional' limits to human excellence, the task of the 'excellent' is to 'excel', to 'outdo', all others as much as possible, and in as many dimensions of living as one can. To this end the use of intelligence and natural endowments provides the highest form of development these human qualities can reach.

Socrates' argument tries to show that this conception of being excellent as a human being must be mistaken. It is quite unlike—indeed, it is antithetical to—how excellent activity is ordinarily understood. Once again we are referred to craftsmen, for they provide us with paradigmatic cases of people doing things well, or of being good at something. The chief complaint brought against Socrates' argument is that it exploits unfairly an ambiguity in the notion of 'outdoing' or of 'wanting to have more' (*ethelein pleon echein*; 349b 3 ff.).[5] Socrates' idea is that if, like the unjust person, your motive in acting is always to want to have more, then you are not being intelligent. In the exercise of crafts, for instance, intelligence is located in knowing what is required and, thus, in not wanting to 'have more' than the expert, or than what is the 'right' amount. The unjust man in wanting to have more than anyone, whether they are just or unjust, is like the ignoramus who cannot understand why he should limit his desires, and who attributes the demand for limitation to the *will* of others, whether they are experts or non-experts, rather than to the objective requirements of the situation.

The alleged ambiguity in Socrates' argument is that between 'wanting to have more' in the sense of being greedy, and 'wanting more' in the sense of doing better. The ignoramus is over-ambitious whereas Thrasymachus' unjust man is simply greedy. There is no reason why Thrasymachus should agree that the greedy must fail to be intelligent *in the same way* that the ignorant fail because, in being over-ambitious, they miss the right mark. This would be so only if the use of intelligence in the acquisition of things was governed by knowledge of what was the 'right' amount. But if there is no such knowledge, because there is no such thing as the right amount of things to possess, then there is nothing to prevent the unjust being clever at obtaining the maximum of possessions and qualifications.

However, I believe the argument is more subtle than the above simple account makes out. For, though its aim is to separate the unjust man's *pleonexia* from the proper exercise of intelligence, it does so by linking intelligence to a certain type of motivation—a type which resembles the motivation of the just more than it does that of the unjust. Thrasymachus cannot but agree to this resemblance, even though he is embarrassed (he blushes at the end of the argument) to find intelligence linked to this type of motivation. The key to the argument is this resemblance or analogy between the motive of the just and the motive of the knowledgeable *qua* knowledgeable.

Before setting out the argument in full, let us observe how Socrates prepares for it. His *first* question to Thrasymachus attempts to extract from him the admission that if *pleonexia* is the motivation of the unjust as he thinks of them, the motivation of those he thinks of as just will be the opposite; that it will be 'anti-pleonectic'. The just man, Thrasymachus agrees, does not want 'to have more' than other just men, *and* does not want 'to have more' than the just action (349b 2–7). It may appear that the ambiguity in 'having more' is introduced at this early stage with the notion of 'wanting to have more than the just action'. What sort of 'wanting' is this, and how does it relate to the innocuous idea of wanting to have more than anyone else, the idea of being greedy? Socrates' point is that wanting to have more than someone else, if understood merely quantitatively, is not a sufficient condition for *pleonexia*. For example, being larger than you I may want to have more food than you because I need the larger quantity. This would not make my motivation 'pleonectic' and productive of injustice. Proportionally, we would say, the amounts of food we each need to consume, though unequal, are nevertheless 'just' amounts to the extent that they meet the need we each have. To be expressive of *pleonexia* the desire to have more has to be understood in a sense which entails disproportion, or some kind of inappropriateness; it must be a desire to have more than what is needed, than what meets an objective need in the context.

It would seem, then, that a 'pleonectic' desire requires a *double* characterisation of the action that expresses it. Since it is a desire to have more than anyone else *irrespective of appropriate needs*, the unjust person's desire is not merely to 'outdo' others in obtaining a larger quantity of *x* (food, riches, honours, and so on) than them; rather, it is a desire to so 'outdo' them *by* outdoing considerations of what, in the context, signifies the 'right', the appropriate, proportion. Consequently, a pleonectic desire is,

(a) the desire to-have-more-than-anyone-else, whether or not the desire of others in the context is that of just *or* unjust persons; and
(b) the desire to-have-more-than-the-just (the right)-amount.

Socrates is suggesting that the structure of the motive underlying greed, acquisitiveness and the wish for aggrandisement is of an over-ambitious kind; to 'surpass', to 'go beyond' what in the context determines the limits of 'right' action. So far, then, from Socrates 'confusing' two senses of 'wanting to have more', he offers an important insight in moral psychology: *pleonexia*, the grasping wish to have more, is a form of excessive ambition, an inclination to 'beat' limits, to act as if there is no objective system of order governing the context of the action. The greedy person would not be satisfied with having more than others (supposing, for instance, that the supply is inexhaustible) unless in doing so he was doing better than the others. Only so could *pleonexia* be seen, as it is by Thrasymachus, as *constitutive* of what makes injustice productive of excellence.

That this is how Socrates thinks of pleonectic desire is confirmed by his somewhat puzzling remarks concerning the relation of the just to the unjust and to unjust action (349b,c). He gets Thrasymachus to agree that the just wish to 'outdo', to 'do better than', the unjust person and action. To some this has appeared scandalous.[6] How can one think of the just and the unjust as competing in the same race? Why should we regard the unjust man as trying unsuccessfully to achieve what the just man achieves? However, Socrates is merely drawing an implication about the structure of the motive of the just; an implication based on the supposition that as a motive it is both at variance with *and* antithetical to *pleonexia*. He rightly takes it that over-ambitiousness is, for Thrasymachus, an essential feature of pleonectic desire. Will the just, asks Socrates, think it fit (*axioi*) to 'outdo' (*pleonektein*) the unjust; will he think it just to do so (349b 8−9)? Thrasymachus, thinking that Socrates is asking whether the just man will dare, or deign, to outdo the unjust, replies that the just will think this way but to no avail (349b 10).[7] Socrates corrects him on this point: 'this is not what I asked', he says, 'I asked whether the just thinks it fit and wishes to have more than the unjust, but not more than the just' (349b 11−349c 2).

The point, though tersely expressed, is of some significance. There must be positive features which characterise the just person's motivation if justice is a quality of mind. These must correspond to the features of pleonectic desire located in the unjust. The just person's motivation cannot simply be characterised as the *absence* of *pleonexia*. For, were it so characterised, we could not distinguish between persons whose actions expressed a wish to *avoid* transgressing the limits of action set (conventionally or otherwise) in some context, and persons whose action expressed a desire to *achieve* the 'right' limits in the circumstances. The former may avoid acting unjustly, but they will not necessarily do so from justice. The motive of the just is not merely *un*pleonectic, it is *anti*pleonectic. With respect to the achievement of the right limits in a situation, the just, while obviously not in competition with other just people, *are* in competition with the unjust. This is because the conduct of the unjust is motivated by a desire not only to have more than others, but to do so by transgressing the 'right' limit. The unjust think fit to 'outdo' both the just person and the just action because, as Thrasymachus confidently says, the unjust think fit to have more than everyone (349c 4−6). The just, therefore, must be concerned to 'outdo' the unjust precisely because the just are concerned to achieve what the unjust systematically want to disregard.

As Socrates says, the just must think it fit and just to 'outdo' the unjust. It is, of course, true that the unjust (and Thrasymachus) see competition in terms of outwitting all others, both the just and the unjust; they desire to come off best in all situations. But this does not prevent the just from regarding themselves as being in competition with the unjust (in the same situation). They also want to come off best—except, of course, that they see this as achieving the right limit in the circumstances, as succeeding in doing what is just. By presenting the just person's motive as antipleonectic, as a positive force, Socrates ingeniously retains the nexus between justice and the desire to excel. It allows justice to be a positive quality of mind, rather than merely the disposition to observe socially established rules or conventions. At the same time the link between *pleonexia*, intelligence, and wisdom which Thrasymachus had wanted to stress is severely threatened.

Socrates summarises the results of this exchange in a general proposition, let us call it (P1): the just 'outdoes' not the like but the unlike, whereas the unjust 'outdoes' both the like and the unlike (349c 11–349d 1). Given the discussion which has led to this point we are meant to understand that 'outdoing the unlike' and 'outdoing both the like and the unlike' refer to the essential characteristics of two types of motivation—those of the just and those of the unjust, respectively. We could put the same point by saying that the motives of *pleonexia* and *antipleonexia* (an invented word) correspond to two positive stances towards 'right' limits of action. The former seeks to 'go beyond' them in an attempt to do better than all other people, while the latter seeks to achieve these limits in opposition to those whose actions aim at frustrating them—the antipleonectic wants to do 'better than' the pleonectic with respect to achieving the right limits of action in some given circumstances.

Socrates turns next to Thrasymachus' contention that the unjust are good and wise, while the just are not. If things are as Thrasymachus claims, then there will be some property by virtue of which the unjust, but not the just, resemble all those who are sagacious and good (349d 6–7). How could it be otherwise, retorts Thrasymachus, since the unjust, being what he is (*ho toioutos ōn*), namely good and wise, must resemble those who are wise and good, while the just, lacking this property, must fail to resemble the good and wise (349d 8–9). Socrates infers from this admission a further general principle, (P2): 'each (type of) person is (such) as the (type of) person it resembles' (349d 10–11). The Greek of the text is awkward to render pithily in English.[8] An alternative rendering would be: 'each (of the just and the unjust) is what those he resembles are essentially'.

The context of the discussion which has led to (P1) suggests that for Thrasymachus wisdom and goodness are not 'accidental' but essential features of the unjust. These qualities belong to the unjust by virtue of the type of person they are. It does not merely happen that in acting unjustly one shows wisdom and goodness; the unjust are wise and good *because* they are unjust. This being so, Thrasymachus must think that the unjust resemble whoever is wise and good by virtue of a property the latter possess essentially. Suppose there is some other type of person, X, concerning whom we also want to say that they are wise and good. There are two different propositions we can assert of the unjust in relation to X:

(a) the unjust resemble X in that they are both wise and good; or
(b) the unjust resemble X in some respect that is essential to X.

The difference between the two propositions can be expressed as the difference between asserting a similarity between two classes on the basis of a shared common predicate and affirming a common predicate of two types on the ground that there is an *analogy* between what is essential to both types. Given that Thrasymachus regards injustice as essential to excellence, he cannot mean that the unjust merely resemble people who are wise and good; he must mean that the unjust are, *as such*, good-and-wise-like. Mere resemblance between the unjust and those who are wise and good would not by itself justify the belief that the unjust are wise and good (if, and when, they are) *because* of their nature.

This interpretation of (P2) links it with (P1). As we saw, the properties *outdoing not the like but the unlike* and *outdoing both the like and the unlike*, are, respectively, the essential characteristics of the motivations of the just and the unjust. Thus, if Thrasymachus believes that the unjust, in contrast to the just, are wise and good, he must believe that the unjust possess this property because of the motivation essential to their nature. For, were this difference in motivation not essential to distinguishing the unjust from the just, there would be no warrant to the belief that the two types of person must contrast with respect to goodness and wisdom. In some contexts the unjust could turn out to be good and wise, while in other contexts the just might be so—a view Thrasymachus could not possibly accept.

Once more (349e–350b) Socrates has recourse to cases taken from the crafts of music and medicine; that is, to acceptable or known ways of attributing wisdom and goodness to a type of person on the basis of what this type of person effects by virtue of what they are. As we saw earlier, the skills specify various areas in which specific benefits ('goods') are knowledgeably (and, so, wisely) effected. The reason we regard craftsmen in the exercise of their skill as wise and good is because of what they, as skilled persons, essentially effect. Socrates extracts a further principle from considering the stance the skilled must adopt towards other skilled persons, and towards the unskilled. This is (P3): 'with respect to the possession of knowledge in general, and the non-possession of it (ignorance), the expert does not wish to outdo or get the better of another expert but only of the ignorant. The ignorant, however, tries to outdo and get the better of both the expert and other ignorant people' (350a 6–350b 1).

Socrates is suggesting that when we consider examples of types of men and of types of actions which are regarded as good and wise because they are embodiments of expertise, we find that they have a motive analogous to that attributed to the just in (P1). Similarly, the ignorant, who act badly and unwisely in various fields, have a motive analogous to the one attributed to the unjust in (P1). Socrates concludes that the man who is good and wise because he is an expert and learned will not try to outdo his like but only his 'unlike and opposite', while the man who is bad and unwise because he is ignorant and unlearned will try to outdo both 'his like and his unlike'.

Socrates is drawing attention here to a resemblance in motivational structure between, on the one hand, the knowledgeable and the just, and, on the other, the ignorant and the unjust. What makes this odd-sounding argument of considerable interest is the way it attempts to extricate the traditionally valued desire to excel from the pleonectic trappings it had become enmeshed in, in the socio-political climate of imperial democratic Athens—a fact cunningly captured, as was suggested earlier, in the portrait of Thrasymachus. How is the desire to excel to be protected from over-ambitiousness and the scramble for power? The only hope, Socrates hints, is to recognise that the motive characteristic of the just is, in relevant respects, analogous to the motive the knowledgeable have in how they respond to other experts and to the ignorant. Excellence in both cases involves knowing what is the 'right' limit to action, and this entails wanting to 'do better' than their opposite.[9]

Socrates can now (350b,c) bring (P2) into operation against Thrasymachus. According to this principle each type of person is what the type it resembles is essentially. The just resemble the knowledgeable in that each wants to outdo not their like but their unlike; each type possesses this property by virtue of what the type is essentially. Similarly, the unjust resemble the ignorant; they are each essentially motivated to outdo both their like and their unlike (350b). But since the knowledgeable are admitted to be wise, and, because of that, good, it follows that the wise and good do not wish to outdo their like but only their unlike and opposite (350b 7—8). The contrary is the case with the bad and the ignorant— they want to outdo both their like and their unlike. It follows that the just resemble the good and wise while the unjust resemble the bad and ignorant (350c 4—5). If further follows that the just are good and wise, while the unjust are bad and ignorant, since, by (P2), each (type of) person *is* what the type it resembles is essentially.

Before commenting on the argument as a whole, it may help to set it out in summary form. To avoid awkwardness of expression I use capital letters to indicate types of person.

(1)   The JUST are essentially antipleonectic: being what they are they wish to outdo not their like but their unlike.

The UNJUST are essentially pleonectic: being what they are they wish to outdo both their like and their unlike—(P1).

(2) The KNOWLEDGEABLE are practically wise (*phronimoi*), and, in that respect, good.
The IGNORANT are practically unwise (*aphrones*), and, in that respect, bad.

(3) The KNOWLEDGEABLE are, as such, antipleonectic, while the IGNORANT are, as such, pleonectic—(P3).
[3' The JUST resemble the KNOWLEDGEABLE and the UNJUST the IGNORANT].
But:

(4) the KNOWLEDGEABLE are, as such, wise (*sophoi*) and good.

(5) The WISE and GOOD are antipleonectic, they wish to outdo not their like but their unlike, while the IGNORANT and BAD are pleonectic, they wish to outdo both their like and their unlike (350b 7 – 8).

Now, given 1, 3 and 5:

(6) The JUST resemble the WISE and GOOD, while the UNJUST resemble the IGNORANT and BAD.
But:

(7) Each type is what the type it resembles is essentially—(P2).
Therefore:

(8) The JUST are wise and good, while the UNJUST are ignorant and bad.

We saw earlier how one might overcome the resistance to accepting (1) against the misgivings of commentators. We also considered an interpretation of (7) which brings out its links with (1). The remaining task is to examine (2), (3) and (4)—in particular, the sort of considerations that lead to (3), and to the acceptance of (3) and (4). It should be noted that in accepting (1) we are not accepting a universal proposition about justice and injustice. The principle sets out to capture only how *Thrasymachus* thinks of justice and injustice, given the way he links power and excellence with injustice. It would not follow that injustice is a manifestation of *pleonexia* in all contexts, and in all social and political arrangements. Anger at an insult, resentment for being passed over or neglected, fear of danger, and a variety of other motives, can lead to unjust acts, not only greed and *pleonexia*. In picking the latter as essential to injustice, Plato is selecting the sort of motive that may plausibly be seen as leading to, as being responsible for, *thinking of injustice as a kind of excellence*. The force of (1), therefore, is dialectical, and does not necessarily represent what Plato, or, perhaps, even Socrates, would regard as an essential feature of justice and injustice.

Nevertheless, the negative argument has a positive implication: that in thinking of justice as a kind of excellence we need to identify a specific kind of motivational structure in the just.[10]

Can we interpret the function of (2) and (4) as similarly dialectical? Does Socrates himself accept it as true that the expert is essentially antipleonectic, and that the sagacity and goodness we attribute to experts flow from their essentially antipleonectic motivation? Or is it, rather, that Thrasymachus' association of injustice with excellence, and with beneficial and sagacious conduct, commits him to the general thesis that no conduct which is not motivated by pleonectic desires can be wise and good? On the latter alternative Socrates would be presenting Thrasymachus with a counter-example: he thinks of expert conduct as a form of wisdom and goodness, yet an antipleonectic motivation seems essential to being a knowledgeable expert. Still, it is difficult to avoid the impression that Socrates believes there is an important connection between, on the one hand, human excellence and the motive characteristic of those who exhibit it; and, on the other hand, the excellence of knowledge and the motive characteristically operative in those who exercise it. The problem, as is often the case with Socrates' arguments in Book I, is how to interpret the premises he employs in such a way that their strategic effectiveness against a particular opponent can be seen as an invitation to deeper reflection about the issues at stake.

A crucial difficulty in this regard is Socrates' introduction of a pleonectic-like motivation for the conduct of the ignorant and, correspondingly of an antipleonectic motivation for the conduct of the knowledgeable. Why should a person of Thrasymachus' outlook accept that the musician in achieving the 'right' tension in the tuning of strings would wish to 'outdo', in this regard, the unmusical but not the fellow-musician? Why, indeed, should anyone accept this point? Why should an expert's concern to 'hit the right mark' entail a particular *attitude* on his part to the non-expert? And why should the bungling efforts of non-experts entail an attitude on their part to experts and non-experts alike? These are problems concerning premise (3). There are further problems with premise (4): can the wisdom and goodness one associates with skill, (premise (2)) be anything like the unqualified goodness and wisdom affirmed in (4)?

Let us examine the issues that generate the first set of problems. The grounds of resistance to Socrates—perhaps Thrasymachus should have espoused them as well—concern the relation asserted between the excellence of the expert and a certain type of motivation. We may, in the first instance, complain that it is not at all obvious that a doctor or musician may not wish to excel their fellow experts in what they can achieve through their skill. Perhaps there are 'better', more reliable and accurate, ways of tuning the strings of the lyre than those currently practised. Perhaps there are diets and drugs which achieve cures more effectively than those currently employed. There is nothing to prevent an expert from wishing to outstrip the current 'state of the art'. Why could not the Thrasymachian unjust person wish, in a similar way, to outstrip what at any given time are seen as ways of being an effective and powerful ruler? In the second place, it is not clear why it should be obvious that the person ignorant of musical or medical techniques should be in competition with experts and non-experts alike in these fields. Could not the 'ignorant' in these fields be indifferent towards 'outdoing' anyone, like or unlike?

In finding out how Socrates might respond to these difficulties we discover some further interesting features of Socrates' conception of expertise and 'ignorance'; they build on to what we have already seen about Socrates' view of craft-knowledge. We met the view earlier that skilful activity in a certain field is both instigated and controlled by considerations of the 'imperfections' in the 'field' of the skill. We now learn that overcoming these 'imperfections' has to do with the discovery of objective 'limits' in the processes and operations constitutive of a particular craft's field. Thus, it is because of certain features of the material out of which strings are made, and because of the type of construction a lyre is, that the musician must know how to achieve the 'right' tension in each of the strings if he is to generate an harmonious sound. Harmony as musical excellence presupposes recognition of the 'right' string tension, of what is more or less than right. Similar points could be made about medicine.

Socrates' answer to the first point above might be, then, that the possible wish of an expert to go beyond current practice will always be governed by what determines doing well in the field in question. And this is not decided by reference to what other experts (or non-experts for that matter) wish or demand; it is decided by reference to the 'rightness' that resides in the facts of the case, upon the knowledge of which the production of a particular kind of excellence (harmony, health, and so on) depends. A craft can be improved or developed to the extent that its capacity to recognise 'right limits' in its field is increased. This can only happen, for example, if we discover something new to be the case about strings, or about bodily functions.

This conception of the knowledgeable contrasts sharply with the idea that the benefits we obtain from a particular expertise depend on the uses to which we put the techniques of the experts. The latter idea may not be entirely free of *pleonexia*-like attitudes. We may, for example, think that because certain manipulative procedures with strings 'work' in music, similar or analogous manipulative techniques will 'work' in dealing, for instance, with human emotions. People may set themselves up as 'experts' in producing 'psychic harmony' by engaging in activities they claim 'tighten' or 'loosen' emotional 'tensions'. The metaphors are not, of course, entirely fortuitous. But this is precisely the point: they remain *metaphors*, fantasy-like conceptions, unless we can show that there resides *in* the facts of human emotional life such a thing as the 'right limit'. Without such factual foundation the supposed 'expert' in emotions does not know what actions in the field do or do not 'overstep' the mark. Consequently, there will be no objective criterion for distinguishing expert from ignorant conduct in the field. In the effort to get people to accept their 'recipes' as 'working better' than those of others, one set of 'emotional experts' will be in competition both with other such 'experts' *and* with the lay person's unknowledgeable attempts to cope with the vicissitudes of emotional life. The presence of objective limits in the object of genuine knowledge prevents any such competitive situation from developing among the possessors of that knowledge. Similar points can be made about social or political 'experts' who purport to tell us how to organise and control people's likes and preferences.[11]

But why should the 'ignorant' be in competition with the genuinely knowledgeable? The remarks in the previous paragraph suggest a conception of 'ignorance' as a positive force, a force which instigates action as distinct from the 'inactivity' commonly associated with the lack of information. Socrates is suggesting that we can come to want things because of our ignorance (= lack of skill). Our wishes for certain 'goods' may be contrary to the type of thing that as a matter of objective fact can be wanted in a field. *A fortiori*, such wishes will be contrary to that which is rationally desirable in that field—the desire of the knowledgeable in that field being the standard of rational desire there. It would seem that since the expert achieves excellence in a field by grasping the 'right limit' operative in it, he or she is committed, *by the very way he or she pursues excellence*, to combat and 'do better' than the actions inspired by the 'positive' ignorance just referred to. This is so because the contrast between expertise and ignorance, thus understood, is an antithesis between, on the one hand, the rationality of a sort of action *and* of the desire for it, and, on the other hand, the irrationality of another sort of action and the desire for it.

The point Socrates is hinting at is important. There may be disagreements among those who seek knowledge in a certain area, and there may be agreements as well as disagreements among those who do not care for a knowledgeable pursuit of activity in that area. But ultimately, and in principle, what joins the former in a non-competitive relation is the value they place on a rational method of deciding what can be wanted in an area. Their desires, *qua* knowledgeable, are rational because they are 'correct'; that is, the knowledgeable are motivated by a desire to fit with what is the case in the situation. In contrast, the desires of the 'ignorant' are pleonectic-like in that they conflict with both 'correct' and 'incorrect' (that is, unrealistic) desires. A desire governed by a fantasy about what can be had in a certain area is necessarily in conflict with realistic desire. But while realistic desires in the field must, in the nature of the case, tend towards agreement and co-operation, there is nothing about an unrealistic desire, a desire based on a fantasy about the situation in a field, to compel it towards agreement with other desires. Wants governed by fantasy are, of their very nature we may say, open to conflict with both rational wants and other irrational wants—the latter being the product of different unrealistic desires, of different fantasies. The knowledgeable are antipleonectic because rational desire is of this nature, whereas the 'ignorant' are pleonectic because this is the nature of irrational desire.

Socrates' complaint, in several dialogues, that the Athenians do not give equal airing to the opinions of experts and non-experts alike in matters that fall within the province of a craft, while they give such airing to moral and political opinions, is the worry that the latter attitude removes the moral and political field from the province of rational desire. There must, he thinks, be a way of combating fantasy-governed wants in these areas, if we are to speak of ethical or political excellence. And whatever these ways turn out to be, they will, if they are knowledgeable, exhibit the antipleonectic feature of rational desire and action.

Both premises (2) and (4) assert a connection between knowledge, wisdom and goodness. But while one can see why Thrasymachus readily assents to (2), it is not clear why he has to accept (4). The two propositions are different, and the truth of (2) in no way compels acceptance of (4). However, it is (4), not (2), which is crucial to the derivation of (5); it supplies Socrates with the key resemblance between the just and those who are wise and good. Thrasymachus, in accepting (2), is agreeing that the actions of the skilled, compared to those of the unskilled, are paradigms of practical wisdom (*phronēsis*). The craftsman's actions follow a rational pattern, and he obtains results, or brings about 'products', through the exercise of intelligence. In the matters, therefore, in which experts show sagacity, they are also good (349e 6). Skill in producing harmonious sound on the lyre, or in bringing health to the ill, makes a person good *as* a musician or a doctor. But skills can be used to bring about things which, from another perspective, may be good or bad. Experts are not, therefore, good and wise human beings by virtue of being experts. Yet, this is what (4) seems to assert. How does Socrates justify (4) and, thus, the inference to (5)?

We should note the dialectical positioning of (2) and (4) in the text: (2) comes *before* the articulation of (P3), the principle that while the knowledgeable wish to outdo their unlike but not their like, the ignorant wish to outdo both their like and their unlike. The impression is thus created that the antipleonectic wishes of the skilled, as well as the pleonectic wishes of the ignorant, are somehow connected with our reason for attributing practical wisdom and goodness to the expert, while finding that the unskilled manifest the opposite qualities. But Socrates does not *infer* the antipleonectic character of the experts from their sagacity and goodness; it is not because they are practically wise and good at producing certain results that the experts are antipleonectic. Therefore (2) merely serves to introduce the general point that we recognise in skilled conduct a circumscribed type of wisdom and goodness, without its being clear what specifically it is about skilful behaviour which makes us accept it as sagacious and good. The fact that skilled actions follow a rational and intelligent pattern does not tell us anything about the wants and desires of those who engage in them. The activity of spiders in building webs exhibits a rational and intelligent pattern, but the attribution of practical wisdom and goodness to them is, at best, metaphorical and anthropomorphic. We do not know anything about the desires of spiders in the context of building webs. But we do know something about the desires of people in the context of their exercising a skill. This is what (P3) tells us: the knowledgeable are antipleonectically motivated with respect to what counts as a skilled action, and in regard to the facts in a given field which make such action possible. The ignorant, as we saw, exhibit the opposite motivation.

Thus while in assenting to (4) Thrasymachus may think that he is only repeating (2), the fact that he has acquiesced to (3), (that is (P3)), means that dialectically he is prepared to accept the antipleonectic motivation of experts as a *ground* for their wisdom and goodness. In stating (4) Socrates uses the word for wisdom (*sophia*), rather than the word for practical wisdom (*phronēsis*) which he used in (2). The former is, traditionally, a word signifying a human virtue, while the latter is more closely tied to notions of being sensible and prudent. But the connection of *sophia* with skill, sound judgement, intelligence and learning would be conceptual for a Greek. In contrast, being sensible, prudent, and in general, alert to aspects of a situation, need not be grounded on skill or knowledge.[12] It is true, of course, that the activities of craftsmen exhibit prudence, good sense, and presence of mind. But in such a context these qualities need not necessarily refer to traits of character, as they normally do in ordinary contexts.

Nevertheless, Socrates' inference to (5) from (3) and (4) (and, perhaps, even (2)) is not valid. The knowledgeable may be antipleonectic, and they may also, *qua* knowledgeable, be wise and good. But it does not follow from these premises that the wise and good are antipleonectic. The inference would go through only if knowledge (as exemplified by crafts) was the *sole* source of wisdom and goodness; that is, if the wise and good were necessarily knowledgeable in the way craftsmen are. In that event they would necessarily be antipleonectic. But may it not be the case that there are some who can live wise and good lives without having the antipleonectic motive characteristic of craft-knowledge? The problem, is of course, a large one for Socratic ethics.[13] But need *Thrasymachus* be committed to a necessary connection between craft-knowledge and being good and wise? The answer to the latter question must be in the affirmative since, as we saw, Thrasymachus bases the excellence and greater strength of the unjust ruler on his skilful manipulation of a *polis* to his own advantage. Thrasymachus must, therefore, believe that the unjust ruler's knowledge in bringing about certain effects makes him wise and good. Socrates' dialectic is effective against

Thrasymachus because it shows that knowledgeable pursuit of an activity imposes its *own*, 'internal', restrictions on a person's desires and wishes; knowledge is antipleonectic by its very nature.

The dialectical force of Socrates' argument, as distinct from questions of formal validity, goes beyond the defeat and shaming of Thrasymachus. It deepens considerably the ordinary Greek view that the craftsman brings about useful and beneficial results by knowing how to discriminate, in a given field, between good and bad states of affairs.[14] In pointing out the antipleonectic character of knowledge, and, hence, its resemblance to justice in this respect, Socrates is making the important point that genuine skill or knowledge is not merely a *clever* means to certain results; it also imposes restrictions and limitations on what the knowledgeable may desire in being knowledgeable and in acting knowledgeably. Consequently, there is an essential difference between the attitudes the skilled and the unskilled have towards a craft. Experts and lay persons may equally value the 'products' of a craft. But the former can also recognise clearly that what makes their actions a rational response to certain aspects of their environment is the *accommodation of desire* to what is truly the case in that environment. The ignorant are precisely those whose actions do not exhibit such accommodation of desire. They consequently have no grasp of this aspect of knowledgeable activity as a general feature of wisdom and goodness. The ignorant can value the products of crafts and, so, find the practitioners worthy of praise and admiration as wise people. The practitioners, however, know that they are wise and good in their actions not so much because of the character of what they produce, but because of the way their desires are shaped *in* the process of their activity. Craft-knowledge, then, provides us not only with a picture of intelligent achievement of certain ends; it also presents us with a general feature of desire in the context of knowledge—a feature which could well be essential to *all* forms of wisdom and goodness, including those we associate with moral excellence.

The negative force of Socrates' perspective on ignorance is considerable. Contemporary societies of the 'advanced' kind are just as much confronted with the dangers of this 'ignorance' as was Socrates' Athens. We approach the moral and political problems raised by our mode of industrial production, our health-care system, our town-planning, our education, our civil administration, and so on, encumbered with dichotomous classifications of people—divisions which are shot through with unexamined and fantasy-ridden ideas about the 'facts' on which these classifications are based. In formulating policies in these areas we separate the masculine from the feminine (as against the male from the female), the active from the passive, the sane from the insane, the normal from the delinquent, the productive from the unproductive, the energetic from the idle, the educated from the uneducated, the creative from the uncreative, and so on. In our practices, we harden the opinions we have about these distinctions into social *dichotomies*, into social 'facts'. But we do so 'ignorantly'; that is, without knowledge of objective features that would ground these dichotomies. How, then, can our social policies recognise the 'right limits' in what can be expected from or imposed upon people? And yet we allow the shape of the mechanisms and of the institutional framework within which our civilisation's self-perpetuating power operates to be determined by such 'ignorance'. In other words, our cultural, social and political activities are governed by ideological and fantasy-ridden wants and demands. If Socrates is right, our practices in this respect run the risk of being cut off from a central source of wisdom and goodness, from the kind of shaping and accommodation of desire to facts vouchsafed only to the knowledgeable.

But is justice antipleonectic in the same way that knowledge is? Though it is true that Socrates' analogy in this argument is limited to a critique of Thrasymachus' view about the knowledgeably unjust ruler, Socrates' questioning succeeds in raising general issues about *pleonexia*; in particular, issues about the relations of *pleonexia* to rational desire which are as relevant to today's moral and political practices as they were to those of Socrates' and Plato's Athens. In concluding this chapter we shall look briefly at the principle (P2) on which Socrates' argument turns. The claim that 'a thing is what the thing it resembles is as such' seems to state, in a rather compressed form, the methodological rule of probable inference. Given that Thrasymachus, in maintaining that injustice is wise and good, was assuming that the powerful ruler is knowledgeable, Socrates is entitled to assume that Thrasymachus accepts that knowledgeability implies wisdom and goodness. What Socrates does is to argue that in recognised cases where knowledgeability grounds goodness and wisdom, the knowledgeability 'carries' with it an antipleonectic motivation. So, since the just also have an antipleonectic motivation, it is probable that in the area where justice and injustice operate it is the just who are wise and good. The argument is based on a sound inductive inference; the ball is now in Thrasymachus' court to show that there are recognised cases of knowledgeability which are *not* antipleonectic.

Now, while this accounts for the *use* of (P2) at 350c 7−8 (our premise (7)), its initial introduction at 349d 10−11 is based on Thrasymachus' answer to a question by Socrates. The latter asked whether the unjust, in being wise and good, resemble the wise and good. In the later passage Socrates moves in the reverse direction; that is, from the fact that the just resemble the wise and good to their being wise and good. There is nothing untoward in this procedure. Socrates treats Thrasymachus' claim that injustice is wise and good as an *hypothesis* to be examined.[15] The view cannot be rejected by appeal to conventional moral notions since it clearly challenges them. The only procedure, therefore, is to see whether the basis of Thrasymachus' claim, namely, that there is a property of the unjust which makes them good and wise, is consistent with what is an essential feature of those who are good and wise in other areas. The unjust, according to Thrasymachus, are essentially pleonectic. If this is the source of their wisdom and goodness should we not expect that the wise and good possess this property wherever we find them? Socrates' introduction of (P2) at 349d 10–11 is merely a reformulation into assertoric form of this methodological question. The only way Thrasymachus could avoid agreeing to it is by being prepared to argue that there are *radically different* forms of wisdom and goodness, and that only some of them are essentially pleonectic. But even if he was prepared to argue this, he could not without contradiction agree that pleonectic forms of wisdom and goodness are not grounded on knowledgeability. Such a denial would leave exposed his contention that the tyrant in being perfectly unjust was rational and intelligent, and his excellence lay in *how* he went about achieving his goals. After all, the question is not whether power, riches and honours are good things, but whether acquiring them justly (or unjustly) is a mark of human excellence.

9

Socrates Sketches the 'Power' of Justice

Having succeeded in throwing doubt on Thrasymachus' association of injustice with wisdom and goodness, Socrates now returns to Thrasymachus' earlier contention that the unjust are 'stronger' (*kreittōnes*) than the just (347e 3–4). Even if the unjust are not wise and good, injustice may make people more powerful than justice (351a 2–3). But how can this be so if justice has been seen to be wisdom and virtue, and injustice ignorance (351a 3–6)? Nevertheless, the argument examined in the last chapter was limited. All it showed was that the just fall on the side of the wise and good because they are more like the knowledgeable than are the unjust. But this does not tell us whether, and in what ways, justice is more powerful, more enabling, than injustice. After all, Thrasymachus' view was that perfect injustice is more profitable to the agent than justice is (348b 9–10). Thrasymachus admires absolute power because it can achieve great material benefits, prestige and social status. It may very well be that in this respect injustice is more 'power-giving' than justice, even if justice is, in some other sense, more 'enabling'. What exactly are the 'powers' of justice, and how do they relate to what is commonly recognised as power? The two arguments which conclude Book I of the *Republic* address themselves to two questions: whether the possessors of justice are made stronger by it than are the unjust by their injustice (350b–352b), and whether it is justice rather than injustice which enables a 'soul' to lead a *eudaimōn* life, a flourishing, happy, and enviable life (352d–354b).

As mentioned earlier, after 350d Thrasymachus loses interest in continuing the argument with Socrates. Plato obviously does not think that the arguments which follow would convince a Thrasymachus, and commentators have found them exasperatingly weak and unsatisfactory. At best, they seem to beg the question; they depend on premises that would be acceptable only to those who already accepted the conclusion. At worst, they owe their force to a rhetoric which has limited scope and would only be effective if one accepted some very contentious ideas.[1] For all that, the arguments succeed in suggesting an alternative conception of power to that implicit in Thrasymachus' doctrine. Plato makes it clear that he does not think the arguments are dialectically effective against Thrasymachus. This does not prevent them, however, from introducing the sort of perspective, quite antithetical to Thrasymachus', from which one may grasp the sense in which justice is an enabling power. Strategically, then, the structure of the three arguments against Thrasymachus in Book I is that while the first argument (discussed in the previous chapter) is meant to undermine Thrasymachus' view, the remaining two are not so much arguments against Thrasymachus as attempts to set right the sort of mislocation of power and excellence that leads to the Thrasymachean view.[2]

In view of this it is beside the point to attack these last two arguments for failing to succeed in rebutting Thrasymachus. The unjust tyrant, given the ends he pursues, may not need justice, but his life may lack what makes a human life effective and flourishing. So, there may be reasons why the prosperity and well-being of cities and individuals require justice. The task is to discover the considerations which show justice to be an objective need of both individuals and cities, even though there are individuals whose desires and ambitions prevent them from seeing such an 'impersonal' need. The generality and abstractness of these last two arguments in Book I are due, I believe, to the fact that Socrates' thought is guided by the intuition that the power of justice resides in its meeting an 'impersonal' need—a need which arises in individuals and communities because of their 'nature'. There being such a 'need' does not mean, of course, that even those who value justice (like Cephalus and Polemarchus) understand that its value consists in meeting such a 'need'. Socrates' task is to explain how and why it is that in meeting this 'need' justice becomes a force responsible for strength and well-being.

Even so, the arguments have some force against Thrasymachus. We recall that the core of Thrasymachus' position was not merely that more benefits accrue, contingently, to persons who make injustice their aim; he views injustice as an ideal of a good and excellent life, one which is in itself superior to justice, 'mightier and freer' (344c 4–6), as well as more profitable. This is confirmed by Socrates' remarks (349a) that Thrasymachus does not regard injustice as more profitable while admitting it is a vice and evil. Injustice for him will be good both in itself—it is 'noble and strong', a virtue, because of what it enables people to achieve—as well as good for what it brings to those who practise it. The 'nature' of injustice is for Thrasymachus such as to entail greater 'powers' than justice. Socrates' sketch of an alternative conception of the 'powers' of justice is meant to counter Thrasymachus' disregard of them. The latter's view runs counter to the common view that justice is a cohesive social force, and that an individual is better off for being just. The essence of the traditional view that a *polis* requires justice, a 'civic virtue', is that it makes for social harmony and cohesion, that it safeguards the *polis* from the dreaded 'disease' of contention and civic strife. However, to produce a plausible alternative to Thrasymachus Socrates must explain how justice 'works', and what it acts upon to produce its effects. He needs to demonstrate in opposition to Thrasymachus, the ways in which justice is a source of power and injustice a cause of weakness.

Socrates begins this task by pointing out that injustice cannot be a source of strength since its practice in a community does not bring men together but sets them apart. It is not a unifying but a divisive force. Even a group of thieves with an admittedly unjust objective will be frustrated in their efforts unless they are just to each other (351c 7–10). Socrates then extends this idea of the essentially divisive character of injustice to the individual. The man who is unjust is at war with himself—the different elements in his soul fight against each other.

It may seem that the extension of the divisive character of injustice to the individual is unwarranted. One may accept the familiar point about the need for honour amongst thieves, that fair dealing among themselves is required if a band of thieves is to be effective in achieving its unjust ends. But what keeps the thieves together may not be motivated by anything other than fear of each other, or of a leader with a strong enough personality.[3] If each of them could achieve their objective on their own they would do so. So, at best, all this shows is that the effectiveness of certain projects depends on co-operation, and that this requires a limited, though variously motivated, suspension of the inclination to outdo everyone else. There is a difference, however, between what is required to make effective the pursuit of some aim, and the force which makes a group cohesive or harmonious. The latter may involve mutual respect, and a sense of obligation to others—a feature not entirely unknown among gangs of criminals.[4] The question, then, is whether there is a characteristic way in which justice and injustice 'work' such that the 'need' for justice and the avoidance of injustice is something that a *band* of people generates, as distinct from what effective common action, such as thieving, may require.

This is the force of Socrates' remark (at 351d 4–6) that injustice brings dissension, hatred, and quarrelling, while justice brings friendship and harmony. Because it causes conflict and hatred injustice makes a group defective as a group, whatever the group's projects. Justice, on the other hand, generates a united group because it brings about harmony and friendliness between people. Thus, fear, or a desire to satisfy greed, may be things shared by a band of thieves. However, it is not these motives which enable them to act in unison but the fact that they recognise injustice within the group to be a weakening of the group. Interference with each other's tasks, the temptation of each to have more than, to outdo, the other, will be destructive of the group's powers as a group. The 'power' of injustice, Socrates hints, is to bring about a double effect: 'wherever it appears (city, tribe, army, and so on) it makes that which possesses it, firstly, incapable of united action, and, secondly, the enemy of itself, of anything contrary to itself, and of the just' (351e 3–352a 3).

The traditional defenders of 'civic' justice would recognise the first 'effect' of the 'power' of injustice; dissension and division makes collective or united action hard. But would they agree that injustice is the cause of the second 'effect'? Is it true that the presence of injustice makes a group an enemy, not only of justice and of its projects, but of itself as well? Socrates is making a challenging and important point here—a point meant to justify his extension of the link between justice and harmony from group to individual. He is saying that if justice and injustice have distinct and opposed 'powers', we should be able to identify their 'work' in any form of behaviour that is caused by them. We should be able to do this whether or not the conduct in question is conventionally recognised as just or unjust. At this stage of the argument Socrates is not dealing with the question of what justice and injustice *are* but with how we identify their symptoms. He is assuming, therefore, something his previous arguments with Cephalus and Polemarchus were meant to make persuasive: namely, that justice and injustice are best thought of as psychic forces operating within individuals or communities. This, as we saw, was in contrast to the notion that justice consists in a kind of social rule or type of relationship. In the present passage he is developing this idea of justice as an 'inner' force. He is arguing that incapacity to act in a co-ordinated fashion, antipathy to co-operative activity, and hatred of the just (thing and person) are 'symptoms' of injustice because its 'power' is to generate hatred and dissension. That injustice has this 'power' may be inferred from the fact that all its symptoms are manifestations of self-destructiveness, of a thing at war with itself.

It may, indeed, be true that in making Socrates say that injustice pulls apart an individual as well as a group Plato has in mind his later *theory* that the soul and the *polis* have analogous parts which need to be co-ordinated. But the point that the unjust man is ineffective because he is always potentially in internal conflict, that he acts against himself and becomes hateful to himself the way he is to others, does not *require* the later theory.[5] The later theory may explain why the point is true; it is not equivalent to its truth. Though the individual is described in terms normally applied to a group, I cannot see that it is a 'strange' or 'extraordinary' idea.[6] Self-conflict, self-hatred, and so on, are ordinary and familiar ways in which people interpret forms of behaviour. The central question raised by this passage is whether Socrates is right in attributing these forms of behaviour to injustice. Is Socrates' moral psychology correct? I believe it can be shown to be so. Nevertheless, in appreciating why he may be right about this we are pressed towards recognising that we need to understand justice in a non-traditional way.

The text (cf. 351d–352a) gives the impression that Socrates extends his characterisation of the 'work' of injustice from groups to relations between two individuals and then, to the individual himself. Injustice causes hatred, revolt, and undermines unified action in both groups and individuals. It is significant that when speaking of the impact of injustice on individuals he makes no reference to 'parts' or 'components' of the soul (cf. 352a 5 – 8). The phenomena of self-hatred and self-rebellion, and of 'disunited' action, are, presumably, identifiable whether or not we can explain why we make the assumptions implicit in these modes of description. The language of our descriptions implies that we regard groups, pairs and individuals as having component parts that come adrift under the impact of injustice. But it does not follow from this that when talking of groups the 'parts' referred to are the members of the group as individuals. It is one thing to say that envy, suspicion, fear, and so on, cause quarrels among members of a band of thieves. It is quite another to say that injustice causes such quarrels. In saying the latter you imply that there is an 'impersonal', a structural, cause of the personal conflict, whereas in saying the former you are attributing the conflict to merely personal factors. Though in both cases the outcome may be the disintegration of the group and what makes it incapable of acting in unison, the causal factors are quite different. Injustice may generate the envy, suspiciousness, and so on, which set one individual against another, but *it* is not these feelings. Though it might be the source of conflict between people, injustice is not itself a mode of personal relation to others; I cannot feel justice or injustice towards another the way, for example, I can envy or resent them. Injustice designates something structural about relationships. Therefore, in judging that the 'work' of injustice in a group is to split it apart we must be viewing the group as a structured entity consisting of individuals *in* various functional relations becoming flawed in the very structure that makes it a whole. Evidently we are able to form such judgements without neccessarily having any clear idea about how to analyse the unifying structure of a group; we may not know whether, for example, it consists in relations of an economic, or a political, or a moral kind, or a mix of all these. We may not know the nature of the forces of social cohesion, but we assume they are there.

The same point emerges when we consider the situation between two individuals. Suppose that *A* acts greedily or egotistically in some situation, and that the action results in *B* being deprived of some benefit that *B* is entitled to. This leads *B* to hate *A*, and they may quarrel. For argument's sake let us further assume that *A*'s act is commonly regarded as a type of unjust act. There are two causal statements we can make about this situation which are quite different in their import. We may say that *A*'s act, which was unjust, caused *B* to quarrel with *A*; and we may say that *A*'s injustice manifested in *A*'s act caused the quarrel between *A* and *B*. It is only the second statement which takes the quarrel between *A* and *B* to be an effect of the unjust character of the act—a reaction quite distinct from, say *B*'s response to how *A*'s action affected him or her. *B* may quarrel with *A* because *A*'s act affected *B* personally, because it deprived *B* of some benefit. But *B* could have so reacted to the deprivation even though *A*'s act was *not* unjust. From the fact that *A*'s act is unjust, and that *B* quarrelled with *A* because of the consequence of the act, it does not follow that it was the act's injustice which was the source of *B*'s quarrel with *A*.

Once again we see that though one and the same act may be both unjust and an act of deprivation, and that the act under either description may be seen as the cause of disintegration of a relationship, we are saying different things when employing either of these descriptions in a causal statement. In the one case the quarrel is seen as the act's potential to hit at the structure of the relationship between two people (whether it is, for example, a relationship based on trust, a formal agreement, a settled division of labour or function, and so on). Seen that way the act disintegrates the relationship because it undermines the 'impersonal' structural factors which make the relationship of the type it is. In the other case the quarrel is seen as a reaction to unjustified personal harm. The difference is registered in two types of remarks we make. We say, 'what you did to me is unforgivable', or 'callous', or, *even*, 'unfair'. But we also say, 'what you did has made our relationship unworkable, impossible, insecure, unprofitable', and so on. We can say both sorts of things about the same act because, quite obviously, the act may affect us personally in both ways. But in saying the second we are indicating that we are upset about what the act did to the relationship itself, to the benefits *of* the relationship, as distinct from the direct damage it perpetrated to our individual interests.

If we grant that the 'work' of injustice has this character of disintegrating social entities in their 'organic' aspect, it is difficult to see how one could deny that the same 'power' is at work in an individual. Whether or not we can give a coherent account of 'parts' of the soul quarrelling or in conflict with one another, there are certainly behavioural phenomena which we want to describe as due to self-destructive, self-incapacitating, and self-disintegrative factors. It need not, of course, be the case that all conduct which exhibits these features is due to injustice. But on the occasions when we do attribute them to an agent's injustice we are thinking of how the orientation of a person's thoughts and desires affects the order or structure of their personality, of the impact of their injustice on their capacity to function as an integrated and effective unit. We are concerned, in other words, to highlight the 'impersonal' aspects of their persona in order to be able to say that the incapacitating effect of injustice *in* them is due to a self-conflicted impulse in their make-up. As Socrates points out (351e 4; 352a 3; 352a 8), the 'natural work' (*haper pephuken ergazesthai*) of injustice has a twofold character: first to make the entity it inheres in (in a group, a relationship, or an individual) incapable of action by stirring revolt and contention within itself; and secondly, to make it an enemy of itself and of the just (352a 6−8).

We may still be puzzled about the second aspect of what Socrates identifies as the 'work' of injustice. Of course injustice can cause strife within a group, and, to that extent, render it incapable of unified action. But what does Socrates mean when he says that it makes people 'enemies of each other and of the just'? It is interesting in this context to note the reference to gods (352a 10–352b 2). The gods are just, says Socrates, and so the unjust will be an enemy, while the just will be a friend, of the gods. Thrasymachus does not really go along with this point (cf. 352a 11 and 352b 3–4), but what exactly is its force? One thing it illustrates is the fact that the presence of injustice generates enmity or antipathy to anything the unjust perceive as antithetical to them. Thus, they loath the very fact that others want things (whether these others are just or unjust people); other people's wants appear to them as obstacles to getting their own way. But they are also antipathetic to those who act justly, to those who exemplify in their conduct a recognition of 'right' limits to action. Traditionally the gods are supposed to be just and powerful. But whether or not a person's injustice affects the individual interest of a god, who may subsequently punish the evil-doer, this is not what makes the unjust enemies of the gods. Being unjust they are, as such, enemies of the gods whether the individual interests of the gods are affected by their injustice or not. Given that the gods are just, and that they are powerful, they represent a force to which the unjust are, of necessity, antithetical. The latter's injustice sets them at odds with the gods because the latter, as divine representatives of justice, desire a particular kind of order in things. It is their going against that order which makes the unjust enemies of the gods.[7]

It would seem, then, that the enmity generated by injustice, though it can lead to personal squabbles, is of an 'impersonal' kind; it is an enmity indiscriminately directed at any order which places limits on action, whether such limitation is imposed by the superior power of another person, or whether it is a limitation objectively required by the situation. A person's unjust action within a group harms the interests of others and may provoke their enmity, but in an important sense the unjust person is an enemy not so much of other people as of the features of the group which hold it together, and whose preservation requires limits to action and desire. It is this aspect of injustice which make individuals enemies of themselves. For, it may well be that in some contexts it is in the interest of the unjust to curb their pleonectic desires, to observe rules, to consider others in what they do. But it is precisely in such situations that the unjust, who tend to abhor limitation, are likely to act against their own interest—to be 'enemies to themselves and to the just'—precisely because the unjust impulse expresses itself as the desire to overstep limits. And it is this impulse which is antithetical to cohesion, whether in groups or individuals; the impulse to 'outdo', left to itself, is of its 'nature' threatening to what makes a group or individual an integrated whole.

Socrates concludes (352b 5–352d 1) that the just have been shown to be wiser, better and more capable of action than the unjust. Indeed, in saying that a band of unjust men brought off some vigorous common action, our attribution of the action to their injustice would not be altogether true. For, had they been thoroughly unjust they could not have avoided damaging each other. A modicum of concord and friendship among themselves—the 'work' of justice— must have kept them from practising on each other the injustice they practised on their victims. A 'sort of justice' enabled them to achieve their unjust ends; their espousal of the unjust deed being based on a 'half-capacity for injustice' (*adikia hē-mimochthēroi ontes*). Had they been total rascals and perfectly unjust they would also have been perfectly incapable of action.

There is an important corollary to Socrates' view that justice and injustice have 'powers' whose characteristic 'work' one can observe in the behaviour of the things in which they operate. To regard the phenomena of concord or dissension, of friendship or enmity, as symptoms of a 'force' that produces them, requires a characterisation of justice and injustice which is *independent* of their tendency to produce these symptoms—a characterisation which can, it is hoped, adequately explain why they are such as to generate this tendency. For, the same effects may come about through the operation of a variety of causes. A not uncommon view of justice is that the source of concord and friendship in a group or a community is the fact that its members regard the rules governing their public behaviour as bearing equally on all of them. Correspondingly, the social dissension prevalent in another group is attributed to the fact that its rules are applied in a discriminatory or unfair fashion to different members of that group.

But to say that this sort of equality or inequality is the nature of justice and injustice (respectively), would not, on the Socratic view, be sufficient. Unless we can show why 'bearing equally (or unequally) on everyone' is *apt* to produce the effects in question, we are not justified in thinking that the 'power' of justice derives from its ensuring that sort of equality. The question is to determine whether the causal powers of fairness, or of an equality of the relevant sort, are those of justice. To decide this question we cannot simply identify justice with fairness, even if we are right in thinking that fairness is a good thing and that it produces concord and social peace. For it to be the case that fairness is justice it would have to be the case that it produces the relevant effects *in the way* that justice does. To know this we logically require a characterisation of justice which explains how these effects are its 'work'. Fairness would be justice only if, or only to the extent that, it satisfied that characterisation. This does not mean, of course, that, in the event that fairness is different from justice, we may not find it a sufficiently worthwhile social good. But it would not be the same good as justice, supposing justice to be a good. The crucial question about justice is not whether it is a good, but whether it designates a unique kind of good, a good that nothing else can bring about.

The last, and closing, argument of Book I of the *Republic* (352d–354b) attempts to show that the just lead a happier and more blessed life than the unjust.

The argument is very abstract and, like some of the other arguments in Book I, it has been found unsatisfactory, and even scandalous.[8] In particular, it has been felt that Socrates' attribution of a 'function' (*ergon*) to human beings is dubious, and that the argument trades on a crucial ambiguity in the notion of 'living well'. Before examining the argument and the charges brought against it, we should note that its most distinctive feature is the introduction of 'the soul' and the application of justice and injustice to it. Socrates does seem to move—'slide', some would say—from the just soul to the just man, and this raises some difficult problems which Socrates leaves unexamined. But the central focus of the argument is the application of justice to the soul.[9]

Socrates' introduction of the soul is intriguing. He has just argued that justice is 'stronger, more capacitating' than injustice, having identified injustice as a cause of the inability to act in an integrated way, as well as a cause of enmity and of social or individual disintegration. He now proceeds to consider whether the just live better and more 'eudaimonically' than the unjust (352d 2–4). Socrates believes that the arguments so far have already shown this, but he claims that there is a better way of arriving at the same conclusion (352d 4–5). It is this 'better way' which introduces the just soul.

The connection of this argument to the previous one may be something like this. We noted above that to regard concord and friendship as the 'work' of justice logically requires a characterisation of justice which is independent of its capacity to produce these effects; we need an account of its 'nature' by virtue of which it possesses that capacity. Now, one general way of approaching such an account would be to look for characteristics of the human form of life which can be taken as the 'field of operation' of justice. The effects of justice (or injustice) can be seen in individuals and in groups of people. But what is it that justice or injustice act upon to produce their characteristic effects? Since the issue is of whether the just or the unjust lead a better and happier life, of how one should live (352d 6), it is natural to identify the 'soul'—living is said to be the *ergon* of the *psychē* (353d 9)—as the 'operational field' of justice and injustice. If the just life is to be shown to be the excellent and happy life, then the causal role of justice upon the 'business' of living has to be that it enables the soul to perform that 'business' in the best possible way. On this supposition justice will be an enabling 'power' in the soul with respect to living. But even if the argument succeeded in showing this, it would not have revealed the nature of justice; it would merely have given us an abstract and programmatic characterisation of *where*, and *what*, to look for in attempting to define justice.

At best, then, the argument we are about to consider offers reasons for the view that an understanding of the nature of justice requires that we investigate its relation to the capacities which enable human beings to conduct the 'business of living' in the best possible way, both individually and collectively. This 'research programme', into what may turn out to be social, economic, political and psychological matters, is required by the thesis that a proper understanding of justice must view it as a causal power within individuals and communities. Such a proposal would be unnecessary if we did not think of justice that way. We may think, for example, that 'justice' signifies the set of rules instituted by society for the mutual protection of the interests and rights of its members. As we saw earlier, such a conception of justice is not a moral one, and consequently it provides no answer to Thrasymachus' claim that living justly is living in a servile and unexcellent way. This last argument in Book I brings together in a highly abstract way the various threads that constitute the Book's unifying theme: to show that justice is essentially connected with the power to achieve human excellence, that it is not merely an inescapable necessity of social existence. The proposition to be countered is the challenging one that the just not only lose out on life but lead a 'low' life, while the life of the unjust is 'high'—a proposition of whose emotional force Plato is thoroughly aware.[10]

Socrates argues as follows:

(i)   The *ergon* (function, characteristic activity, or 'way of working') of a thing is that which it alone can perform, or which it performs better than anything else—353a 10 – 353b 1. The point is illustrated by reference to horses, eyes, ears, and pruning knives (cf. 352e – 353a).

(ii)   To each thing to which there is an *ergon* there is a corresponding virtue or excellence without which the thing would not perform its *ergon* well— 353b,c.
        Therefore:

(iii)   things perform their *ergon* well by reason of their proper virtue, and badly by reason of the corresponding vice—352c 6 – 10.
        Socrates uses this as a general principle and applies it to the soul. Thus:

(iv)   the *ergon* of the soul is to live, to superintend, to control, to rule, to deliberate, and such like. We cannot assign such activities to anything other than the soul—353d 3 – 7.

        So (by ii):

(v)   there is a virtue or excellence proper to the soul—353d 11.

(vi)   Given (by iii) that the soul cannot perform its proper *ergon* well if deprived of its proper virtue—353e 1 – 2—it follows that:

(vii)   it is necessarily the case that a bad soul performs the activities of controlling, ruling, and superintending, badly; while the good soul, necessarily, does these things well—353e 4–5.

But:

(viii) it has been argued that justice is a virtue of the soul and injustice a vice— 353e 7–8.

Therefore:

(ix) the just soul and the just man will live well, while the unjust will live badly—353e 10–11.

But:

(x) Those who live well are happy and blessed; those who do not, are the opposite—354a 1–2.

Therefore:

(xi) the just are happy and the unjust miserable—354a 4.

But:

(xii) being happy, not miserable, is what is profitable—354a 6.

Therefore:

(xiii) injustice can never be more profitable than justice—354a 8–9.

The word '*ergon*' is usually translated as 'function' but it is not the best translation. An *ergon* is what a thing does as the kind of thing it is. When applied to people's activities, it means 'job' or 'work', and when applied to natural kinds like men and horses it means the 'characteristic behaviour' we associate with the kind. The word is used for the craftsman's activity as well as for the product of that activity. But even when applied to artefacts made for a purpose, there is no essential reference to purpose in the use of the word. Reference to purpose is absent from Socrates' criteria in (i).[11] The range of meanings of '*ergon*' has already been fully exploited in Book I: as *product* of activity at 330c; as the *activity* in respect of which the just help friends and harm enemies at 332e; as what *something does* relative to what it is (the *ergon* of cold is to cool, of the good to benefit, of the bad to harm) at 335d; as *characteristic end*, goal or achievement at 346d 5–6 (the end of each craft is to benefit its 'object'). It is this last idea that comes closest to our notion of 'functioning' as applying, for instance, to organisms, machines, institutions or states.[12]

Is Socrates fallaciously moving between these meanings of '*ergon*' in the argument? It has been claimed that Socrates uses *three* criteria for assigning an *ergon* to a thing: that which it alone can perform, that which it can perform better than anything else, and the use which has been assigned to it. 'The notion of function presupposes purpose—the purpose for which we use a thing which we find, or the purpose for which we have the thing designed'.[13] The accusation is that Socrates moves from saying

(1)   that living (which could be living well or badly) is the function of the soul; to

(2)   if the soul is performing its function well, it lives well.

Cross and Woozley contend that Thrasymachus could argue that in living in a bad way the soul performed its function by the first criterion—it is that which it alone can do. He could argue, further, that injustice is the excellence of the soul which enables it to perform that function, and that, therefore, it is the unjust soul which performs its function best.[14]

   This misunderstands Socrates' argument and his use of *ergon*. Socrates does not refer to purposes, to anything like the alleged third criterion above. Nor is premise (i) meant to split into *two* criteria for assigning an *ergon* to a thing. Socrates is merely saying that the *ergon* of a thing is the 'product', the 'job', the activity, or the end—thus covering the full range of the use of '*ergon*'—which it alone can achieve, or which it achieves better than anything else. The point is that excellence of a kind is built in to the very idea of an *ergon*; it refers to what a thing characteristically or typically *achieves*. Thus, as we saw earlier (341d; 342b; cf. above p. 112), crafts do not need a virtue (*aretē*) to perfect them, the way eyes in order to be perfect as eyes need sight, and ears need hearing. The fact that organs can become deficient with respect to their 'excellence', that is, to what they perform best, brings crafts into existence. What is crucial to Socrates' argument is not so much the fact that only eyes can see; rather, the point is that in relation to sight considered as something achieved by an organ, it is the *ergon* of eyes only if there is no other thing that can perform it better. If it is true that only eyes can see, then it follows that nothing can achieve that activity better than eyes. In the case of activities such as pruning, tools other than pruning knives can perform the task. But the activity would not be the *ergon* of a kind of knife unless there was nothing which achieved that activity better. If a different tool was invented that pruned better, then pruning would cease to be the *ergon* of pruning knives, even though one could still prune with them tolerably well. The crucial point about the soul is not whether there are some activities (among which is living) which it alone can perform, but whether concerning these activities there is anything other than the soul which can achieve them better. For, if there was, the activities could not be said to be the *ergon* of the soul.

   It is because the *ergon* of something indicates an area of activity where things can be done better or worse, that Socrates asserts premise (ii). This applies to eyes just as much as to artefacts. Thus, it is not because it is the 'purpose' of eyes to see, and of pruning knives to prune, that we speak of 'excellent' or 'inferior' eyes and pruning knives. Rather, it is because we believe that seeing and pruning are activities which nothing can do better than eyes and pruning knives, that we judge particular eyes or particular pruning knives in terms of how well they achieve their respective tasks. In other words, the criteria of excellence in these cases are 'internal' to the activity considered as the *ergon* of the item in question. This would not be the case if *ergon* referred to 'purpose'. An artefact could be designed to perform a certain function and, if well-designed, the purpose of the maker could coincide with the purpose of the user—the designer's purpose being to enable the user to meet *his* purpose. But the two 'purposes' could fall apart. The user's conception of 'excellent' or 'inferior' as applied to the artefact could be determined by purposes other than those of the designer.

But this is not a possibility with the *ergon* of something. A pruning knife could be used for purposes other than pruning, and the user could find it 'excellent' in this respect. But it would not be what made it excellent or inferior as a pruning knife. Similarly, a designer could have invented the pruning knife for the purpose of pruning. But what makes the knife excellent or otherwise is not that it satisfies the inventor's purposes, but the fact that what pruning achieves could not be done better by anything else. The inventor's purposes could have been based on a mistaken apprehension of what pruning achieves and, so, he could have thought of his invention as the best because it met his purposes. But he would be mistaken. It is because the *ergon* of something indicates a sphere of achievement in which the thing is *unsurpassable* that it provides us with criteria for the excellence of that thing's performance in that regard. Consequently, we judge whether an eye or a pruning knife is excellent by determining whether it possesses or lacks the 'excellences' which enables it to achieve the *ergon* of its kind. Premise (ii) asserts that assigning an *ergon* to *x* entails that there is an excellence proper to the kind *x* without which a particular *x* cannot perform well the activity regarded as 'proper' to the kind it falls under.

The crucial issue with respect to the soul, then, is whether living, and the other activities assigned to it by Socrates, can be thought of as *erga* of the soul. If they can, then there will, of necessity, be an excellence of the soul without which it could not perform these activities well. These points are made in propositions (iv), (v) and (vi). The inference to (vii) is unavoidable. It is worth noting that the argument so far cleverly exploits an assumption essential to Thrasymachus' position. The latter holds that the injustice of the powerful and successful person is responsible for that person's excellence. In calling the unjust 'wise' and 'sagacious' Thrasymachus builds into injustice the *skilfulness* Greeks standardly associated with wisdom (*sophia*). The unjust is *sophos* because he succeeds in bringing off something skilfully. His success, therefore, is evidence of excellence. But is the unjust person's 'success' in life evidence of genuine excellence, of the sort of excellence proper to human beings and their lives?

The notion of an *ergon* of the soul enables Socrates to press that question on Thrasymachus because that notion is none other than the idea of an excellence proper to a kind of thing. Socrates is facing Thrasymachus with an implicit dilemma: either the unjust man is 'doing well' in a sense which implies his excellence as a human being—that is, excellence in performing the specifically human activities—or he is 'doing well' in a sense divorced from such human excellence. But the first alternative entails the idea of an *ergon* of the soul: that there is a 'field' of activities (superintending, ruling, deliberating, controlling, and so on) which are achievements of the soul. The excellence of a soul, therefore, is determined by reference to that feature of it which enables human beings to perform these activities best. Previous arguments (with Polemarchus and, later, with Thrasymachus himself) have shown this to be justice or, at least, more like justice than injustice (this is the force of proposition (viii)). Therefore, either the unjust person's 'doing well' is different from this sense of 'living well' which connects it with justice, and Thrasymachus loses the connection between the unjust man's success and wisdom, or he has to deny that the excellence of the unjust is tied to the characteristic activities that constitute the *ergon* of the soul. But if he opts for this latter alternative Thrasymachus loses the link he wishes to stress between injustice and living excellently as a human being. It could be granted to him that there may be a sense of 'excellence' in which one can say that the unjust person showed excellence at 'living'. But the crucial question would be whether *that* sort of 'excellence' characterised a sort of life in which activities regarded as characteristic human achievements were given little or no value. If the activities with respect to which we judge the excellence of human beings as human do not figure in our estimation of what makes a human life excellent, then it is difficult to see the relevance of this notion of excellence to assessing the worth of the life of a human being.

This last point is of great moral significance; it connects the present argument with the considerations Socrates was urging on Thrasymachus in the previous two. The link is captured by the question, 'does the excellent performance of all the activities proper to human beings require justice?' Socrates clearly believes that it does, but it is worth seeing how the various things he has been saying in response to Thrasymachus lead to this belief. Having determined the grounds of this belief we can then say with precision what issues Socrates leaves undiscussed, and what, according to Plato, is the central task of an adequate theory of justice.

Thrasymachus, we saw earlier, bases his praise of injustice on the ground that a life which intelligently seeks to satisfy the desire to have more and to achieve more than anyone else is, by its nature, a superior and excellent life. Those who lead it are considered blessed and happy. By contrast, those who accept the limitations on action imposed by justice do not do so well. The sort of challenge Thrasymachus issues to conventional morality implies that in order to assess the excellence or otherwise of a way of living one has to fall back on what characterises human life as such. For, if the life of injustice is the best for human beings this must be because it enables them to perform the 'mind-full' operations recognised as distinctive of human nature in ways which promote to the full the human potentialities for happiness and well-being. Socrates' reference to the soul's 'work' in this context is perfectly in order: living, the life-activity of any organism, comes under the control of the functions 'natural' to the kind of organism it is. The good performance of the life-activities of a living thing, then, will depend on the factors which enable the instrumental functions that control life-activity to be performed well.[15] In the case of human beings these 'instrumental' functions include such 'mind-full' operations as overseeing, ruling, deliberating, and so on ; that is, rational and intelligent operations. But, as we have seen in this and the previous chapter, the exercise of rationally controlled intelligence—paradigmatically exemplified in a craft—involves the recognition of the limits that operate within some region of the world of nature. It is only by grasping such limits that the craftsmen can knowledgeably bring about a good (or bad) *proper* to the thing which is the 'object' of the craft.

Now, if by 'an excellent life' we mean the good performance of the life-activity of human beings, then we are logically compelled to accept that the soul's work of the person who leads an excellent life is performed well. But such work involves the 'mind-full' and rational control of life-activities. And, as we saw in the first of the last three arguments against Thrasymachus, it is of the nature of rational control in general to recognise limits. Given, therefore, that human life-activity is part of nature, its rational control will involve a knowledgeable grasp of the limits operative within it. Only so can we knowledgeably obtain the good proper to the human life form. That first argument also suggested that the just are motivated by considerations which are analogous to those which govern the exercise of rational control in general: to do better and to achieve more than what a non-rational ('fantasy-ridden' we called it) approach to control aspires to, and not to 'outdo' what can be realistically had in a given area. In this respect the unlimited *pleonexia* of the unjust resembles the non-rational approach to control that the ignorant have in comparison with the knowledgeable. It is more likely, then, that it is living in a just rather than an unjust way which more truly satisfies the 'mind-full' and rational control of life activities. This is because it is justice, not injustice, which seeks to discover and observe the objective limits operative in human living.

The second of the three arguments brought out is that it is justice and not injustice which enables groups and individuals to achieve unity, strength and internal harmony—benefits whose absence makes social and individual life frustrating. The life of the unjust is self-conflicted, the life of those who are enemies to themselves. Nevertheless, these effects of injustice are its 'symptoms' in the *human* life-form. It could be that in a different life-form what counts as injustice among humans (*pleonexia*) was not really injustice, and, so, did not produce these 'symptoms'. It follows that as far as human beings are concerned the 'symptoms' of injustice in them indicate that its 'power' is to interfere with, to disrupt, the good performance of the instrumental functions which control human life-activity—it prevents the soul from performing its work well. Therefore, injustice is the vice which makes the soul work badly by depriving it of its proper virtue. And since justice is a humanly beneficial 'power' (its 'symptoms' benefit people *as* human beings) it is the virtue which makes the soul do its 'work' well. It is thus responsible for the good performance of human life-activity. But this is precisely what was agreed to be the meaning of 'excellent life', of 'living well'.

The last argument in Book I collects together the various threads whose main aim was to link justice with the rational and intelligent capacities of human beings, those which can secure the good of what they control. If what permits these capacities to achieve this result in the various crafts is a 'just-like' approach to the 'objects' of the crafts, then is it not likely that the goodness of human living is ensured by the fact that it is justice itself which enables the soul to do its work well? Is it not also likely that the badness specific to the human life-form comes about because of injustice? Having the 'power' *opposite* to justice, will it not of its 'nature' thwart the proper functioning of intelligence and rationality?

These questions are not rhetorical. To answer them in the affirmative we need to be confident that the person who lives well, that is, the person whose soul, being just, performs its work well, is also the just *person*. But in spite of Socrates' slide in proposition (ix) ('the just soul and the just man will live well') we have not been given any conclusive reasons for accepting that the just person is identical with the person whose soul is just. Pending such a demonstration, our agreement with propositions (ix)–(xiii) in Socrates' argument must be provisional. To be really convinced—Plato makes it obvious that Thrasymachus, at any rate, is not—that justice is more profitable to human beings than injustice we need to be shown that the person with the just soul who lives well is the person who lives justly in the *ordinary* sense of that expression.[16] Socrates may have succeeded in throwing doubt on whether Thrasymachus' unjust person is likely to be a well-functioning human being. None the less, Thrasymachus could retort that it is the benefits of the unjust life which make human life worth living as a human life, not the fact that a person's specifically human faculties are functioning effectively. He need not deny that the latter factor yields benefits of a kind; all he needs to assert is that these benefits are not all that a human requires to be happy. So, even if it is true that justice of a kind is related to the 'species-benefit' of well-functioning rational capacities, this does not show that the sort of benefits ordinarily regarded as constitutive of human happiness are more linked to justice than to injustice.

Socrates' argumentation in Book I leads to, but does not accomplish, a basic task: to redefine justice, to show that the nature of justice is to be a 'power' in the soul which is good for humans to have because they are the type of being they are, *and* that it is good for them because of what it enables them to do and become in the world as it is. It should be obvious that no such account is possible unless it can be shown that in spite of the great variety of ways human beings have of achieving fulfilment, enjoyment and satisfaction, they all involve an intelligent grasp of limits proper to human life. For, it is only by showing this that Socrates can demonstrate persuasively the advantage to anyone of bringing under the control of reason the great variety of human desire and motivation. Socrates must show that justice is the sort of 'power' which enables human beings to meet *all* the requirements of living happily. He can only show this by proving that controlling human action in accordance with justice is the same as having basic human capacities ordered in a certain way, and that the benefits of the former are none other than the benefits of the latter.[17]

Plato indicates clearly that Socrates' arguments so far have not begun this central task of defining justice. As the latter points out ironically (354b,c), he has behaved like a greedy man who snatches at and tastes every dish that goes by without experiencing the measured or proper enjoyment (*metriōs apolausai*) of a meal. The task of defining justice was abandoned for the dialectical examination, first, of whether it is vice and ignorance or wisdom and virtue, and secondly, of the contention that injustice is more profitable than justice. Socrates is quite right in saying that without a definition of justice the question whether justice is a virtue, and whether he who possesses it is happy, cannot be conclusively (knowledgeably) settled. Socrates' questioning of Thrasymachus, though negatively successful in exposing the moral and political misrecognitions underlying Thrasymachus' evaluation of justice, has focused on the necessity to investigate whether and why justice contributes *uniquely* to the excellence of the lives of human beings. By juxtaposing Socrates and his interlocutors in the way he has in Book I, Plato has effectively invited his contemporaries to reflect on the suggestion that the need for justice is a human need, not merely a contingency of social existence. Socrates' dialectic exercise reveals in these contemporaries their systematic misunderstanding of the nature of that need and, consequently, of the very power inherent in living and acting justly.

10

Conclusion: the Socratic Vision

PREAMBLE

The analysis of Socrates' examination of his interlocutors about justice is now complete. It has not yielded a theory of justice, nor, as we saw in the last chapter, have all the issues been resolved. Nevertheless, Socrates' discussion prepares the way for such a theory. It does so by suggesting a new perspective on justice; a perspective which takes seriously the idea that justice is a human virtue, not merely an 'artificial' or a social one. Socrates clearly believes that justice is an essential component of what enables human beings, whether as individuals or as groups and communities, to lead a good and flourishing life. In this regard 'Socratic' justice departs from ordinary or conventional ideas about it. The aim of this, the concluding, chapter is twofold: to examine the merits and implications of the Socratic challenge to commonly accepted views; and to raise some questions about the relevance of that challenge to some pressing contemporary issues. There are many difficult and important philosophical questions about Socratic ethics which I do not attempt to deal with; in particular, I am not concerned to argue that the Socratic perspective on justice is morally superior to that which guides more conventional views of it. But I am interested in whether the Socratic inquiry into justice succeeds in raising worthwhile questions that the conventional perspective neglects or cannot perceive as questions of justice.

A preliminary observation seems in place before the discussion begins. It concerns the relation between Socrates and Plato. On the whole I agree with those who see important differences between them, in temperament, in orientation, and in particular doctrines. Though it is unlikely that the historical Socrates would have held all the views Plato represents him as articulating in the *Republic*, it seems to me evident that Plato shares the same perspective on justice as Socrates. It is important, therefore, to distinguish between this perspective and more determinate views or theories of justice such as the one Plato develops in the *Republic*. Undoubtedly Plato had his own reasons for presenting his theory; reasons which may not have prompted Socrates' thinking. And one may find fault (as many have) with Plato's views without thereby thinking that the perspective which inspired it was worthless. My concern is with the general perspective Socrates and Plato shared, not the particular theory Plato constructed within it—

a theory which some regard as containing politically unsavoury or morally unacceptable proposals.

SOCRATES' CHALLENGE TO 'CONVENTIONAL' JUSTICE

It was claimed in the Introduction (cf. above, Chapter 1, p. 18) that the Socratic insistence on an 'internal' view of justice was part of the intellectual movement which sought to gain for philosophy a socio-political role. Philosophy, representing the power of reason to apprehend intelligible order, must confront views of justice in the *polis* which hold it to be a matter of observance of cultural norms and rules whose function is to secure peaceful social co-existence. Or, views which regard it as an outcome of a political accommodation between conflicting demands and interests in the *polis*. Thus, though on the surface Socrates' arguments appear mainly directed at moral issues, the political implications of an 'internal' conception of justice are certainly there. Morals and politics are difficult to disentangle in the Athenian democratic context, and the jurors in Socrates' trial were quite aware of the political implications of Socrates' preoccupation with the moral welfare of his fellow Athenians. It is worth considering what it was about this preoccupation that Socrates' contemporaries may have found objectionable. Such an investigation may reveal what are the sources of resistance to an 'internal' conception of justice—then as well as now.

Our discussion in the early chapters of this book revealed three main ideas about justice, each of which, Socrates believed, led to 'looking for justice in the wrong place'. All three are expressions of Greek conventional wisdom at the time. First, the idea that justice consists in fulfilling obligations to gods and people, obligations contracted in the course of living with others, and obligations imposed on one by virtue of living in a *polis* with a distinct culture, with its own customs and norms. Secondly, the idea that justice consists in doing what is appropriate or fitting to others, the criteria of appropriateness being laid down by the type of social relation in which the agent stands to the receiver of the just act. Thirdly, the idea that justice consists in submerging one's self-interest out of consideration for the good or benefit of another, whether that 'other' is an individual or a plurality of individuals in a group, ultimately the body of citizens in the *polis*. I suggested that Plato builds into his characterisation of the upholders of these three ideas a diagnosis of the factors which in his view made his contemporaries incapable of appreciating the true 'power' of justice.

A crucial element in this diagnosis is the judgment that all three of the ideas assess justice and its benefits from an 'external' perspective. I mean by this that the upholders of the three ideas do not see justice as transmitting or communicating, to both agent and recipient, a specific benefit inherent in justice itself. They recognise that justice is 'a good thing', and that peace and harmony between people make it reasonable to expect them to act justly. But what they value primarily are actions which are in conformity with the demands of what is socially deemed as just, not the capacity to recognise what is just. Justice, thus, becomes primarily a social value rather than a mark of excellence in individuals and communities. So long as the observance of certain maxims of conduct, suitably translated into moral and legal norms, is secured, the members of a *polis* can be satisfied that justice 'is done'. What matters is that the way they 'give' to, or 'receive' from, others in the *polis*, and especially the way this 'transaction' is supervised and regulated by those in positions of power, does not result in anyone feeling 'done down', or 'done out' of the things they regard as 'due' to them. The general perspective governing this conception of justice is that of fairness, though what is thought of as 'fair' at any given time or place may vary considerably. The benefit of fairness is that it increases the degree of social peace. The presence of social harmony will, of course, contribute to the general well-being, but this is not to say that being just is a *constituent* of anyone's *eudaimonia* or, if this makes sense, of the flourishing of the *polis* itself. Under some circumstances being just may involve choices and decisions which cannot please everyone. But justice is not meant to ensure the absence of disappointment or frustration, only the removal of reasons for feeling angry and indignant at the decisions which cause the disappointments. As a recent writer has put it, justice tries to make clear that people *ought* not to be angry at certain decisions or outcomes, since they *should* recognise the cogency of the reasons behind the decisions or outcomes.[1] But, as the same author recognises, this view of justice does not reveal it as constitutive of human excellence but only as a precondition of a sort of 'peace which enables the individual to identify with society, and brethren to dwell together in unity'.[2] This means that,

> I can be just and lack many moral virtues. I may be fair-minded and yet lack love. Justic by itself is not enough. It does not make a man happy or fulfilled, and is no guarantee of salvation in this world or the next.[3]

Socrates, as we saw, is opposed to this view of justice, though he does accept that justice has the 'power' to effect social cohesion. But he derives the reasons for thinking so from adopting an 'internal' perspective on justice; that is, from the thought that the features which constitute the capacity to be just are identical with, or are generative of, *the power to render people good*.[4] It becomes evident from Socrates' cross-examination of his interlocutors that he believes this 'power' to reside in reason, in an exercise of intellect and intelligence which aims at the realisation of, and 'care' for, the capacities which define the human 'soul'. As I shall argue below, Socrates' proposal was meant to counter what he (and Plato) saw as the dangers of a nascent individualism fostered by the democratic ethos. The existing political arrangements in Greek city-states and especially democracy, they thought, were undermining the power to render people good. If justice is identical with, or a component of, this power, the political arrangements of the Greeks were making them powerless to 'care for the soul'.[5] As we shall see, this notion becomes in Socrates' and Plato's hands interestingly anti-individualistic. It introduces the impersonal perspective, as distinct from the idea of impartiality, into the moral and political field. It is this adherence to the project of achieving an impersonal 'view of things' which both fascinates and exasperates Plato's readers. Nevertheless, there are issues of deep moral and political significance involved in the choice of whether to adopt an impartial or an impersonal perspective on human affairs. Let us consider briefly what is involved in this choice.

To seek to adopt the standpoint of impartiality is to be concerned with fairness; with resolving conflicts and disputes among people that arise from different claims people feel entitled to make. The making of these claims depends, of course, on what interests or demands are, at any given time, thought worthy of pursuit. But the *having* of these interests or demands depends on the socio-cultural and psychological factors which, at that time, shape people's beliefs, perceptions, aspirations, feelings and desires. The impartial 'adjudicator' is primarily concerned to find an accommodation between the conflicting interests of individuals and groups by considering whether the situation and circumstances of those involved provide good reasons for acceding to their claim. The fair-minded can be aware, of course, of what shapes the beliefs and desires of those making the claims, and they can be sympathetic or antipathetic to some of these beliefs or desires. But to be impartial requires that one attends to what in a situation creates *relevant* differences between the contending parties. How people perceive, or feel about, things may be similar or widely different. But differences of this kind may not generate differences relevant to an impartial judgment; just as similarities in outlook do not prevent people from finding themselves in situations of conflict. The impartial judge must attend to differences in how individuals or groups are placed, rather than to their views and attitudes, except, of course, where the latter themselves become the object of contention. There could, for example, be disagreement between rival parties as to the type of beliefs and attitudes that ought to be fostered in a certain institution. Even in this case, however, impartial judgement requires investigation not so much of the beliefs or attitudes themselves but of whether there are important and relevant differences between the contending parties as *parties*. It is not to beliefs, desires, and aspirations that one renders justice but to those (individuals or groups) who, because of their situation, regard themselves as entitled to make claims on their basis.

There are two interconnected respects in which adopting the standpoint of impartiality differs from opting for the impersonal perspective. I am assuming that we incline to the latter when what is at stake is that we need to understand what makes a situation a good or a bad one. We do this irrespective of whether we think the situation itself is bad, or whether we think it is bad for those who find themselves in it. The two differences (there are more) between the perspectives I wish to highlight are these: they conceive differently what is important about individuals; and, as models for dealing with human situations, they exemplify contrasting structures. With regard to the first difference, we have already noted that the impartial person must attend to how an individual is placed, rather than what kind of individual he or she is. This is because impartiality has to deal with claims individuals may make (or have made on their behalf), not with whether such individuals are happy, fulfilled, or frustrated. From the impersonal perspective, however, what matters in a situation of conflict or competing demands is why individuals feel the need to make certain claims, rather than the mere fact that they make them. The impersonal perspective, thus, *reverses* the priorities implicit in the impartial standpoint; it is individuals as possessors of needs and the forces which generate them, rather than as initiators of claims and possessors of entitlements, which is of fundamental importance. It is not, of course, the case that being impartial prevents one from being sensitive to people's needs and what generates them, any more than adopting an impersonal standpoint prevents one from taking into account the fact that people feel passionately about the claims their situation entitles them to make. Nevertheless, what each perspective considers a priority is structurally determined by the kind of perspective it is.

This introduces the second point of difference between them. Impartiality and fair-mindedness is structurally individualist even where the situation involves groups or nations rather than individuals. This is because it is committed to attending to what in a situation of competing claims constitutes a relevant difference between the parties. The primary value of the fair-minded is not to treat similar cases differently, or different cases similarly, unless there are good reasons for doing so; unless, in other words, there are reasons that make a difference. By contrast, the impersonal perspective is structurally holistic. What one looks for, whether in individuals, groups, communities, or social movements, are *similar* forces and impulses. This is because one hopes to detect the patterns in human living, wherever they are found, that are responsible for enhancing or diminishing the powers of such living, and thus, makes it good or bad living.

It is as part of a strategy to make room for a conception of justice from the impersonal standpoint that Socrates employs the analogy between justice and craft. In the process of deploying this strategy Socrates provides himself with a sustained critique of the conventional view of justice on the grounds that it allows only an 'external' value to it. Before assessing Socrates' contribution let us review some key features of his attempt.

DIKAIOSYNĒ AND TECHNĒ

The analogy between virtue and craft-knowledge is a key feature of Plato's 'early' dialogues. As Alcibiades says in the *Symposium* (221e), the matters concerning crafts and craftsmen were forever in Socrates' mouth. The employment of this analogy by Socrates has been much commented upon. It is, at once, the object of much of the criticism directed at Socratic ethics and of lively debate about its interpretation. Though the scholarly consensus is that Socrates meant to capture through the parallel an important feature of the exercise of intelligence in moral conduct, there is much less agreement about how successful Socrates was in his effort.[6] There is also difference of opinion as to whether Plato came to abandon the analogy because of the difficulties he saw in the idea that virtue is a skill or like a skill.[7] It is indeed true that Socrates was extremely impressed by crafts and craftsmen. In the *Apology* he says that craftsmen know what they are doing, and can give an account of what is good or bad about the 'product' or 'outcome' of their skill.[8] He constrasts this ability with the shakiness of the claims others, such as poets, sophists, politicians, and so on, make to moral knowledge. In other dialogues, he explores the idea that virtue, or a particular virtue, is or resembles a skill. But though he clearly means to suggest that virtue is a kind of knowledge (*epistēmē*), his confidence in the analogy, and in what is the *object* of the skill of virtue, varies considerably from dialogue to dialogue.[9]

It would take us too far afield to discuss all the logical ramifications of Socrates' and Plato's employment of this analogy.[10] Our analysis of how Socrates uses it with Polemarchus and Thrasymachus (cf. above, Chapters 5 – 8) suggested that the way Socrates regarded *technai* was not the same as the ordinary or standard view. For, while the standard view sees in skills an organised body of knowledge of means to achieve a certain end, it is not so much their instrumental character that Socrates emphasises, but the fact that they exemplify the power to render the relevant or appropriate good to whatever is their specific 'object'. It is, of course, true that the doctor delivers health to the body, the shoemaker usable shoes to people, and the navigator safe passage to travellers. And it is also true that they do so knowledgeably, through mastery of certain techniques and an understanding of the principles governing their craft. But while what makes the craftsman useful, from the point of view of a user of a craftsman's products, is the fact that the 'products' enable the user to achieve certain ends, this is not what makes a craft, and the activities of its practitioners *qua* such practitioners, an exemplification of excellence. Passengers want to reach their destination and they dictate that destination to the navigator. The nature of the destination, thus, seems 'external' to the navigator's skills, as something that does not necessarily fall within the scope of his judgement. A particular navigator may be good *for* getting people from A to B, but what he is good *at* is getting a boat from A to B safely. Therefore, the 'strict' or primary object of the navigator's skill, the item to which the navigator renders the benefits specific to his craft, is not the satisfaction of the various individual interests, desires and aims of his passengers (perhaps a task impossible to accomplish). Rather, the object of his concern is safe passage for the particular boat under his command, to which the subordinate functions of various crew-members contribute and, must, therefore, come under the craft's control.

We could put this point by saying either that the navigator renders a good (safety) to the activity of sea-passage, or that the navigator renders sea-passage good (safe). This good is quite distinct from the benefit, the *advantage*, that the passenger gains from the navigator. The navigator exercises his skill for the sake of a safe passage, even though, to the passenger, the skill is an instrumental means to reaching his destination. This distinction between 'goods' generates the possibility that they can come into conflict. Certain destinations are incompatible with safe passage. Therefore, from the fact that the choice of destination is not initially the navigator's it does not follow that *ultimately* he cannot authoritatively determine it with a view to what is or is not antithetical to the good 'internal' to his craft.[11] It is also worth noting that where a more specific craft (plough-making or armour-making) is, or is made, subordinate to another craft (farming or the craft of the *hoplite*, the foot-soldier), it is the *for the sake of* relation, not that of instrumental-means-to-an-end, which comes into play.[12] It is not *any* want that some farmer or hoplite has in mind which dictates what the plough-maker or armour-maker is to produce. It is the good 'internal' to farming or fighting on foot which subsumes the good 'internal' to making ploughs or armour. The hierarchy of goods thus generated forms a series of 'nested' goods, linked by the relation of *for the sake of*. At any level of the hierarchy the good 'internal' to a craft indicates what is rational to aim for in that sphere. But in the case where such goods form a nested series, the rationality of the aim at any given level is relative to that of the level above it. Thus, ultimately, it is the rationality of the aim of the 'top' craft which 'transmits' itself down the chain; the good 'internal' to the 'ruling' craft in the hierarchy becomes the standard in relation to which the more specific goods down the hierarchy are determined. It is an understanding of the features which make fighting on foot good or bad that rationally determines why a good armour for a hoplite should be such and such.

It is this model of craft-knowledge which Socrates proposes we should apply to virtue and justice. It repays to observe how the analogy simultaneously performs a critical and a positive function. From the discussion of Socrates' arguments we can extract a number of general propositions which constitute the negative force of the analogy; but we can also derive from them its positive force. Using 'N' and 'P' to stand, respectively, for 'negative' and 'positive', we can sum up Socrates' use of the analogy in the following theses:

(1N) On the conventional view of justice what makes actions just is the fact that they conform to certain rules or maxims of conduct. But this cannot be correct since, in some cases, the person who acts contrary to such a rule or maxim is considered just. On the assumption that a person so acting acts for the sake of justice, and does the just thing, we have to infer that he knows the kind of good to be achieved by the action. But if this is so, the knowledge in question cannot be identified with knowing the content of the rule or maxim (compare Chapters 2 and 5, above).

(1P) So, though, contrary to the conventional view, we may not know in advance what in some particular situation is the just thing to do, there is, in our recognition that an action is just, a built-in *presumption* that there exists a knowable good for the sake of which the action is undertaken. It is not the case that an action is just because recipients of it find it good or advantageous to themselves; rather, the just agent regards an action as good or advantageous in itself because he knows it is just.[13] Thus, what makes a just action useful or beneficial *to* its recipients is not the same as the good which acting justly renders to them. There is a good inherent in justice, 'internal' to acting justly, in a way analogous to that in which the good inherent in a craft is 'internal' to its exercise. Analogously, any other advantage which may accrue to the recipient of a just act is 'external' to the good inherent in acting justly, the way in which the benefit obtained from the *use* of the 'works' of a craft is 'external' to the good for the sake of which the craft exists. There is, thus, a good specific to acting justly. But what is it, and how is it related to the benefits people expect to obtain from acting or being treated justly?

(2N) On the conventional view, to do the just thing is to render to each person his or her 'due'. The idea is that the performer of just actions dispenses goods ('rewards') or evils ('punishments') to people on the basis of how such 'dispensers' perceive their relation to the 'receivers'. Dispensing a good or an evil becomes 'fitting' or 'appropriate' depending on whether the receiver is a friend or an enemy. But this cannot be a general principle of justice if the just person acts for the sake of justice. Such a person must ensure that in distributing rewards or punishments the 'good of justice' is *thereby* transmitted. Existing social relations may dictate certain things as 'due', but it will not be just to deliver them if in so doing the 'good of justice' is undermined or destroyed. On the assumption that just persons want to see justice realised in their relations to others, we have to infer that they know what it is in the recipients of their act which renders their act an appropriate response. However, such knowledge cannot be identical with the knowledge that the recipients are, for example, friends or enemies; rather, it is knowledge of why justice demands that people should be treated in certain ways and not in others which dictates who is a genuine friend or enemy (compare Chapters 2 and 6 above).

(2P)   So, though contrary to the conventional view, there can be no general social criterion of what makes a person deserving of justice, there is in our recognition of just 'deserts' a built-in *presumption* that acting justly is a response to something in the recipient which is such as to make the response fitting or appropriate. But, now, the 'something' in the recipient to which the just person responds cannot be 'external' to the good of justice which the just person perceives, and for the sake of which he or she acts. Advantaging a friend or disadvantaging an enemy will be 'external' to justice if in the process the justice 'in' the friend *or* the enemy is sacrificed for the sake of some other benefit or advantage. With respect to recipients, the 'power' of justice must be to render them just; for this is what, from the point of view of the just agent, is 'due' to the recipients. To think otherwise is to fail to distinguish between the way the actions of a just person benefit and the ways other actions do so. The latter may do so non-justly (that is, in a way 'external' to justice), and they may do so unjustly (that is, in a way contrary to justice). But just actions which only benefit in these latter ways cannot be just. As we saw in Chapter 7, there is an important link, in Plato's view, between what makes one a 'fit' recipient of justice in this sense and the craft of statesmanship. The just rulers respond appropriately to what in their subjects calls for justice, and in doing so they 'communicate' the character of justice to them. But what precisely is it 'in' subjects which makes them 'fit' recipients of justice? And how does this 'communication' of justice between ruler and subject take place?

(3N)   On the conventional view of justice, to be just is to be disposed to do 'another's good'. The idea is that justice often requires us to submerge our strong individual wishes and desires for the sake of a 'common' good. To be just is to be motivated to act unselfishly by having due regard for other people's reasonable claims. As we saw in Chapters 3 and 4, it is this view of justice and of the motivation to be just which leads Thrasymachus to criticise the just as 'simpletons', as necessarily advancing the interests of the 'stronger' who do not want to miss out on the greatest amount of benefit they can secure for themselves. The conventional view implies that the just (in contrast to the unjust) will always get less in a given situation where both operate, even though it is thought that the overall and long-term benefits of justice make such sacrifice worthwhile. Thrasymachus' objection is that because of their orientation towards the good of another the just act irrationally: to want to achieve for oneself less than it is possible to achieve in the circumstances is not reasonable or intelligent. To the extent that those (say, leaders) who declare what is just are disposed to generate such motivation in others, they are, in fact, asking that people be disposed to act unintelligently. The demand to do 'another's good', implicit in the conventional view of justice, makes it susceptible to Thrasymachus' complaint. This susceptibility cannot be allowed in a true view of justice. The just person is motivated to achieve the best outcome possible compatible with the good of justice. But this is not the same as the outcome which least offends the principle of 'fair shares', or one which exemplifies the principle of maximum satisfaction for everyone concerned, or one which preserves as far as possible the freedom of choice of those concerned, or one which equalises the opportunity for everyone concerned to obtain some 'goods', and so on.[14] All these principles may, in various contexts, represent worthwhile objectives, and the motives to pursue them can differ widely from individual to individual (sympathy, calculated self-interest, altruism, benevolence, 'social conscience', and so on). However, neither these objectives, nor the various motivations for pursuing them, are those *of* justice unless the objectives are pursued for the sake of realising 'the good of justice'. The desire 'to do another's good' cannot be the motive to be just unless it has the structure which characterises *desiring justly* (compare Chapters 3 and 4 with 8).

(3P) So, contrary to the conventional view, we cannot identify 'wanting to do the just thing' with 'wanting to do the good of another'. Nevertheless, in our recognition of the 'other-directedness' of justice, there is a built-in *presumption* that wanting to be just involves a distancing from, or a rising above, the motives with which people ordinarily pursue a variety of objectives. The idea is that we have to do this in order to assess how and whether such pursuits either promote or undermine the 'good of justice'. The desire to be just, therefore, must involve a characteristic way in which thought relates to desire. But what exactly is this way?

The suggestion that emerged in Chapter 8, was that the just person's desiring is *anti-pleonectic* in a way similar to that exhibited by the genuine craftsman. The practitioners of the various *technai* are not merely paradigms of acting knowledgeably. By virtue of the fact that they want to achieve the 'right' thing in the field of their activity, through discovering the correct limits of what can be had in that field, they are also paradigms of acting wisely and well. The craftsman's concern to combat 'excessive' or 'inadequate' action in his field, his desire to do 'the best by' the object of his craft, constitute what we may well call a sort of 'just desire'. The craftsman wants to 'do justice' to what his craft deals with, and he can only do so if he is capable of identifying and neutralising the factors which are likely to subvert his efforts. Not least among these factors, as we saw, are beliefs, perceptions, and desires concerning the 'product' or 'outcome' of the craft whose sources lie in interests and demands that are irrelevant to what the 'product' or 'outcome' is objectively. This irrelevance renders the possession of such beliefs, desires and perceptions detrimental to the excellence that the craft is capable of.

Restriciting the analogy between justice and craft to the aspect of acting justly which concerns how thought relates to desire, we have a constraint on how to interpret the conventional idea that to want to be just is to want 'to do the good of another'. Though the constraint relates primarily to the 'dispensers' of justice, its observance has consequences for the 'recipients' of justice. The constraint is that acting justly involves an objective assessment of how the satisfaction or non-satisfaction of potentially conflicting demands and interests will affect the distinctively human capacities of those who make the demands or have the interests. Thus, for the desire to do the good of another to be a just desire it has to be *at least* a desire to act intelligently *vis-à-vis* the interests and demands of others. Socrates hints that to act intelligently in this regard requires that we know not only that certain desires, perceptions and beliefs shape people's demands and interests; we must also discover what effects the satisfaction of certain demands and interests has on how people desire, perceive, and judge. In wanting to do the good of another, the just cannot merely give impartial and due attention to competing demands; they must also impersonally assess whether the *having* of these demands is, in the circumstances, a good thing, and whether their satisfaction would make people good or bad. The just renders good to another by making sure that the other is, by that action, made good as a human being, or, at least, is not diminished in this respect. But what is it to be good as a human being, and how must one think of justice to regard its exemplification in human affairs as a form of 'making things good'?

IMPLICATIONS OF 'SOCRATIC' JUSTICE

The Socratic perspective, then, leads to certain important questions. But is Socrates fair to the 'fairness' model of justice? Why must a concern for justice be a concern with what makes good human beings? Granted that the latter concern is of fundamental moral and politicial importance, is it not politically dangerous to extend the scope of justice to embrace that concern? 'Socratic' justice is unlikely to convince everyone. It has implications which will appear to many to go against the liberal temperament of the prevailing social and political thought in modern Western societies.[16] From the moral point of view also, Socrates' view will seem to transgress the primacy of individuals and their autonomy—the idea that respect for persons and their right to make moral choices (however wrong) is of fundamental importance. These criticisms are important, but do they meet the Socratic challenge? I shall conclude with some considerations which may incline us to reconsider the Socratic proposal. Certain moral dimensions of social issues which have increasingly come to occupy a central place in modern life seem, curiously enough, to make this ancient Socratic conception of justice a serious contender to the idea of it that has become dominant since the eighteenth century. The analysis of why this may be so, or of how it has come to be so, lies, of course, well beyond the scope of this study. Nevertheless, it is worth considering what makes the Socratic ideal a powerful one.

I shall discuss the questions which opened this section in the light of the remarks made earlier (in the section 'Socrates' challenge to "conventional" justice' above) on impartiality and on the impersonal perspective. We need to notice at the outset a fact that may have escaped notice. Though the Socratic perspective on justice is at some distance from how people conventionally regard justice, it is by no means the case that the 'fairness' model captures what underlies conventional ideas while the Socratic perspective does not. Certainly, people expect those who *dispense* justice to be fair-minded and impartial. But the conventional view is considerably vague as to whether what *makes* a situation, an arrangement, or a transaction, just is the fact that it establishes or restores a structure of fairness among those involved. The common intuition about justice may well be that there is more to justice than fairness, even though it is not clear what is this 'more'.

Be that as it may, the questions we extracted (in the previous section) from the positive force of Socrates' use of the craft-analogy compel our attention (if at all) precisely because they flow from Socrates' attempt to make explicit certain presumptions built-in to the *ordinary* notion of justice. However radical and surprising Socrates' conclusions, he evidently believed that he was refining and building upon a common notion of justice. The ideas introduced by the questions Socrates asks are: first, that there is a good specific to justice; secondly, that there are certain features of the interaction between people, or between people and their situation, which make them 'fit' recipients of justice, and that this fact must be 'communicated' by the just action; thirdly, that there are aspects of human living which are made excellent by justice and rendered inferior by injustice. Both the 'fairness' model and the Socratic perspective attempt to develop these ideas, but do so in very different ways. Those who consider justice to be fairness locate the good specific to justice in the fact that it preserves a fundamental human good—that every human being has, as a person, as much right to things considered good as any other. Differential treatment of individuals or groups *always* requires justification in terms of reasons which do not transgress respect of persons as persons, of human beings as possessors of a will which can be good or bad. Correspondingly, what, on this model, makes people 'fit recipients' of justice is primarily the fact that, for whatever reasons, there is conflict or competition between wills such that non-adjudication between them will result in some being treated unfairly. Finally, the idea that justice makes certain aspects of life better than injustice is interpreted by the 'fairness' model along the lines that it secures social harmony and integration to a degree compatible with the fundamental respect for persons; life in a society where fairness prevails is, on the whole, better and happier, even if people do not have all they desire, or do not have their desires satisfied to the fullest extent.

Fundamental to Socrates' alternative way of developing these ideas is a central intuition: that no act or arrangement is fully just which does not render its 'recipient' good in precisely those respects which made that recipient a 'fit' subject of such an act or arrangement. Without wishing to repeat points made earlier in this chapter (and in the book as a whole) I want to stress that it is this intuition which sustains Socrates' conviction that justice requires a special kind of knowledge. Perhaps the nearest that a common view of justice comes to this intuition is the sense that dealing with situations of injustice in the manner required by the 'fairness' model, though perhaps the best that can be achieved in societies as they have developed, is not 'fully' or 'ideally' what we can expect of justice. In particular, there is the uneasy feeling that acting fairly is compatible with leaving untouched the ultimate springs or causes of injustice. A fair decision may leave the conflicting parties, as well as observers of the situation, satisfied that there is no justifiable cause for complaint at the decision by anyone concerned. Yet, it may be the case that we are unsure whether it was the best way of dealing with the original situation. Symptoms of an illness can be so unbearable that their removal appears imperative. Yet, they are *symptoms*; and we may not know whether the way we attempt to remove them does not generate worse ills, or does not perpetuate the disease by forcing its 'displacement' to a different region of the organism. This is only an analogy, of course. But its point is that if acting justly is an exemplification of goodness, then its aim must be to discover and deal with the *causes* that generate and sustain injustice, not merely with the fact, and the manner, that injustice 'manifests' itself in the social conscience. 'Causes of injustice', in this sense, may be present even though people do not recognise them in the prevailing forms of social conduct; and, conversely, acts and decisions may be judged 'unjust' or 'unfair' when, in fact, they are dealing with factors which generate injustice.

Considerations of this kind incline towards adoption of the impersonal perspective on justice. If fairness in dealing with injustices is only a necessary but not a sufficient condition of a just act, then, perhaps, a further necessary condition is that the act issues from knowledge of the deeper springs of injustice in the human condition, and of how to neutralise their effects. At any rate, this is the direction of 'Socratic' justice. To desire the 'good of justice' is to want to deal knowledgeably with those features of being human which 'feed' and generate destructive patterns and injustice in people's thought, feeling and desire. And what makes anyone, or any situation, a 'fit' recipient of justice is the fact that these 'roots of injustice' within people and their arrangements have been allowed to grow and threaten to get out of control. The respect, therefore, in which justice makes human life better than injustice, whether for an individual or a group, is that it is inseparable from a way of living which is fully conscious and in control of the forces within it that enhance its flourishing and the factors that undermine it. Living well as a human being requires knowledge of what it is to be human; and being just is a crucial aspect of the desire to acquire such knowledge.

As we saw in Chapter 9, there is an important argument, or sketch of an argument, by which Socrates seeks to justify this last claim. It also brings out a respect in which the analogy of justice with craft-knowledge is only an analogy. The force of the analogy is that since the power to render good in any domain requires knowledge and understanding of that domain, then, if justice is the power to render good in the domain of human living, justice requires knowledge of that domain. Socrates designates this domain as that which is under the control of the 'soul' (*psychē*). Though he does not give us, in Book I, a full account of the human *psychē*, Socrates does indicate that he regards the capacity to deliberate, and to organise things rationally, as most distinctive of human living. This does not mean, of course, that there are not other aspects of the 'soul' which humans share with other living things. It does mean, however, that it is essential to human beings that these other aspects of living be brought under the control of the capacity to reason. It follows that the concern with justice is, for human beings, peculiarly self-referential. For, to know and understand the domain of the human 'soul', of what in that domain is responsible for goodness or badness, entails that one knows the factors in it which promote or frustrate the rule of reason over other aspects of human living. But the desire for knowledge and understanding is itself an aspect of the desire to ensure that reason is not swamped by other forces in the *psychē*. Therefore, to inquire whether in some area of human life reason maintains its rightful dominance over other aspects of living is itself an exemplification of the desire to make sure that what is most distinctive of human living, rationality, does not become eclipsed. In the case of beings endowed with reason and intelligence, the capacity to question whether they live in a way that best achieves the potential they have as the type of being they are itself partly defines the kind of being they are.[17] Consequently, if the concern with justice is to render human living good, then this concern ought, necessarily, to be part of the process whereby humans can hope to gain knowledge of what makes their life good.

This is why the analogy of justice with *technē* is only an *analogy*. In the case of ordinary crafts the processes which constitute the exercise of the craft are not part of the 'object' of the craft. For though as we saw, the excellence of the 'object' of a craft is subject to some constraints the craft itself imposes, what makes that 'object' good is not determined by reference to excellences in the exercise of the craft. That the body whose health is secured is the doctor's, or that the person whose safety is secured is the captain's, is only incidentally related to the proper exercise of the skill of healing or navigation. But the fact that it is the 'soul' that is to be made just means that there cannot be a similar distinction between 'practitioner' and 'recipient' of justice. No one *can* be incidentally related to the exercise of justice. To be just may involve dealing in certain ways with other people, or with the relations they have to each other, but these ways are essentially self-applicable. Justice cannot be achieved without the actions through which it is achieved rendering just both those who perform them and those who 'receive' them. The just not only *do* just things, they make themselves and others just *by* doing things which are just. It is as if in the case of justice the popular injunction 'physician heal thyself' has not only a moral but a conceptual force.

There remain, of course, the misgivings about the political implications of the Socratic proposal. We saw earlier (in Chapter 4) that Socrates and Plato were perturbed by the fact that democracy had created a growing gap between the political process on the one hand and, on the other, the desire and the capacity of Athenian citizens to concern themselves with questions of moral excellence. In a climate where the primary consideration was that every citizen was given the opportunity to express his opinion of how the affairs of the *polis* were to be run, the competition to achieve political power led to moral corruption. Aspiring leaders could secure political support by proposing policies which promised to increase the material prosperity of the majority, or that appealed to national pride and filled the hearts of citizens with self-aggrandising desires and thoughts. This climate left little room for cool reflection on how the adoption of a policy, ostensibly aimed to secure advantages for everyone, was going to affect the capacity in citizens rationally to control other aspects of their 'soul'. The democracy was replacing conceptions of human *aretē* with ideas of 'doing well' which were dictated by political expediency. The emphasis on succeeding as an individual, with its natural extension to an individualistic conception of the success of a *polis* over rivals, was undermining the 'power in the soul' of both leaders and citizens to look for what made their living good as an instance of human living.

Even so, it cannot be denied that acting justly in the way the Socratic perspective demands is bound to come into conflict not only with the right of people to be heard, but also with their right to assert their will so long as they do not interfere unfairly with the opportunity for others to do likewise. 'Socratic' justice requires that not only beliefs but also practices, aspirations, and desires, be vetted to ensure that they do not set up patterns generative of injustice. This requirement is not compatible with according primary importance to being an individual, to being a self-contained and distinct source of will set against other such sources of will. It is not difficult to see how this latter kind of thinking about persons can be extended to groups, to institutions, and to collective entities such as nation-states. It forms an essential part of the ideas of a 'group-identity', of a 'corporate identity', of an 'institutional identity', of a 'national identity', and so on. These ideas have an enormously powerful hold on people's imagination, even though there are forces that go against them and, in more recent times, signs that they may be becoming disfunctional.

The modern emphasis on the autonomy of the individual is not, of course, the kind of individualism Socrates was criticising. The former depends on a conception of fundamental rights human beings have *qua* persons, while the latter did not. Nevertheless, the question whether considerations of justice should remain 'external' to what makes for goodness in individuals can be raised once more. Modern individualism, as much as its ancient prototype, carries an 'individualised' conception of doing well; what matters is to succeed as an individual, not whether a person, perhaps in concert with others, succeeds in mastering the conditions which make for goodness in human living. The contrast is crucial to how we think about justice. Valuing success as an individual demands that the chances of everyone to such success are not impaired or unfairly interfered with. It is left to each individual to determine what will count as success for them, and to compete with others in securing it. Thus, justice is seen as a limit externally imposed on what individuals may do in pursuit of such success, as fashioning a stucture aimed at securing the highest possible degree of 'free play' between individual interests. Valuing success in human living, by contrast, requires discovering which areas of life are essential to living *qua* a human being, and what is the best form of interaction between the human life-form and its environment which includes other life forms. Justice from the latter perspective, thus, involves an indefinite process of adjustment of how people live in relation to a set ideal or standard. It also involves a constant critical *revision* of how one thinks of the ideal or the standard itself in the light of new aspects of human living that may emerge.

This is a key difference in the two models of justice. The individualistic model sees justice as involving the task of solving the problem of co-ordinating conflicting interests of individuals in a manner that the individuals concerned will accept as fair and reasonable. Justice does, therefore, require continuous adjustment in the light of what people will accept as reasonable. Nevertheless, the goal of justice remains static: to co-ordinate interest for the sake of social cohesion and peace. The Socratic model, by contrast, while accepting that social cohesion and peace are effects of justice, does not recognise them as its essential goal. It is *how* social peace and cohesion are achieved which matters, not merely the fact that they are achieved. The all-important question is whether the manner of achieving peace and cohesion preserves *the human power to discover and implement what makes human living good.* The guiding thought is that if it is true that human beings have to find out through the exercise of intelligence what it is about themselves which makes them good it will be to commit an injustice against human nature itself to allow that activities are pursued in a manner which undermines this capacity of reason. The danger with emphasis on individual will, and the accompanying notion of justice as a co-ordinator of the interests of such wills, is that it cannot comprehend how there can be 'injustices against humanity' which may not necessarily be offences against individuals and their rights. Here are some examples:

(1) Safeguarding the right of people to social 'goods' such as health, education, leisure, a comfortable standard of living, and so on, does not by itself determine how a 'fair' distribution of these goods in a community affects the power in people to discover what makes them good. That it may do so adversely is not thought to be a matter of justice. To be the cause of *alienation* in individuals is not to do an injustice to any particular individual. Yet, does not the production of such alienation commit an injustice against that *in* individuals which makes them capable of not being alienated?

(2) Safeguarding people against their unequal treatment by others, or by the state, is considered a primary function of justice. Applying the due process of law equally to all individuals, irrespective of their cultural, social, educational and racial background, is the pride of the liberal conception of justice. Yet, how the application of a system of justice affects the capacity of those who receive it to assess its benefit is not thought to fall within the province of justice. What matters is that people receive justice, not whether the administration of justice is *educative*. To be the cause of confusion or obfuscation in people is not to commit an injustice against any particular individual. But is it not unjust to diminish the power in individuals to understand the point of how they are dealt with? Yet, this is precisely what may happen when those who are dealt with 'equally' by the law differ markedly from each other in the respects mentioned above.

(3) Every one has a right to a fair return on the contribution they make to the production of material wealth, be they workers, managers or investors of capital. It is a matter of justice how such 'fair return' is determined and implemented. But how a system or 'mode' of production affects the power of those within it to judge its suitability or functional appropriateness to human well-being is not considered to be a matter of justice or injustice. If the processes of capitalist production *mystify* those who take part in it, no individual can complain on the grounds of justice that things are not as they are represented to be. If the workers receive a 'fair wage', their cry of 'exploitation' does not entail that they are being done an injustice; only that they were under the illusion that they were independent partners to a contract when, in fact, they had very little choice whether to enter it or not.[18] But while social mystification is not an injustice against any particular individual, is it not an injustice against the capacity of producers to judge the suitability to human well-being of their mode of production, to mystify them about is nature?

(4) Every one has the right not to be discriminated against on irrelevant grounds. Performing the same task and possessing the same relevant qualifications entitles you to the same rewards, whether you are a woman, a foreigner, a person with a different colour skin, and so on. It is a matter of justice to combat discrimination of this sort. But the measures taken to ensure the absence of such discrimination against individuals do not ensure that the *oppression* of sexism, racism, class-snobbery, elitism, and so on, are removed. To perpetrate these forms of oppression is not considered as committing an injustice against the individual, so long as their rights have not been denied in the process. But is not the systematic down-grading of the power people have to make special contributions by virtue of being women, blacks, 'working-class', 'ordinary folk', and so on, an injustice against the *range* of human resources?

One could lengthen this list indefinitely.[19] The point is that if we view justice as having the aim of guarding those features of human life which contribute to its goodness, then it also becomes a matter of justice whether the proceess of discovering new ways in which life can be made excellent, or of finding fresh aspects of old ways of doing so, is encouraged or discouraged by our practices and arrangements. It does, of course, seem odd to talk of injustices against capacities or powers. But is is only odd within the framework of individualistical-ly conceived justice. If the logically primary subject of injustice is thought to be the individual because injustice is an offence against the *will* of such an entity, then, naturally, the perpetrator of injustice must be shown to have deliberately or irresponsibly acted against that will. But from the fact that the will of a person has been transgressed it does not follow (though it may often also be the case) that any of his or her human capacities has been impaired. And, equally, harm to the latter capacities does not entail a transgression against an individual's will. This is why on the individualistic model of justice considerations of justice must be *individualised*, must exhibit a detached care for the individual. 'Detached' because justice requires an impartial treatment of individuals, treating similarly placed individuals in a similar manner. And 'care' because justice requires that singular or unique features of cases be taken into account. For the individual to feel justly dealt with he or she must be satisfied that his or her case has been given adequate attention by the dispenser of justice, even if failure to do so may not entail any diminution in their powers.

By contrast, on the Socratic model of justice the logically primary subject of injustice is the 'soul', the ensemble of distinctively human capacities. Consequently, it need not be the case that the perpetrator of an injustice deliberately sets out to damage some such capacity. It is enough if it can be shown that the perpetrator's actions do in fact have that effect. The will of the individual thus becomes secondary to the question whether their actions damage or enhance human capacities. This is why, on this model, considerations of justice demand an *impersonal care* for the human good. The just person's care for the individual must 'go through' a care for the condition of various human powers in that individual, and for the way in which that individual's activities affect that condition both in themselves and in others. The differences between the two notions require a much deeper and detailed investigation than I can give them here. They involve different conceptions of reason and of its relation to the other mental functions which make up the human personality in the context of action.[20] They also differ radically about the sort of entity an individual is and, consequently, they differ about what it is to care for another person.[21] Our modern conception of the individual presupposes that each human being is a 'subject', a consciousness located in a body aware of itself as the locus of experiences and as the source of a particular will. The idea, therefore, that justice consists in not 'doing down' another human being is interpreted in terms of the mutual recognition between human beings that for all their substantial differences, in ability, in character, in aspirations, and in the material conditions of their existence, they are all 'subjects' or 'selves'. To be just is to realise that we cannot, at one and the same time, cherish our selfhood and demand that it be recognised by others while acting in a way which refuses to acknowledge that others are selves too. It is such selves or subjects which are also regarded as 'objects' of love, as recipients of a kind of care which is warmer and differently concerned with the flourishing of another self than is required by justice.

The notion of the 'self' or 'subject' is absent from the thought of Socrates and other Greek thinkers when they refer to 'the soul'. Without entering into the difficult question of how they thought about this 'soul', it would seem that a *psychē* denoted the ensemble of capacities, perhaps hierarchically arranged, by reference to which one kind of being could be distinguished from another.[22] The 'soul', therefore, is not 'a subject of consciousness' but an integrated *form of living*. Consequently, the idea of justice as being 'fair to others' and 'not doing them down', when Socratically re-interpreted, becomes the notion of doing or failing to do what is required by the flourishing of the integrated form of living as it is instantiated in a human being, in a specimen of humankind. Socrates' message to his contemporaries was that the manner in which they lived and thought about their relations to each other was deficient to the extent to which it remained 'external' to what truly constituted the flourishing of the form of life peculiar to humankind. Justice had to be 'internal' to this flourishing in the sense that it involved the application of reason, a distinctive capacity of the human life-form, to the life-form itself and to its relation to other life-forms. In other words, justice for Socrates involved the rejection of certain choices about how to live and act on the ground that they undermined what is distinctively human. To be just is to realise that one cannot at one and the same time value a pattern of living under the control of reason while acting in a way which undermines the achievement of such pattern in others or in oneself. To be unjust is, thus, an indication of a tension or conflict within the 'soul' itself. And, since reason is essential to this 'soul', what undermines reason must undermine how the 'soul' shapes the life of the being whose 'soul' it is. To be unjust, therefore, is to diminish the power of the human 'soul' to organise living.

Because the two conceptions of justice we have considered involve radically different views of how 'caring for a human being' is to be understood, they can come into conflict.[23] They can seem to each other to view justice in a way which makes it 'external' to what each considers important about persons. Decision as to which is more acceptable cannot, I believe, be divorced from the difficult question of what constitutes personhood. The way our ideas on this issue have developed since the seventeenth century place them in marked contrast to those of Socrates. We put stress on the individual will and its autonomy whereas Socrates emphasised an impersonal case for the 'soul', for the development of human capacities and their effective integration in a well-functioning individual. Aspects of our current situation in the world are forcing us to attend to the global nature of social, economic, technological, environmental, and political problems. It is beginning to look as if confining questions of justice to relations between individual wills, or to individualistically conceived nation-states, is fast becoming inadequate and problematic. It is becoming apparent, once again, that we need to consider *structural* questions about how personalities, groups, institutions, and so on, are shaped. This suggests that we ought to take seriously the Socratic perspective on justice.

The aim of this study has been to elicit what the Socratic ideal of justice involved, and why it should be taken seriously. It was not my purpose to argue that it is, or should be, the only one. It seems to me, however, that if we are to think of justice as an *enabling* condition in human beings and communities, we cannot limit justice to the role of guarding the rights of individuals; we have to include within justice a knowledgeable concern with how our actions and arrangements affect the realisation of human capacities in people. There is, after all, a sense in which it is unjust not 'to render to each what is due'. And the factors which sustain our present perilous world-situation prevent us from rendering 'what is due' to human beings as such—the *power*, not merely the right, to flourish and realise their potential. It was Socrates' merit to have been the first to draw attention to this implication of justice. Let us hope that Plato's attempt to construct a theory of justice on this basis does not remain the last.

Notes and References

1 INTRODUCTION: 'TURNING THE SOUL AROUND'

1. 'Justice' and 'happiness' are the standard translations of the Greek words *dikaiosyne* and *eudaimonia*. As most commentators on Plato and Aristotle point out these translations are not entirely satisfactory. Concerning *dikaiosyne* it should be noted that although it refers to the 'rightness' of conduct towards others and towards one's city-state (law-abidingness, observing moral and legal norms), it is the name for one of the cardinal moral virtues or excellences. It is the individual and his dispositions (his 'soul') who are primarily just (the way we speak of a person being courageous, temperate, kind or just), just actions being a manifestation of that excellence whose opposite is *pleonexia* (graspingness, greed). Aristotle in his *Nicomachean Ethics*, Book V, chs 1–4, distinguishes between two senses of the word, one applied to law-abidingness and virtuous behaviour to others in general, the other for the more specialised virtue to do with various aspects of *pleonexia*. Some commentators take Socrates to be talking about justice in the broader sense where it is equivalent to virtue as a whole in its relation to others. Thus, Frietdländer (1964), vol. 2, no. 13, p. 307; Cornford (1941), p. 1. But Annas (1981), pp. 11–13, is correct in pointing out that Socrates' discussion both in Book I and the rest of the *Republic* concerns the narrower notion, though Plato wants to make justice more important than people would expect. For a useful summary account of ordinary views of morality at the time Plato is writing, see Irwin (1977), ch. 2 and notes. K. J. Dover's *Greek Popular Morality in the Time of Plato and Aristotle* is invaluable.

   Concerning *eudaimonia* we should note that it is the word used by Greeks to refer to whatever sort of life is the most desirable and satisfying. *Eudaimonia* is not a state of feeling, or of enjoyment or content, something one *could* sacrifice for a greater good. It signifies the condition where one *likes and enjoys what one has got* (whether it be possessions, social role, mental, physical and moral attributes, etc.) rather than the condition of getting what one wants. For this distinction and an interesting discussion see J. Austin in Schneewind (1968), pp. 234–50. *Eudaimonia*, thus, has the force of 'doing excellently in one's life', 'flourishing or excelling as a human being'—something which misfortune can affect but which is not simply a result of good fortune. People not only admire and praise the person whose life is *eudaimon*, they also call him 'blessed' (*makarios*). Aristotle in *Nicomachean Ethics*, I, 4, 1095a 18–20, refers to the common view that *eudaimonia is* 'living well' (*eu zēn*) and 'acting well' (*eu prattein*). Cf. J. L. Austin in Moravcsik (1967), especially pp. 279–83. *Eudaimonia* primarily characterises *lives* or life-activities, rather than states of mind or feeling.

2. On this question see Frietdländer (1964), vol 2, ch. 3, and n. 1, pp. 305–6 and references there.

3. This is how Cross and Woozley (1964), p. 61, look at the relation of the rest of the *Republic*, from Book II on to Book I. Annas (1981), p. 59, also takes *Republic*, II to express dissatisfaction with the methods of Book I. Irwin (1977), pp. 183–4 takes

the transition to *Republic*, II to indicate Plato's rejection of the analogy of justice to craft-knowledge. White (1979), p. 8, is excessively dismissive of Book I, suggesting that its only worth consists in anticipating or foreshadowing later discussion. Hopefully, the present study is a corrective to this attitude.

4. Thus, Cross and Woozley (1964), p. 61, Annas (1981), p. 57 on the ineffectiveness of Socrates' method for discussing 'the powerful claim of the moral sceptic'. Irwin (1977) looks upon Book I as exposing weaknesses and limitations in Socrates' conception of justice and virtue, because it relies on the craft analogy, while Cross and Woozley (pp. 12–16) take Socrates to be *exposing* the weakness of the analogy, as does Gould (1955), ch. II.

5. See, for example, Annas (1981), ch. 2; Cornford (1941), p. xxvi.

6. For example, White (1979), p. 8, Cross and Woozley (1964), p. 52 and p. 58.

7. This is substantially Irwin's thesis about the relation between Plato and Socrates. Cf. Irwin (1977), ch. vi, pp. 174–6, ch. vii, 184.

8. In this respect I differ from M. J. O'Brien (1967) who claims that there is continuity between 'the Greek mind' and the Socratic/Platonic 'intellectualism' in ethics. The case against a continuity between Socrates and Plato is forcibly argued by Irwin (1977), especially III, n. 59, IV, n. 7, V, n. 21. The account of the craft-analogy presented here is radically different from Irwin's, though he *may* be right about the rejection of the analogy being part of the development of Plato's ethical theory. I suspect, however, that the situation is much more complex than Irwin makes out.

9. It is not clear whether gender and status came into this. Meno refers to there being different virtues for women, children and slaves, *Meno*, 71e, 72a 5.

10. See, for example, Laches' view of courage in *Laches* as 'standing firm in battle' (190e 4–6) or 'endurance' (192a 9–c1). Cf. Irwin (1977), p. 19.

11. *Phaedo*, 68d–e on 'slavish' virtue, cf. Irwin (1977), pp. 160–1.

12. The task is pursued at length both in the *Republic* and in the *Nicomachean Ethics*.

13. This issue forms the substance of Socrates' discussion with Polus and Callicles in the *Gorgias*.

14. Cf. *Republic*, 518d 3–7.

15. Cf. Annas (1981), pp. 256–9, for an interesting discussion of the Cave allegory.

16. Cf. Nettleship (1937), pp. 20–1. It seems that the Socratic critique was part of the general intellectual movement in the latter part of the fifth century, BC, which included the work of some Sophists such as Antisthenes and the historian Thucydides. On this Kerferd (1981) contains valuable discussion. Cf., also, Guthrie (1969), Part I.

17. See Finley (1974), pp. 3–5, especially p. 5.

18. See Finley (1963), pp. 62–3. Finley bases this judgement on the fact that the size of Athens was limited, that it lacked resources in men and materials, that its rudimentary economy and technology were incapable of expanding, and that the Greeks were incapable either to transcend the *polis* or to live at peace with themselves within it.

19. Finley, (1974), p. 22.

20. For details see Forrest, (1966), chs 6 to 10 inclusive.

21. For a judicious assessment of what pressures democracy placed on its leaders, see Finley (1974), pp. 9–19.

22. Illuminating contributions can be found in Finley (1963), Andrewes (1956), Jones (1957), and de Ste Croix (1981).

23. In this context it may be worth quoting Plato's attitude to his contemporary

conflicts at some length. The translation is Morrow's in G. R. Morrow (ed.) *Plato's Epistles*, revised edn, Bobbs—Merrill, (1962). Cf. also Morrow's introductory essay to this volume, 'Plato and Greek Politics', pp. 118—44. Plato, or whoever was the author of the letter, says,

'When I was a young man I had the same ambition as many others: I thought of entering public life as soon as I became of age. And certain happenings in public affairs favoured me, as follows. The constitution we then had, being anathema to many, was overthrown and a new government was set up . . . . I thought that they were going to lead the city out of the unjust life she had been living and establish her in the path of justice, so that I watched them eagerly to see what they would do. But as I watched them they showed in a short time that the preceding constitution had been a precious thing. . . . The more I reflected upon what was happening, upon what kind of men were active in politics, and upon the state of our laws and customs, and the older I grew, the more I realised how difficult it is to manage a city's affairs rightly . . . the corruption of our written laws and our customs was proceeding at such an amazing speed that whereas at first I had been full of zeal for public life, when I noted these changes and saw how unstable everything was, I became in the end quite dizzy; and though I did not cease to reflect how an improvement could be brought about in our laws and in the whole constitution, yet I refrained from action . . . At last I came to the conclusion that all existing states are badly governed and the condition of their laws practically incurable . . . , and I was forced to say, in praise of philosophy, that from her height alone was it possible to discern what the nature of justice is, either in the state or the individual, and that the ills of the human race would never end until either those who are sincerely and truly lovers of wisdom come into political power, or the rulers of our cities, by the grace of God, learn true philosophy' (324b—326b).

24. Cf. Aristotle, *Politics*, Book III. 17, 1288a 15ff.
25. Perhaps the tendency to elitism was part of the democratic system as it had developed, a necessary consequence of a direct, as distinct from a representative, democracy. As Finley points out, '[the] leaders in Athens had *no* respite. Because this influence had to be served and exerted directly and immediately—. . .—they had to lead in person . . . '(Finley, 1974, p. 16). This applied just as much to leaders with democratic sympathies as to those with aristocratic or oligarchic tendencies.
26. This may well have been the reason for the reaction of Athenians against Alcibiades (and, perhaps, people like Callicles in the *Gorgias*). Cf. Thucydides, VI, 28—1, and the incident of the Hermae statues.
27. Cleon says, for instance, 'Bad laws that stay unchanged are better than good laws which are unstable; stupidity continued with restraint is better than unbridled cleverness. It is the ordinary man, not the clever one who manages a city well. The latter always wants to seem wiser than the laws . . . but the former mistrusts his own cleverness . . . and acting as judge rather than competitor, arrives more often at the true answer. So we must not let ourselves be carried away by ingenuity or intellectual rivalry into offering ideas to you the people simply for effect' (*Thucydides*, III, 37).
28. Aristotle, *Politics*, 3, 4—5 (1278b—79b) and 4, 6—7 (1293b—94b), thinks that monarchy becomes tyranny when an individual rules in his own interest rather than

in the interest of the whole state, aristocracy similarly becomes oligarchy, and polity becomes democracy. The first items of these pairs are the 'right' forms of government ('according to absolute justice') while the second items of the pairs are their degenerate forms. Cf., also, Finley (1974), p. 7.

29.   Cf. Finley (1974), pp. 5–6 and further references given there.

30.   Solon, for example, was urged to become a tyrant. For an analysis of his reasons for refusing and for the expectations of those who wanted him to become a tyrant, see Andrewes (1956) pp. 89–91. On tyranny in general, cf. Andrewes (1956) chs I and II, and pp. 147–50, Forrest (1966), chs 4–7, and Finley (1963), p. 43.

31.   Cf. *Republic*, IV, 435e, and in VIII, 545d–e, Plato suggests that a change (for the worse) in the constitution of a city reflects the lack of unity or dissension within those who rule.

32.   Cf. Finley (1963), p. 52.

33.   Ibid., p. 47.

34.   Cf., ibid., pp. 49–50, for Finley's characterisation of the nature of this inescapability.

35.   For the effects of this on law-courts and the style of litigation in the latter part of the fifth century BC Athens, cf. Adkins (1972), pp. 119–26.

36.   As Finley (1963; p. 51) expresses it,

> The citizen felt he had claims on the community, not merely obligations to it, and if the regime did not satisfy him he was not loath to do something about it—to get rid of it if he could. In consequence, the dividing line between politics and sedition (*stasis* the Greeks called it) was a thin one in classical Greece, and often enough *stasis* grew into ruthless civil war'.

37.   On the political role of the tyrants, cf. Forrest, (1966), ch. 6 and 7 and 8. Also, Andrewes, (1956) chs III, IV, and V.

38.   Cf. Adkins' discussion of Attic drama in Adkins (1960), ch. IX.

39.   In *Republic*, II, 368e–369a.

40.   *Merit and Responsibility*, Oxford, 1960; and *Moral Values and Political Behaviour in Ancient Greece*, Chatto & Windus, 1972.

41.   Though see his discussion of justice, moral 'pollution', and the gods in Adkins (1960), chs V, VI and VII.

42.   Cf. J. E. Harrison, *Themis*, Cambridge University Press, 1927, ch. XI, pp. 514ff. The notion of justice as a cosmic force has a prominent role in pre-Socratic thought. Anaximander, for example, thought that the opposites encroached upon each other and were then compelled to render 'justice and reparation to one another according to the ordering of time' (Frag. 36.3). It is important to realise here that *dikē* (justice) operates in a context which suggests a cyclical process, a process of natural regeneration. 'Disturbances' of what is apportioned have the role of regenerating an order. Analogously, man, god and everything else, have a place in the order of 'honour' (*timē*) established by *moira*. The essence of justice is to deal with others in accordance with that order, not to encroach upon it. Cf. also Parmenides, Frag. 8. 36–8 and Frag. 1. 13–4; Cf. also Heraclitus, Frag. 94.

43.   Solon's conception of what is the appropriate share of wealth and privilege for each class operates with the same notion of *dikē* as Anaximander's (cf. previous note). He thinks that only 'excess' and *hybris* will disturb this arrangement, but while the traditional view included birth in the prerequisites of status, Solon equates it with

property (cf. Solon, Frags. 34 and 36). Aristotle says in *Athenian Constitution*, 7.3, that 'to each class he [Solon] awarded political office in proportion to their rateable property'. Cf. Vlastos' 'Solonian Justice'. *Classical Philology*, vol. XLI, no. 2, April 1946, p. 80.

44. As Demosthenes put it, echoing the spirit of Solon's great innovation, 'every deed of violence is a common injury, affecting those also who are not directly concerned' (Demosthenes, XXI, 45). It is this spirit which lies behind the most radical institution of fifth and fourth-century Athens, the introduction of public courts and the gradual removal from aristocratic hands of the exclusive hold over judiciary powers.

45. Cf., (for example), Protagoras myth in *Protagoras*, 320c–322d.

46. As Vlastos shows admirably in 'Solonian Justice', cf. pp. 75ff.

47. Ibid., p. 75.

48. Ibid., pp. 76–7. Cf. also, Greene (1963), ch. 1.

49. Vlastos, 'Solonian Justice', p. 69.

50. Ibid., p. 74.

51. For a discussion of the traditional restraints on injustice, cf. Adkins (1972), pp. 75–98 and, especially, pp. 95ff. for Orphic beliefs. Cf. also Adkins (1960), pp. 140ff.

52. J. Harrison says in *Themis*, p. 482: 'Zeus himself cannot summon his own assembly. He must "bid Themis call the gods to council from many-folded Olympos' brow. And she ranged all about and bade them to the house of Zeus" [Homer *Iliad*, XX, 4–6]. . . . It is the meed of Themis to convene and dissolve the agora; it is hers too to preside over the equal, sacramental feast'. Cf. Greene, *Moira*, p. 401.

53. In Harrison (1927).

54. Vlastos 'Solonian Justice', p. 62.

55. Cf. Vlastos' references to different cases in 'Solonian Justice', p. 63.

56. The Greek attitude to *Themis* as Harrison (1927), pp. 483–4, suggests, comes out very vividly in the account of the Cyclopes. In Homer's *Odyssey*, IX, 106, they are represented as god-fearing, they are earth-worshippers and earth brings forth her increase, but they are *athemistes*, they have no customs, no conventions, binding by common consent, they have no *agora*, no public place. 'That', says Harrison 'for the Greek was the last desolation. . . . Themis was the use and wont of full-grown men, citizens, made effective in the councils of the agora.'

57. *Odyssey*, XVIV, 225.

58. Harrison (1927), p. 516.

59. Harrison (1927), pp. 484–5, says,

Themis was of course at first of the tribe, and then she was all powerful. Later when the tribal system, through wars and incursions and migrations, broke up, its place was taken less dominantly, more effectively, by the *polis*. The *polis* set itself to modify and inform all those primitive impulses and instincts that are resumed in Earth-worship. It also set itself, if unconsciously, as a counterbalance to the dominance of ties of near kinship . . . Themis and the actual concrete agora are barely distinguishable . . . Here the social fact is trembling on the very verge of godhead. She is the force that brings and binds men together, she is 'herd instinct', the collective conscience, the social sanction. She is *fas*, the social imperative. The social imperative is among a primitive diffuse, vague, inchoate, yet absolutely binding. Later it crystallizes into fixed conventions, regular tribal customs; finally in the *polis* it takes shape as 'Law and Justice'.

We may add that the nearer the social imperative comes to this last stage the more *externalised*, 'objectified', it appears to those ruled by it. Witness, for instance, the conflict between Antigone's emphasis on kinship and Creon's patriarchal emphasis on law and convention in Sophocles' play. It is at this last stage that what is meant to bind men may also divide them. *Themis* is threatened by the lack of civil order whose source lies in the lack of social and economic knowledge. Cf. Solon's remarks on ignorance as a cause of 'bondage' in Frags. 9 and 10.

60.   This is, of course, the central message of the *Republic* as a whole. Cf., also, *Gorgias*, 521d, where Socrates claims he is probably the only Athenian who practices 'The real political craft'.

2 OLD RECIPES ABOUT JUSTICE

1.   The conversation is apparently continued the next day in the *Timaeus* cf. *Timaeus* 17a–20c.

2.   The religious festival Socrates is attending is probably the 'foreign' one of the goddess Bendis. The reference to the 'Thracians' at 327a 5 probably refers to the resident aliens in Piraeus. Adam (1965), n. 5, p. 2, suggests that it was Athenian policy to encourage commercial settlers by allowing them to exercise their own cults. The worship of the Thracian goddess Bendis was brought to Piraeus by Thracian merchants. For Cephalus' family ruin see Lysias' *Against Eratosthenes*. Lysias was sent to exile when Polemarchus was executed. Cf. Allan (1944), pp. 18–21.

3.   Plato would have been in his teens when the scene of the dialogue is taking place. Scholars usually place it some dozen years before Socrates' death in 399BC. See discussion in Allan (1944), pp. 20.

4.   For example, Annas (1981), pp. 18–19.

5.   *Protagoras*, 320d–328d. For an excellent analysis of the speech see Kerferd (1981), ch. 11.

6.   Cf. *Republic*, II, 357a–d. Glaucon there raises the question of what kind of good justice is, having distinguished three types. Note also that on Glaucon's view the common opinion about justice is that it belongs to the class of onerous goods which are pursued for the sake of other rewards but are not welcome in themselves. Socrates locates the ground of Thrasymachus' attack on justice in this common opinion (358a 4–9).

7.   Cf., for example, Annas (1981), ch. 2, and White (1979), p. 8.

8.   In Irwin (1977), ch. VII, pp. 177ff. the view is advanced that in the 'middle' dialogues Plato had abandoned the Socratic analogy between virtue and craft-knowledge, and that his purpose in reviving it in *Republic*, I is 'meant to expose the weaknesses in Socrates' views on justice' (p. 178). Irwin grants that Socrates' conclusions are defended later in the *Republic*, but with different arguments (p. 183). Irwin's view depends on an interpretation of how Socrates views *technē* which is at variance with the one presented here. On the latter view there is much more continuity between Plato's conception of knowledge (*epistēmē*) and Socrates' view of craft-knowledge; Plato's problem is how to characterise a second-order kind of craft which is that of the statesman. For the notion of a second-order craft, and the issues involved in how Plato thinks of it, see Kent Sprague (1976), chs 1 and 3.

9. Adam (1965), p. 33, for example, says that the principle that rulers *qua* rulers always seek the good of their subjects (342e 6–10) though practically exemplified by Solon and the early lawgivers, was first elevated and developed into a principle of political science by Plato.

10. Cf., for example, Socrates' remarks to young Hippocrates in *Protagoras*, 312a–14c. Cf., also, Anytus' attitude in *Meno*, 91c–92d.

11. By the 420s BC full democracy was something to be taken for granted. But the generation entering politics at the time, particularly those of aristocratic background, had to face the claim of non-aristocrats like Cleon for recognition. They also belonged to the generation which was the first to feel the full impact of the new intellectual revolution, the growth of the so-called Sophists, who began to apply the principles of Ionian science to fields more relevant to politics, to rhetoric and to moral and political theory. Trained by such men the young aristocrats could form their distaste for Cleon into a critique of democracy. Cf., Forrest (1966), p. 224, and on one of these young men, the 'old Oligarch', who builds his case against democracy on the principle 'every man has the right to look after his own interests', see, ibid., pp. 102–3. For 'The Old Oligarch', cf. Ps.—Xenophon, *The Athenian Constitution*, i, 6–8.

12. Socrates gives expression to these attitudes in his trial and in his conversation with Crito in gaol. Cf. *Apology*, 29d,e, *Crito*, 50a–54d.

13. The latter view is to be found in Annas (1981), p. 19.

14. Cf. *Apology*, 38 a 5–6.

15. Cf. *Republic*, IV, 444d 13–444b 4.

16. The word Socrates uses for 'creation' is *'ergon'*. The translation 'production' or 'creation' is not entirely satisfactory. The reference to poets and fathers suggests a social role with its own characteristic activity or 'product'. Perhaps Plato is suggesting that those who view money-making as their social role regard the making of money as their 'own' specific product (*hōs ergon heauton*), at 444d 5–6.

17. Cf. Greene (1963), chs 1 and 2.

18. Cf. Thucydides, *The Peloponnesian War*, 5, 85–111. For a discussion of the 'Melian Debate' cf. Guthrie (1969), vol. III, pp. 84–8.

19. Thus, Annas (1981), p. 34.

20. Annas (1981), p. 28, suggests that Cephalus and Polemarchus share a conception of justice which, though it elicits respect from both of them, does not play an important part in their lives. This is both dubious and misleading. It is not clear that what Polemarchus respects is the *same* as what Cephalus respects. Though Socrates shows that justice as Polemarchus conceives it cannot be important in his life, Cephalus is presented as faithfully observing the obligations which spell out justice for him.

21. The saying is literally (331e 3–4): 'The rendering to each what is due is just'. The context, however, suggests that Polemarchus takes Simonides to be talking about justice in general, not merely identifying a particular type of just act.

22. For an interesting discussion of the nature of political changes in the administration of law in Athens around 462 BC, cf. Forrest (1966), ch. 9. Cf., also, Finley (1963), chs. 3 and 4. On the evolution of the Greek conception of justice that attended the political changes see the discussion in Adkins (1960), chs 4, 5, 7 and 10; also Adkins (1972), chs 3–5. On Solon and justice, cf. Ehrenburg (1968), Thomson (1972), chs. 9 and 10, and Vlastos (1946), pp. 65–83.

23. For a satirical picture of this 'busybody' attitude of the juries in the Athenian popular courts, cf. Aristophanes' *Wasps*.

24. Young (1980), p. 409, n. 19, takes the dictum in the latter sense.
25. Cf., for example, the conflict between Antigone and Creon in Sophocles' play *Antigone*.
26. Cf., Young (1980), p. 406.
27. Socrates says 'If someone says that it is just to render each what is owed, and *by this he means* (*touto de noei auto*), that harm is owed to enemies by the just man and benefit to friends . . .' (my emphasis). Cf., Young (1980), n. 17, p. 408.
28. This suggestion is made in Young (1980), p. 406.
29. Ibid., pp. 408–9.
30. Unless, of course, it is tempered by a general respect for the law, independently of who administers it. There is reason to think that, broadly speaking , this was the case in Athens following the democratic reforms of 462 BC. Cf., Forrest (1966), pp. 209–20. Socrates recognises the supremacy of law in *Crito*, 50e–51c. Plato's view, perhaps jaundiced by the events that followed the loss of the war by Athens, seems to have been that neither of the *political* factions, oligarchs or democrats, had genuine respect for law, however much such respect was part of the ideology of democracy. On the connection between *isonomia* ('equality under the law') and democracy, and of Plato's attitude to this connection in *Republic*, Book VIII, cf. 'Isonomia Politikē' in Vlastos (1973), pp. 164–203.
31. For the idea that moral qualities are objective characteristics of people and social movements, cf. Anderson (1962), Essays 21 and 22.
32. On the political role of the tyrants, cf. Forrest (1966), chs 6–8, and Andrewes (1956), chs 3, 4 and 5.
33. In the *Republic* (Books VIII and IX), Plato presents tyranny and the tyrannical character as degenerate forms of democracy and the democratic character, thus *reversing* the historical development. Plato is, of course, discussing the ways in which the choice of objectives is manifested in political arrangements and life-styles which depart from those which are truly just. But he could be hinting that, *morally speaking*, the tyrant's blatant disregard of justice as part of human excellence is implicit in the democratic *idea* that justice requires that an equal voice (and weight) be given to the various competing interests within a *polis*, independently of their true merit. In *practice*, of course, Athenian democracy did no such thing. Cf., for example, Pericles' stress on *aretē* and merit in the distribution of honour within the democratic state, in his 'Funeral Oration'—*Thucydides*, 2.37.1 On a comparison of Pericles' speech with Socrates' views in the *Menexenus*, cf. Vlastos (1973), pp. 188ff.

3   THRASYMACHUS ON JUSTICE AND POWER

1. The literature dealing with Thrasymachus is both large and complex. I make no attempt in this study to comment on the rich and varied scholarly opinion which, in English at least, stretches back to the nineteenth century, and the early part of this century. My comments on both older and more recent commentators will be confined to points where my interpretation owes something to them, or where it helps to explain why I find a comment to contain only a partial insight. Needless to say, the wealth of scholarly and philosophical thought on Thrasymachus contains

important contributions from which I have profited greatly. The bibliography lists the works that have served most to shape my views. For fuller bibliographies, cf. Guthrie (1969), Kerferd (1947), and Nicholson (1974).

2. Guthrie (1969), pp. 91–2.
3. The reference is to the feast of Bendis which Socrates and Glaucon had been attending. Cf. Appendix 1 in Adam (1965), vol. I, p. 62.
4. For historical details, cf. Guthrie (1969), pp. 294–8.
5. For example, Maguire (1971), pp. 142–63 and, in a different sense, Harrison (1967), pp. 27–39.
6. Cf., for example, Annas (1981), p. 35. Kerferd (1981), pp. 123–5 puts the matter well.
7. Cf. Guthrie (1969), pp. 291ff.
8. For the view that Thrasymachus is not a Sophist, cf. Irwin (1977), n. 32, p. 291. For the contrary view, cf Guthrie (1969), p. 295, and Kerferd (1981), pp. 51–2.
9. Cf. Kerferd (1981), chs 11 and 12.
10. For these cultural and political developments, cf. Forrest (1966), ch. 10, and Jones (1978), pp. 41–72.
11. Cf. Adkins (1960), ch. III, esp., p. 52ff, and n. 16, pp. 58–9.
12. Cf. Adkins (1960), chs IX and X, esp. pp. 198–214.
13. The conflict between the two conceptions is exemplified in Socrate's discussion with Polus in *Gorgias*, 466b–81b.
14. Cf. Adam (1965), n. on 337a, p. 25. Maguire (1971) argues that in this presentation of 'Thrasymachus', Plato adds a *moral* dimension to Thrasymachus' essentially *political* doctrine about justice.
15. Cf., Guthrie (1969), pp. 94–5 and notes.
16. Cf. reference to the view of Max Salomon in Guthrie (1969), n. 3, p. 91, and pp. 94–5.
17. On Socrates and 'definitions', cf., below, ch. 5.
18. Cf., for example the differences of interpretation in Kerferd (1947), pp. 19–27, Hourani (1962), pp. 110–20, Maguire (1971), pp. 142–63, and Dorter (1974), pp. 25–46.
19. Cf. Nicholson (1974), pp. 211-16 for a good summing up of the differences in interpreting Thrasymachus in recent literature. For the debate among earlier scholars, cf. Kerferd (1947).
20. For example, Hourani, Kerferd and Nicholson, though they disagree among themselves.
21. For example, Maguire (1971) pp. 150–1, Cross and Woozley (1964), pp. 38–41, and others, but not Kerferd (1947) or Nicholson (1974).
22. Yet this is how the majority of interpreters had understood Thrasymachus. Cf. for example, Adam (1965), p. 25 ('the natural history definition of justice'); Cornford (1941), p. 14, Hourani (1962), p. 110, and earlier by Grote, Gomperz, Lindsay, Bosanquet and others.
23. Cf., Nicholson (1974), p. 211; also Young (1980), pp. 410–17.
24. Cf. Adkins (1960), p. 238 and Adkins (1972), p. 119.
25. Hourani's view in Hourani (1962). Cf. Kerferd's reply in Kerferd (1964), pp. 12–16; also Hadgogoulos (1973), pp. 204–8.
26. On this point Sparshott (1966), pp. 421–59, is right; cf., also, Young (1980), pp. 416–17.
27. I cannot see why 'just for the subject' *must* refer only to the *weaker*; cf. Kerferd (1947) p. 25, and Henderson (1970), p. 220.

28. *Laws*, 714c.
29. Plato's attitude to this view is found in the Athenian's remarks at *Laws* 715b,e. Cf., especially 714d.
30. Aristotle, *Politics*, III, ch. 7, 1279b 4ff, makes it the distinguishing mark of his three 'perverted' forms of constitution that they seek their own, not the common advantage (*to koine sumpheron*).
31. This is what makes the attribution of a 'naturalistic' definition of justice to Thrasymachus (for example, by M. Salomon and Adam) implausible.
32. Cf. Adkins (1960), ch. IV.
33. Cf., Kerferd (1947), p. 25ff; Hourani (1962), p. 116.
34. Cf. Young (1980), pp. 415–16.
35. Maguire (1971), p. 151.
36. Ibid., pp. 148–9.
37. Maguire (1971) accepts the second alternative, cf., op. cit., pp. 156–63.
38. As Kerferd (1947), p. 26, and Nicholson (1974), sec. III, recommend.
39. Cf. Young (1980), pp. 415–17.
40. This used to be the standard view among scholars. Cf., for example Nettleship (1897), p. 17, Barker (1906), p. 95, Cross and Woozley (1964), p. 16, Allan (1964), p. 29, Cornford (1941), pp. 14–15. Kerferd (1947), Nicholson (1974), Young (1980) and Henderson (1970) disagree with this older view.
41. A thesis originated in Kerferd (1947) and defended by Nicholson (1974), and amended by Young (1980).
42. This is, in essence, the account in Nicholson (1974), pp. 227ff.

4 THE FUNCTION OF 'THRASYMACHUS' IN PLATO'S TEXT

1. Henderson (1970), p. 221, suggests that 'the ruler "in the strict sense" is defined by Thrasymachus as one who always makes laws which are to the ruler's advantage . . . He is *defined*, be it noted, neither as an unjust, nor as a strong man'. This leaves the injustice of the stronger a general contingent fact about the stronger in the *polis*. But at 340e 8–341a 2 (to which Henderson refers) Thrasymachus explicitly links the formula for justice 'doing what is advantageous to the *stronger*' with the ruler's prescribing infallibly what is best for himself (*to hauto beltiston tithesthai*). The subjects, in other words, in doing what serves the interest of the ruler (laid down infallibly by the ruler in the strict sense) are *thereby* doing what is advantageous to the stronger. The ruler in the strict sense, therefore, must be 'the stronger', otherwise doing what is just (on the part of subjects), doing what is in the interest of the ruler, would not necessarily be doing what is advantageous to the stronger. But this is precisely what Thrasymachus wants to claim from the start.
2. This is well brought out in Henderson (1970), p. 220.
3. For example, by Henderson (1970), p. 219ff, and by Nicholson (1974), pp. 227–9.
4. *Ethica Nicomachea*, V, ch. 3, 1130a 3ff.
5. This might provide the beginning of an answer to the questions raised in Nicholson (1974), p. 232, about the relation between the phrases 'the advantage (*sumpheron*) of the stronger' and 'the good (*agathon*) of another' in Thrasymachus' two speeches.
6. This is often taken to be the case. Cf., for example, Irwin (1977), pp. 28–30 on Callicles and Thrasymachus.

7. Cf., Jones (1978), pp. 99–133. Cf., also, Guthrie (1969), vol. III, pp. 117–33.

8. Cf., Jones (1978), 127–9, for a sober assessment of the sort of power leaders like Pericles and Cleon had.

9. For Thrasymachus as 'a disillusioned moralist', cf. Guthrie (1969), vol. III, pp. 96–7, and references to other scholars in the footnotes.

10. Cf. *Epistle VII*, 325b, if this is a genuine Platonic work.

11. *Ps-Xenophon, Constitution of Athens.* This is a pamphlet by an anonymous writer of the latter half of the fifth century containing a crude pro-oligarchic attack on democracy along the lines that its system is a bad one because its actions are dictated by the interests of the poorer and inferior sections of the citizenry. Finley, in Finley (1974), p. 8, acutely observes that the special interest of the pamphlet is its conclusion, that 'the strength of the Athenian government comes from what many criticize, namely the fact that it is government by a faction acting unashamedly to its own advantage'. Finley comments that '[t]he great difference between political analysis and moral judgement could not be better exemplified. Do not be misled says the Old Oligarch in effect: I and some of you dislike democracy, but a reasoned consideration of the facts shows that what we condemn on moral grounds is very strong as a practical force, and its strength lies in its immorality. This is a very promising line of investigation, but it was not pursued in antiquity.' I am suggesting that it *was* so pursued by Plato in his characterisation of Thrasymachus.

12. Cf. Socrates' characterisation of democracy, in Book VIII of the *Republic*, 557d–e, as 'a handy place to look for a constitution' because it is an 'universal provider of constitutions'. Cf., also, comments on the 'isonomic man' at 561d–e.

13. Cf., Kerferd (1947), pp. 19–21 for an account of the different positions attributed to Thrasymachus by different scholars.

14. Cf. Callicles' speech in *Gorgias*, 482e–86d. Guthrie, vol. III, pp. 85ff suggests that association between the assertion of power by the strong over the weaker with justice, illustrated in Thucydides, 'supply the necessary background to . . . Thrasymachus in the *Republic* . . . '. But as Maguire (1971) points out, pp. 158ff. this fits the position of Callicles in the *Gorgias* more than it does Thrasymachus who merely thinks that being just is being simple-minded.

15. As Kerferd (1947), p. 19, maintains. Nicholson (1974), 216–17, is right to separate this claim from Kerferd's interpretation of what Thrasymachus says.

16. Such link between *'sumpheron'* and *'euboulia'* is made by Cleon and Diodotus in *Thucydides*, iii 40 and 42–8. On this topic cf. Adkins (1960), p. 223 and ch. XI as a whole.

17. The implicit contrast is between two ways of understanding the 'power' of justice. Cf., 366d–67b for Adeimantus' summing up of the difference between what he expects Socrates to defend and what people like Thrasymachus hold. The latter 'reverse' (*metastrephontes*) the power inherent in, respectively, justice and injustice (367a 5–8).

18. This disagreement, as we saw, forms part of Thrasymachus' *entry* into the discussion (366c,d). Contrast with this method of investigation Socrates proposes to Glaucon and Adeimantus in *Republic*, II (368d–69a). The important difference is between locating 'powers' *in* justice and injustice, and seeing justice and injustice as conduct which places people in different *relations* of power (being dominated or dominating). If Adeimantus is right that Thrasymachus mistakenly *reverses* the 'powers' inherent in justice and injustice, it follows that his view that acting justly places people in the position of being dominated by the strong (and unjust)

mistakes the 'power' of justice. It is justice, not injustice, which has the 'power' to place people in a position of true control—a view elaborated at length in the rest of the *Republic*.

19. There is, thus, some plausibility in the suggestion in Maguire (1971) p. 150ff that we should distinguish Thrasymachus' essentially *political* conception of justice ('advantage of the stronger and ruler') from the moral dimension ('the good of another') Plato *adds* to that conception in Thrasymachus' second speech. Where I differ from Maguire is in thinking that in Plato's mind the moral downgrading of justice is *implicit* in Thrasymachus' conception of justice as a relation of power. Cf., pp. 63–70 of this chapter.

20. Cf., the fragments of the historical Thrasymachus in Guthrie, vol. III, n. 294–8 and, also, p. 97.

21. Cf., Jones (1978), pp. 66–7.

22. Cf., for example, Adkins (1960), ch. IV.

23. Cf., Forrest (1966), chs. 6 and 7; also, Andrewes (1956), pp. 114–15 on the relation between tyranny and democracy.

24. Cf., for example, Pericles, in *Thucydides*, II. 37–41 and Cleon in *Thucydides*, III. 37.

25. For the functional dependence of the democracy on demogagues see, e.g., Finley (1974).

26. This theme is explored by Plato in the *Gorgias* from 506d till the end of the dialogue.

27. It is not clear whether the notion of political equality (*isonomia politikē*) was confined to democracy, even if it gained ideological prominence in the democracy. Plato criticises it in *Republic*, VIII 558c, where it is said that democracy distributes a 'peculiar kind of equality alike to equals and unequals impartially'. Both Plato and Aristotle disapprove of this principle, Plato making much of the distinction between 'numerical equality' (*isotēs kat' arithmon*) and 'proportional equality' (*isotēs kat' axian*) in *Laws* 757b–c, and Aristotle questioning the value of the former, arguing that wealth should be taken into account in the distribution of political rights (*Politics*, 1318a 11ff.; Cf., also, 1280a 8ff.). However, *Thucydides*, III 62.3 mentions that the Thebans referred to their political system as 'equalitarian oligarchy' (*oligarchian isonomon*), and Plato, in the Seventh Letter speaks of a 'just and isonomic constitution' when he is hardly likely to be referring to democratic *isonomia*. On this topic, see Vlastos (1973) pp. 164–203 and Ostwald (1969), esp. part II, chs 2 and 3.

5 DEFINING JUSTICE

1. On this, see the excellent articles by A. R. Lacey and K. J. Dover in Vlastos (1971), pp. 22–77.

2. This image of Socrates finds its sharpest expression in the *Apology* and *Crito*. Cf. Vlastos' assessment of Socrates in his Introduction to Vlastos (1) (1971), pp. 1–21.

3. It is significant, for instance that an *old* friend of Socrates like Crito could have misunderstood what his friend stood for (to the extent of arranging for his escape from prison) so that people would not blame *him* for not trying to save his friend. Cf. *Crito* 44b–c.

4. Plato's efforts to draw a line of demarcation between philosophic method (Socrates' *elenchos* and, later, the notion of dialectic) and other forms of persuasion is almost obsessive. The matter is discussed at length in the *Protagoras* and the *Gorgias* (cf. *Meno* 75d) as well as in later dialogues such as the *Phaedrus* and the *Theatetus* (esp. 171d–77b). The topic of the *Sophist* is the nature of the Sophist and his difference from the dialectician. On the topic of differences in method between philosophy and the Sophists, see Kerferd (1981), ch. 6. Kerferd includes Socrates as part of the Sophistic movement. Cf. Kerferd (1981), pp. 55–7. On the Socratic *elenchos*, see Irwin (1977), ch. III.

5. To Xenophon Socrates is so persuasive that '. . . whenever he spoke, he, of all men that I have known, most readily prevailed upon his hearers to assent to his arguments' (*Memorabilia*, IV, 6, 16). But such 'persuasion' did not convince the 501 jurors in Socrates' trial, even though the decision was a close one—cf. *Apology*, 36a.

6. Most scholars are satisfied that we can group Plato's dialogues into three groups, the 'early', written probably in the 390s, the 'late', most of which were written in the 350s and the 'middle' written in the period in between. For a useful discussion on this question, cf. Crombie, (1962), vol. I, pp. 9–14. Cf., also, Irwin (1977), ch. II, n. 33, pp. 291–2.

7. For a recent work, cf. Rawls (1972), esp. chs 1 to 3.

8. Socrates claims, *Apology*, 31c–32a, that his concern with justice of necessity meant keeping clear of politics. In the *Gorgias* Socrates adverts to his ineptitude in political life (473e) and, later, is scornfully attacked by Callicles for preferring to 'talk to youths in a corner rather than engaging in public life like a man'.

9. Cf. Vlastos (1) (1971), pp. 18–19 on Socrates as a 'reformer of conscience' which 'in the long run has power to make or break social institutions'.

10. Vlastos, ibid., pp. 16–17 accuses Socrates of 'a failure of love' towards his fellow citizens.

11. Irwin (1977), ch. III, n. 69, pp. 303–4, doubts that Socrates thought of virtue as valuable in itself, in contrast to Plato (cf. *Phaedo* 68d, *Republic* 362e). Other scholars (for references cf. Irwin's note referred to above) would disagree. The assumption that it is not the 'work' of justice to harm anyone is explicitly stated in Socrates' discussion with Polemarchus (cf., below pp. 95f.). For the assumption that virtue is self-sufficient and ensures *eudaimonia*, cf. *Meno*, 88b and *Charmides* 175c–76a. The view that virtue is knowledge of the good seems to pervade most of the 'early' dialogues as well as the *Protagoras* and *Gorgias*.

12. This issue comes up in an interesting way about piety in the *Euthyphro*—cf. 5c–6c. Cf., also, Meno's confidence about what virtue is in *Meno* 71e–72a.

13. Cf. Irwin (1977), pp. 68–71.

14. *Meno*, 71b.

15. Irwin (1977), ch. III.7, to which the account given here is heavily indebted.

16. Socrates often assumes a connection between these three; cf. , for example, *Euthyphro* 7c–d; *Crito* 47c; *Gorgias* 459d; *Republic*, 493c, 520c. Cf. Irwin (1977), V, 2.3, pp. 117–18, and notes.

17. Cf., for example , *Apology*, 29d–30b, for Socrates' assessment of his mission.

18. Cf. Robinson (1953), pp. 15–17; cf., also, M. F. Burnyeat in Vlastos (1) (1971), pp. 213–14.

19. This assumption is evident in a number of 'early' dialogues, for example, *Lysis*, *Laches*, *Charmides*.

20. For a parallel point about courage and endurance, cf. *Laches*, 192b–3d. For the distinction between an estimation of facts and an estimation of values, cf. Santas' essay in Vlastos (1) (1971), 177–208, esp. 192–5.

21. For Socrates' conception of virtue as something capable of dominating and organising the whole pattern of a man's life, cf. M. F. Burnyeat's essay in Vlastos (1) (1971), pp. 209–34. Cf., also, Irwin (1977), ch. III, pp. 43–6.

22. Cf. Irwin (1977), pp. 73–4 about 'products' of craft. Cf. also, Kent Sprague (1976), pp. xiv for putative crafts (rhetoric, sophistry, statecraft) where we cannot specify a 'product' in a sense which is different from the cases of flute-playing or chess-playing.

23. At 333a 13 Socrates asks Polemarchus whether by deals or agreements (*sumbolaia*) he means co-operative ventures (*koinonēmata*). Cf. entry for '*koinonēma*' in Liddell and Scott's *Greek–English Lexicon*.

24. Cf. Irwin (1977), chs III to V. Cf., also Gosling (1973) ch. IV, Gibbs (1974), pp. 23–41.

25. For the difficulties, cf. Irwin (1977), III, 11, pp. 75–101, IV. 5, pp. 127–31.

26. Cf. Annas (1981), pp. 25–7.

27. So, Annas (1981), p. 27, is wrong to suggest that Polemarchus could have suggested that justice is a skill aiming at *eudaimonia*. Annas assimilates too much Polemarchus' view to that of Cephalus.

6 LIMITS ON THE JUST

1. In a number of books: cf., for example, Illich (1971), (1973) and (1975).

2. *Republic*, 433a, introduces the idea that justice in its social aspect consists in each citizen 'doing his own' (that is, what they are naturally fitted to do) and not meddling in things for which he is not fitted. At 433b 7–433c 2 justice is said to be the remaining virtue, having examined how temperance, courage and practical wisdom (*phronēsis*) are located there. Socrates claims that justice is what provides the power (*dunamin pareschēn*) to the other virtues to come into being to preserve them into being once they have appeared, so long as it is present in the city. Justice therefore, is *productive* of the qualities identified as the traditional virtues or the excellences of character. It is not merely an additional item in the traditional list, not even the most general or comprehensive item in the list; it is causally responsible for the other items in the list. Plato's view of justice and its relations to virtue has moved a long way from the traditional understanding of them.

3. '*Chrēstos*' means 'useful, good of its kind, serviceable'. When applied to people it can mean 'good', 'valiant', 'true', and generally, 'good', 'honest', and 'worthy'. It would seem to have the latter sense in Socrates' argument, though one cannot rule out its 'instrumental' use altogether. Cf. *Liddell and Scott* entry.

4. As, for example, Hume does, cf. Hume's *Enquiry*, Sec. III, Part I; cf., also, *Treatise*, Part II, sec. 1 for justice as an 'artificial' virtue. One could, of course, attempt to give an utilitarian defence of justice as a moral good. For a criticism of such defence, cf. Rawls (1972), ch. III, secs. 29 and 30.

5. Cf., for example, Irwin (1977), p. 324, who distinguishes between 'i-harm' (damaging some thing's interest) and 'e-harm' (damaging some thing's excellence). On this argument cf. Annas (1981), pp. 31–4; Allan (1944), pp. 24–5, Cross and Woozley (1964), pp. 20–2.

6. As Annas (1981), p. 32, suggests.
7. So, Annas (1981), p. 32. Cf. also, Irwin (1977), p. 324.
8. Protagoras, in *Protagoras* 322b–23c, makes a similar claim.
9. Cf., for example, Socrates' view of punishment in *Gorgias*, 472d–481b.
10. For different cases where conventional justice may lack this concern, cf., below, ch. 10.
11. Quine (1969), pp. 114–38, suggests that the discovery of new dispositional states proves new standards of similarity between things whose states they are. On Socrates' use of 'power' cf. Irwin (1977), pp. 44–6; Burnyeat in Vlastos (1) (1971), pp. 225–8 and Penner (1973), pp. 35–68.

7 POWER, SKILL AND RULING

1. The separation of a craft from what it is *of* applies just as much to crafts which produce an artefact, shoe-making, ship-building, saddle-making, etc., as to those which do not, such as flute-playing, calculating. Cf., for example, *Charmides*, 166a–b. On this point, cf. Kent Sprague (1976), XIV–XV, Irwin (1977), pp. 73–4.
2. The notion of an 'object' of a craft needs a good deal more philosophical elaboration than I give it here. Put bluntly, my view is that we should not allow the fact that some crafts have distinct 'things' (artefacts) as 'products' to be confused with the general conceptual point Plato is reaching for in claiming that a *technē*, like *episteme* and other cognitive and 'mental' verbs such as thinking, hoping, worshipping, imagining, etc., are, in Kent Sprague's phrase, '*tinos*-words'. Craft-verbs are 'intentional' verbs and the phrases that give us the 'object' of a craft are like phrases that give the direct object of intentional verbs. But, as Anscombe argues in 'The Intentionality of Sensation: A grammatical feature' (in Butler, 1965), pp. 158–80, esp. 166–8), the direct object of an intentional verb does not necessarily give an 'intentional object', an object whose existence is 'mental' or special. The identity of the intentional object of a mental act or state can be reduced to the identity of what Ascombe calls the 'material object' of that act or state (by which phrase she does not mean what modern philosophers mean, physical objects like tables, planets, and so on). Her point is simply that *given*, for example, that someone has contracted a debt of five dollars his thought 'that debt of five dollars' would have as its material object something described and indicated by the phrase giving the intentional object of his thought. In the case where the debt is imaginary there would, of course, be no such reduction of intentional to material object. Analogously, I am claiming, the phrase 'a malfunction of the liver', which indicates the intentional object of the physician's activity in relation to a patient, would give the material object of healing given that the malfunction exists. But the phrase indicates an intentional object of medical activity even where no such malfunction exists. The existence of the patient or, even, his liver is not in question here; the object of the physician's activity *is* the *condition* of the liver, not the liver or the patient. The intentionality of *technē*-words raises the interesting question of how to separate genuine from pseudo 'technical' activity—a problem that greatly concerned Plato. I hope to pursue this question elsewhere.
3. Cf., for example, Annas (1981), p. 49.
4. Cf. Cross and Woozley (1964), pp. 49–51.
5. Cf. *Republic* 2, 369b 5–7 and *Republic*, V, 473dff.

6. Cf. Henderson (1970), p. 222.

7. Henderson (1970), p. 225, misses this point when he says that Thrasymachus need not have accepted Socrates' 'suppressed premise', namely, that the only deviations from perfection in ruling must be in the form of unintentional errors, due to the ignorance of the true nature of ruling'. Though the inexperienced physician and the unscrupulous expert (who removes healthy organs for a fee) differ in their *intentions*, from the point of view of the 'object' of medicine they *both* fail in 'perfection'; they do not meet the 'needs' medicine is supposed to deal with.

8. The text does not contain this distinction, but Thrasymachus' point about shepherds and sheep seems to require it.

9. The analogy of justice to mental health, and of the political craftsman as a healer of the body politic is prominent both in the *Gorgias* and in the *Republic*. On this analogy, cf. Kenny (1973), pp. 1–27.

10. As Annas (1981), p. 49, claims.

11. Marx's sense of 'production' when he speaks of 'modes of production' in *Capital* is to be sharply distinguished from a Socratic *technē*.

12. A remark of Freud's about the electrical treatment of War neurotics captures this attitude admirably. Freud says, 'This therapeutic procedure, however, bore a stigma from the very first. It did not aim at the patient's recovery, or not in the first instance; it aimed, above all, at restoring his fitness for service. Here medicine was serving purposes foreign to its essence. The physician himself was under military command and had his own personal dangers to fear—loss of seniority or a charge of neglecting his duty—if he allowed himself to be led by considerations other than those prescribed for him' (Introduction to *Psychoanalysis and the War Neuroses*, S.E., vol. 17, p. 214).

13. The 'productive' city—'the city of pigs'—of *Republic* Book II sees labour as aimed at the mutual satisfaction of the needs of its members. This is a far cry from Locke's conception of the relations of labour to property in *Two Treatises of Government*, (ed. with Introd. by Peter Laslett, 2nd edn, Cambridge U.P., 1970), Second Treatise, ch. V, pp. 303ff.

14. It is interesting in this context to consider Marx's critique of political economy. Cf. *Capital*, vol. I, ch. VII, secs. 1 and 2.

15. Cf., for example, Plato's description of the timocratic and oligarchic cities in *Republic* Book VIII, 545c–48c, and 550c–52e.

16. On Plato's 'impersonal' conception of goodness, cf. White (1979), Introduction, Sec. 4.

17. Cross and Woozley (1964), pp. 49–51, miss this point.

18. Plato uses different arguments as to why in a good city those fit to rule might be prepared to rule. Cf. *Republic* Book VII, 519d–21b; cf., also, White (1979), pp. 189–96.

8   EXCELLENCE AND THE MOTIVATIONAL STRUCTURE OF THE JUST

1. For the view that Thrasymachus represents a return to the basic framework of Homeric values in spite of the 'infiltration' of the 'quieter' virtues into fifth-century morality, cf. Adkins (1960), pp. 235–40.

2. On the connection between *kalon* and *agathon* and their opposites *kakon* and *aischron* cf. Adkins (1960), pp. 179–89. Polus in the *Gorgias*, 474c–d, denies that

whatever is *kakon* is *aischron*. Cf. Irwin (1977), II. 6.2, III. 3.3, VI, 12. 3–5, and the references given there.

3. Cf., for example, Cross and Woozley, pp. 52–3; Annas (1981), pp. 51–2.

4. Cf. *Republic* Book IV, 422e–23d and the comment on this pasage in White (1979), pp. 109–11.

5. Cf., for example, Annas (1981), pp. 50–2; Irwin (1977), pp. 181–2.

6. For example, to Annas and to Cross and Woozley.

7. Socrates is clearly thinking that the just man *thinks it fit* of himself as a just man to 'outdo' the unjust person and the unjust action. Thrasymachus takes it that it is *expected* of the unjust man to 'outdo' every one and, by parity, that it is expected of the just to try to 'outdo' the unjust though he is unable to do so. For the meaning of *axioi*, cf. Liddell and Scott. Lindsay's translation 'presume' is not quite right, since it captures only one of the senses of 'think fit to', viz. 'think it worth attempting'. But there is also the sense 'think it worthy (of one) to'. It is the latter sense Socrates has in mind.

8. Cf., Cornford (1941), p. 32, who omits the argument from his translation 'because only a very loose paraphrase could liberate the meaning from the stiff and archaic form of the original'.

9. This notion of knowing the right limit to action is echoed in Plato's characterisation of justice in the soul in *Republic*, Book IV, 441e–42b, 443c–e.

10. If we assume that the essence of justice for Plato is captured in the notion of 'psychic order' (cf. *Gorgias* 506c–507c) or 'psychic harmony' (cf. *Republic* Book IV, 441d–44c), then the avoidance of *pleonexia* will be *one* manifestation of justice in the soul. But is not the specific *anti*-pleonectic intent of justice built-in to the idea of psychic harmony, the proper treatment of the other parts of the soul by the rational part?

11. It is instructive to compare Socrates' attack on rhetoric on moral grounds in the *Gorgias* (cf. 463a,b, 464b–465e, 479e–481b, 499b–503d) with a possible criticism of the values governing such alleged kinds of expertise as 'aversion therapy', 'market research', 'welfare economics', and so on.

12. Cf. Liddell and Scott entries for *sophia* and *phronesis*.

13. Cf., for example, the criticisms in Irwin (1977), III. 11 and V. 5.

14. Cf. Gosling (1973), pp. 55–71.

15. Irwin (1977), pp. 158–9, claims that 'Plato offers definitions in *Republic* IV more freely than Socrates ever did, because he does not claim they are more than hypotheses'. The method of arriving at hypothetical accounts of virtues, for example, which pass the *elenchos* test of consistency of beliefs without including a full account of the final good, was introduced in the *Meno* 86e ff., elaborated in the *Phaedo*, 99e ff., and distinguished from dialectic in *Republic* VI, 510c–511c. However, if my interpretation of Socrates' argument against Thrasymachus is correct, we find something very much like a hypothetical method in this use of 'resemblance' by Socrates. Plato connects the use of hypotheses with the use of perceptible objects as *images* of non-perceptible entities (cf. *Republic*, VI, 511a).

9 SOCRATES SKETCHES THE 'POWER' OF JUSTICE

1. This is the assessment in Annas (1981), pp. 53–6.

2. A similar structure is found in Socrates' discussion with Callicles in the *Gorgias* after

the argument which ends at 499b.

3. Even the avoidance of public lawlessness among Athenians is referred to fear by Pericles when he says (*Thucydides*, II, 37–41) that 'fear teaches us to obey the government and the laws . . .'.
4. Cf. Cross and Woozley (1964), p. 56.
5. As Annas (1981), p. 53, points out.
6. As Annas (1981), ibid, seems to think.
7. For a similar point, cf. *Theatetus*, 176a–177a.
8. Cf. Annas (1981) developed at greater length, pp. 53–5, Cross and Woozley (1964), pp. 57–60.
9. Cf. Annas (1981), pp. 54–5.
10. Cf. Annas (1981), p. 56.
11. On *ergon*, cf. Annas (1981), p. 54.
12. Cf. De Lacy (1976), pp. 63–6.
13. Cross and Woozley (1964), p. 58.
14. Ibid.
15. Cf. Irwin (1977), ch. VII, n. 7, p. 325.
16. A similar problem arises in the *Gorgias* in relation to the well-ordered soul. Cf. *Gorgias* 506e–508e. On this cf. Irwin (1979), notes on 506e–507a, 507ab 507b, 507c, pp. 220–4. Cf., also, Irwin (1977), V, 4.2 and 4.3.
17. This, of course, Plato attempts to do in the rest of the *Republic*, particularly in Books IV to IX.

10   CONCLUSION: THE SOCRATIC VISION

1. Lucas (1980), p. 68. Lucas' book presents a contemporary version of the conventional view of justice, and the way in which its value has to be limited by other values such as freedom.
2. Ibid., p. 263.
3. Ibid.
4. As Kent Sprague (1976), p. 51, n. 5 points out, commenting on *Euthydemus*, 292d 5–6, Plato's phrase *ē allous agathous poiēsomen* is probably *deliberately* ambiguous between '[the knowledge whereby] we shall make other men good' and 'whereby we shall make other good men'.
5. Note Socrates' admonition in the *Apology*, 30 C–E.
6. Contrast, for example, Bambrough's views in Bambrough (1956), pp. 98–115, Vlastos' own Introductory Chapter in Vlastos (1971) and, Irwin's views in Irwin (1977) with Kent Sprague (1976) and Tiles, (1984), pp. 49–66.
7. A point argued at length in Irwin (1977).
8. *Apology*, 22a.
9. Contrast, for example, the *Protagoras* account with those found in *Charmides*, *Hippias Minor*, and *Euthydemus*.
10. On this issue, cf. Kent Sprague (1976), Tiles (1984), Gosling (1973), ch. IV.
11. It remains, of course, an open question whether, and how, this point carries over to the craft of ruling. For further discussion cf., Bambrough (1956), Versenyi (1971) and Tiles (1984).

12. This distinction needs to be made otherwise we misunderstand the notion of the 'good' a craft aims at. The notion of *for the sake of* is, of course, central in Aristotle's *Nicomachean Ethics*, Bk I, chs 1 and 2. Cf. Ackrill's essay in Rorty (1980), pp. 15–33.
13. For a parallel point about piety (*to hosion*), cf. *Euthyphro*, 10a–11a.
14. Cf., for example, the issues that surround the contemporary discussion of the Prisoner's Dilemma and its converse the Altruist's Dilemma. Cf. Lucas (1980) ch. 3.
15. It is noteworthy that in *Republic*, Book II, 358a, Socrates connects Thrasymachus' attack on justice with the conventional view, that which the 'many' have of it.
16. It is part of this tradition to restrict the scope of justice to certain areas of life. Cf., for example, Lucas (1980), pp. 38–9. This point may underlie Hume's idea that justice is an *artificial* virtue.
17. For an excellent discussion of the point as it arises in Aristotle's ethics, cf. McDowell's essay in Rorty (1980), pp. 359–76.
18. For a discussion of the relation of 'mystification' and 'exploitation' to justice in Marx's thought, cf., Wood (1972), pp. 244–82, Buchanan (1979), pp. 121–39, Holstrom (1977), pp. 353–69, and G. A. Cohen's article in Ryan (1979), pp. 9–25.
19. Perhaps an important area which is beginning to emerge is that of 'miscommunication', that is, the systemic distortion of acts and processes of communication within a society.
20. On Plato's conception of reason and rationality, cf. *Republic*, Books IV, VIII and IX. On this, cf. Annas (1980), chs 8 and 10, and Irwin (1977), VII, pp. 191–248.
21. For Plato's views on this cf. *Symposium* and *Phaedrus*. Cf. Irwin (1977), pp. 267–72.
22. Cf. Aristotle's *De Anima*, II, chs 1 and 2, and compare with Plato's 'tripartite' theory in *Republic*, Book IV.
23. A modern version of such a conflict arises over the adequacy of the utilitarian view of justice. Cf. Smart and Williams (1973).

Bibliography

The bibliography contains only the books and articles which played a part in the writing of this book.

Text, Editions and Translations

Adam, J. (ed.), *The Republic of Plato*, with critical notes, commentary and appendices. 2nd edn, with an Introduction by D. A. Rees (Cambridge University Press, 1963).
Allan, D. J. (ed.), *Plato: Republic Book I*, 2nd edn (London: Methuen, 1944).
Burnet, J. (ed.), *Platonis Opera*, vol. 4 (Oxford: Clarendon Press, 1902).
Cornford, F. M., *The Republic of Plato*, Transl. with Introduction and Notes (Oxford: Clarendon Press, 1941).
Lindsay, A. D., *Plato, the Republic*, translation. Introduction and notes by R. Bambrough (London: J. M. Dent, 1976).

Historical and Political Background

Adkins, A. W. H., *Merit and Responsibility* (Oxford: 1960).
Adkins, A. W. H., *Moral Values and Political Behaviour in Ancient Greece* (London: Chatto & Windus, 1972).
Andrewes, A., *The Greek Tyrants* (London: Hutchinson's U.L., 1956).
Barker, E., *Greek Political Theory* (London: University Paperbacks, Methuen, 1960).
Dover, K. J., *Greek Popular Morality in the Time of Plato and Aristotle* (Oxford: Basil Blackwell, 1974).
Ehrenberg, V., *From Solon to Socrates* (London: University Paperbacks, Methuen, 1968).
Finley, M. I., *The World of Odysseus* (London: Chatto & Windus, 1956).
Finley, M. I., *The Ancient Greeks* (London: Chatto & Windus, 1963).
Finley, M. I., 'Athenian Demagogues' in *Studies in Ancient Society*, ed. M. I. Finley (London: Routledge & Kegan Paul, 1974).
Forrest, W. G., *The Emergence of Greek Democracy* (London: World University Library, Weidenfeld & Nicolson, 1966).
Greene, W. C., *Moira, Fate, Good & Evil in Greek Thought* (New York: Harper & Row Torchbooks, 1963).
Guthrie, W. K. C., *A History of Greek Philosophy*, vol. III (Cambridge U.P., 1969).
Harrison, J. E., *Themis: A Study of the Social Origins of Greek Religion* (Cambridge U.P., 1927).
Jones, A. H. M., *Athenian Democracy* (Oxford: Basil Blackwell, 1957).
Kerferd, G. B., *The Sophistic Movement* (Cambridge University Press, 1981).
Morrow, G. R., *Plato's Epistles*. Translation with Critical Essays and Notes (Indianapolis: Bobbs–Merrill, 1962).
Ostwald, M., *Nomos and the Beginnings of the Athenian Democracy* (Oxford, 1969).
De Ste. Croix, G. E. M., *The Class Struggle in the Ancient World* (London: Duckworth, 1981).
Struever, N. S., 'The Background of Humanist Historical Language: The Quarrel of Philosophy and Rhetoric', ch. 1 in her book *The Language of History in the Renaissance* (Princeton U.P., 1970).
Thomson, G., *The First Philosophers* (London: Lawrence & Wishart, 1972 edn).

Thucydides, *The Peloponnesian War.* Translation by R. Warner (Harmondsworth: Penguin Classics, 1954).

Vlastos, G., 'Isonomia Politikē' in *Platonic Studies*, Part I, ch. 8 (Princeton U.P., 1973).

Vlastos, G., 'Solonian Justice', in *Classical Philology*, vol. XLI, no. 2, April 1946.

Plato and the Republic: Books and Collections of Essays

Annas, J., *An Introduction to Plato's Republic* (Oxford: Clarendon Press, 1981).

Bambrough, R., 'Plato's Political Analogies' in P. Laslett (ed.) *Philosophy, Politics and Society* (Oxford: Basil Blackwell, 1956).

Crombie, I. M., *An Examination of Plato's Doctrines*, 2 vols (London: Routledge & Kegan Paul, 1962).

Cross, R. C. and Woozley, A. D., *Plato's Republic* (London: Macmillan, 1964).

Friedländer, P., *Plato*, translated by H. Meyerhoff, Bolingen Series LIX, Princeton University Press, vol. 2 1964, vol. 3 1969.

Gosling, J. C. B., *Plato* (London: Routledge & Kegan Paul, 1973).

Gould, J. P. A., *The Development of Plato's Ethics* (Cambridge University Press, 1955).

Grote, G., *Plato and the other Companions of Socrates*, 3 vols (London: John Murray, 1975).

Joseph, W. H. B., *Essays in Ancient and Modern Philosophy* (Oxford University Press, 1935).

Irwin, T., *Plato's Moral Theory* (Oxford: Clarendon Press, 1977).

Irwin, T., *Plato: Gorgias*, trans. with notes (Oxford: Clarendon Press, 1979).

Nettleship, R. L., *Lectures on the Republic of Plato* (London: Macmillan, 1937).

O'Brien, M. J., *The Socratic Paradoxes and the Greek Mind* (Chapel Hill: University of North Carolina Press, 1967).

Robinson, R., *Plato's Earlier Dialectic*, 2nd edn (Oxford: Clarendon Press, 1953).

Sesonske, A. (ed.), *Plato's Republic: Interpretation and Criticism* (California: Wadsworth, 1966).

Sprague, R. K., *Plato's Philosopher-King* (University of South Carolina Press, 1976).

Taylor, A. E., *Plato; the Man and his Work*, 4th edn (London: Methuen, 1937).

Vlastos, G. (ed.), *The Philosophy of Socrates*, A collection of Critical Essays (New York: Doubleday Anchor, 1971 (1)).

Vlastos, G. (ed.), *Plato II*, A Collection of Critical Essays (New York: Doubleday Anchor, 1971 (2)).

White, N. P., *A Companion to Plato's Republic* (Indianapolis: Hackett, 1979).

Articles dealing with topics relevant to Republic, Book I

Davis, L. P., 'The Arguments of Thrasymachus in the First Book of Plato's *Republic*', *The Modern Schoolman*, 47 (May 1970) pp. 423–32.

De Lacey, P., 'The Concept of Function in *Republic I*, *Paideia*, Special Plato Issue ed. by G. C. Simmons, State University College at Buffalo (1976), pp. 63–6.

Dorter, K., 'Socrates' Refutation of Thrasymachus and Treatment of Virtue', *Philosopy and Rhetoric*, vol. 7, no. 1 (1974) pp. 25–46.

Dover, K. J., 'Socrates in the *Clouds*', in Vlastos (ed.) (1971 (1)) pp. 50–77.

Hadgopoulos, D. J., 'Thrasymachus and Legalism', *Phronesis*, 18 (1973) pp. 204–8.

Henderson, T. Y., 'In Defence of Thrasymachos', *Amer. Phil. Quart.*, 7 (1970) pp. 218–28.

Hourani, G. F., 'Thrasymachos' Definition of Justice in the *Republic*', *Phronesis*, 7 (1962) pp. 110–20.

Harrison, E. L., 'Plato's Manipulation of Thrasymachus', *Phoenix* 21 (1967), pp. 27–39.

Joseph, W. H. B., 'The Argument with Polemarchus', ch. 1 of *Essays in Ancient and Modern Philosophy* (see above).

Kerferd, G. B., 'The Doctrine of Thrasymachos in Plato's *Republic*', *Durham University Journal*, N.S. 9 (1947–8) pp. 19–27.

Kerferd, G. B., 'Thrasymachus and Justice: A reply', *Phronesis* 9 (1964) pp. 12–16.

Maguire, J. P., 'Thrasymachos . . . or Plato?', *Phronesis* 16 (1971) pp. 142–63.

Nicholson, P. P., 'Unravelling Thrasymachus' Arguments in "The Republic"', *Phronesis*, 19 (1974) pp. 210–32.

Sparshott, F. E., 'Socrates and Thrasymachus', *Monist* 50 (1966) pp. 421–59.

Tiles, J. E., 'Techne and Moral Expertise', *Philosophy* 59 (1984) pp. 49–66.

Vlastos, G., 'Introduction: The Paradox of Socrates' in Vlastos (ed.) (1971 (1)) pp. 1–21.

Young, C. M., 'A Note on *Republic* 335c 9–10 and 335c 12, *Philosophical Review*, vol. 83, no. 1 (January 1974).

Young, C. M., 'Polemarchus' and Thrasymachus' Definition of Justice', *Philosophical Inquiry*, vol. 2, no. 1 (1980) pp. 404–19.

Other Books and Articles

Anderson, J., *Studies in Empirical Philosophy* (Sydney: Angus & Robertson, 1962).

Anscombe, G. E. M., 'The Intentionality of Sensation', in R. J. Butler (ed.), *Analytical Philosophy*, 2nd Series (Oxford: Basil Blackwell, 1965) pp. 158–80.

Austin, J., 'Pleasure and Happiness', in J. B. Schneewind (ed.) *Mill: A collection of Critical Essays* (London: Macmillan, 1968) pp. 234–50.

Austin, J. L., *Agathon* and *Eudaimonia* in the *Ethics* of Aristotle', ed. J. M. E. Moravcsik (New York: Doubleday Anchor, 1967) pp. 261–96.

Buchanan, A., 'Exploitation, Alienation, and Injustice', *Canadian Journal of Philosophy*, vol. IX, no. 1 (1979) pp. 121–39.

Burnyeat, M. F., 'Virtues in Action', in Vlastos (ed.), 1971, (1) pp. 209–34.

Cohen, G. A., 'Capitalism, Freedom and the Proletariat' in A. Ryan (ed.), *The Idea of Freedom*: Essays in honour of Isaiah Berlin (Oxford: Clarendon Press, 1975) pp. 9–25.

Gibbs, B. R., 'Virtue and Reason, *PASS*, 48, (1974) pp. 23–41.

Hall, D., 'Techne and Morality in the *Gorgias*', in *Essays in Ancient Greek Philosophy*, ed. by J. P. Anton and G. L. Koustas (State University of N.Y. Press, 1971), pp. 202–18.

Hume, D., *Enquiry Concerning the Principles of Morals*, 2nd edn, ed. L. A. Selby-Bigge (Oxford: Clarendon Press, 1902).

Hume, D., *A Treatise of Human Nature*, ed. L. A. Selby-Bigge (Oxford: Clarendon Press, 1888).

Holstrom, N., 'Exploitation', *Canadian Journal of Philosophy*, vol. VII, no. 2 (1977) pp. 353–69.

Illich, I., *Deschooling Society* (Calder & Boyars, 1971).

Illich, I., *Tools for Conviviality* (New York: Harper & Row, 1973).

Illich, I., *Medical Nemesis* (Lothian Publishing Co., 1975).

Kenny, A., 'Mental Health in Plato's *Republic*' in A. Kenny, *The Anatomy of the Soul* (Oxford: Basil Blackwell, 1973) pp. 1–27.

Leys, W. A. R., 'Was Plato Non-Political' in Vlastos (ed.), (1971 (2)) pp. 166–73.

Locke, J., *Two Treatises on Government*, ed. with Introduction by Peter Laslett, 2nd edn (Cambridge U.P., 1970).

Lucas, J. R., *On Justice* (Oxford: Clarendon Press, 1980).

McDowell, J., 'The Role of *Eudaimonia* in Aristotle's Ethics' in A. O. Rorty (ed.) *Essays on Aristotle's Ethics* (University of California Press, 1980), pp. 359–76.

Marx, K., *Capital*, vol. 1 (New York: International Publishers, 1967).

Nozick, R., *Anarchy, State and Utopia* (New York: Basic Books, 1974).

Penner, T., 'Socrates on Virtue and Motivation', in *Exegesis and Argument*, ed by E. N. Lee, A. P. D. Mourelatos and R. M. Rorty, (New York: Humanities Press, 1973) pp. 133–51.

Quine, W. V., 'Natural Kinds', in *Ontological Relativity* (New York: 1969 Columbia University Press, pp. 114–38).

Rawls, J., *A Theory of Justice* (Oxford University Press, 1972).

Smart, J. J. C. and Williams, B. A. O., *Utilitarianism, For and Against* (Cambridge University Press, 1973).

Sparshott, F. E., 'Plato as Anti-Political Thinker' in Vlastos, ed. (1971 (2)) pp. 174–83.

Wood, A. W., 'The Marxian Critique of Justice', *Philosophy & Public Affairs* (1972), pp. 244–82.

Young, G., 'Justice and Capitalist Production: Marx and Bourgeois Ideology', *Canadian Journal of Philosophy*, vol. VIII, no. 3 (1978) pp. 421–55.

Versenyi, L. G., 'Plato and his liberal opponents', *Philosophy*, 46 (1971) pp. 222–37.

Index

Ackrill, J., 192
Adam, J., 180, 181, 183, 184
Adeimantus, 23, 24, 180
Adkins, A. W. H., 12–13, 42, 178, 181, 183, 186, 190
Allan, D. J., 180, 184, 188
Anaximander: Frag. 36.3, 178
Andrewes, A., 176, 178, 186
Anderson, J., 182
Annas, J., 175, 176, 180, 181, 183, 188, 189, 190, 191, 192, 193
Antisthenes, 176
Apology, 181, 186, 187, 192
Aristotle, 4; *Ath. Const.*, 7.3, 179; *De An.*, II, 1–2, 193: I, 1–2, 193; *Eth. Nic.*, V, 1–4, 175: V, 3, 184; *Politics*, III, 17, 177: III, 4–5, 177: III, 7, 184: IV, 6–7, 177: VI, 3, 186
Aristophanes, 9, 181
Athens: democracy in, 7–8; empire of, 8; Plato's critique of democracy in, 8, 10; political elitism in, 9; Socrates and, 76; Thrasymachus and, 63, 66–7
Austin, J., 175
Austin, J. L., 175

Bambrough, R., 192
Barker, Sir E., 184
Buchanan, A., 193
Burnyeat, M., 187, 188, 189

Charmides, 187, 189, 192
Cephalus, 4, 21; on character, 28–9: and justice, 82–3; on law-abidingness, 23–4, 27, 30–1; on old age, 27–8; on wealth, 28, 29–30; portrait of, 26–31; Socrates' argument with, 80–3
Cleisthenes, 69
Cleon, 68, 177, 181
Cohen, G. A., 193
Cornford, F. M., 175, 176, 184, 191

craft (*technē*): analogy of justice with, 84–9, 90, 93, 103–4, 159–69; critical use of, 160–4; criteria of success of, 87: distinguished from usefulness of, 87; 'field' of a, 84–5: distinguished from 'product' of, 85; infallibility of, 112; is not 'in need', 112–13; as knowledgeable response to a need, 109; as manifestation of power, 108–9; 'object' of, 109, 110, 189: achieving its good the value of, 111
Crito, 181, 182, 186
Crombie, I. M., 187
Cross, R. C. (and A. D. Woozley), 148, 175, 176, 183, 184, 188, 189, 191, 192

De Lacey, P., 192
Demosthenes, 179
dikaiosynē: translation of, 175; see also justice
Dikē, 15–18 *passim; see also Themis*
Dorter, K., 183
Dover, K. J., 175, 186

Ehremburg, V., 181
elenchos: aims of Socratic, 74–5; assumptions of, 78–9; as conversion of mind, 6; as cultural critique, 7, 76, 79–80; negative and positive function of, 77; personal character of, 80
Epistles, 176–7, 185, 186
ergon (characteristic work, 'function'), 86, 147–9, 181; living as the *ergon* of the soul 145, 149–51; and living well, 146–7, 150; of injustice, 140–3; of justice, 76-7, 90, 100, 104–5; of the soul and justice, 150–3; translation of, 147
eudaimonia (human flourishing): justice constituent of, 156; justice in the soul and, 152–3, 173; life of justice is that of, 145–53; meaning of, 3–4,

198